EGYPT

in the time of the pharaohs

CIVILIZATIONS THAT SHAPED OUR WORLD

EGYPT

in the time of the pharaohs

Reader's
Digest

THE READER'S DIGEST ASSOCIATION, INC.
PLEASANTVILLE, NEW YORK / MONTREAL

CIVILIZATIONS THAT SHAPED OUR WORLD *was developed by Reader's Digest.*

EGYPT *in the time of the pharaohs*
is part of the CIVILIZATIONS THAT SHAPED OUR WORLD collection

Editorial
GÉRARD CHENUET, PATRICE MENTHA,
VIVIANE KOENIG, YVAN KOENIG, RÉMY
COTON-PÉLAGIE, CAMILLE DUVIGNEAU,
THOMAS VON JOEST, CLAUDINE ANTONIN

Design
DOMINIQUE CHARLIAT, VÉRONIQUE
ZONCA, COLMAN COHEN

Illustrations
JEAN-BENOIT HÉRON

Cartography
EDITERRA

Picture Editing
MONIQUE TRÉMEAU,
DANIELLE BURNICHON

**U.S. READER'S DIGEST
PROJECT TEAM**

Contributing Project Editor
FRED DuBOSE

Designer
JENNIFER R. TOKARSKI

Production Technology Manager
DOUGLAS A. CROLL

Art Production
PATRICIA HALBERT

Translation
MOLLY STEVENS

Proofreading
JANE SHERMAN

Indexing
NAN BADGETT

READER'S DIGEST BOOKS

Editor-in-Chief
NEIL WERTHEIMER

Editorial Director
CHRISTOPHER CAVANAUGH

Senior Design Director
ELIZABETH L. TUNNICLIFFE

Associate Marketing Director
DENNIS MARION

Vice President and General Manager
KEIRA KUHS

**GLOBAL BOOKS & HOME
ENTERTAINMENT RIGHTS
& PERMISSIONS**

Director
ALFREDO G. SANTANA

Asssociate Director
LISA GARRETT-SMITH

**READER'S DIGEST
ASSOCIATION, INC.**

Editor-in-Chief
ERIC W. SCHRIER

**President, North American Books
and Home Entertainment**
THOMAS D. GARDNER

**READER'S DIGEST EDITORIAL,
INTERNATIONAL**

GARY Q. ARPIN, IAIN PARSONS

FIRST EDITION
© 2002 The Reader's Digest Association, Inc.
© 2000 Sélection du Reader's Digest, S.A.

This volume includes material from THE EGYPTIANS *by Cyril Aldred,* © *1961, 1984, 1987, and 1988 Thames & Hudson Ltd.,
London. First published in Great Britain in 1961 as volume 18 in the* Ancient People and Places *series. Second edition 1984.
Third edition revised by Aidan Dodson, 1998. Exerpted by arrangement with Thames & Hudson.*

ISBN 0-7621-0415-5

Address any comments about *Civilizations That Shaped Our World* to:
Editorial Director, Reader's Digest Home Division
Reader's Digest Road, Pleasantville, NY 10570-7000

To order additional copies of *Civilizations That Shaped Our World*, call 1-800-846-2100.

You can also visit us on the World Wide Web at **rd.com**

Printed in the United States of America

UK 0074/G–US   1 3 5 7 9 10 8 6 4 2

TABLE OF CONTENTS

MAIN TEXT IS THE CONDENSED VERSION OF *THE EGYPTIANS*
BY CYRIL ALDRED, FIRST PUBLISHED IN 1961.

ANUBIS'S PREPARATIONS
The jackal-god Anubis, god of mummification, is preparing the mummy of Sennedjem for eternity. Tomb of Sennedjem (19th Dynasty, Deir el-Medina)

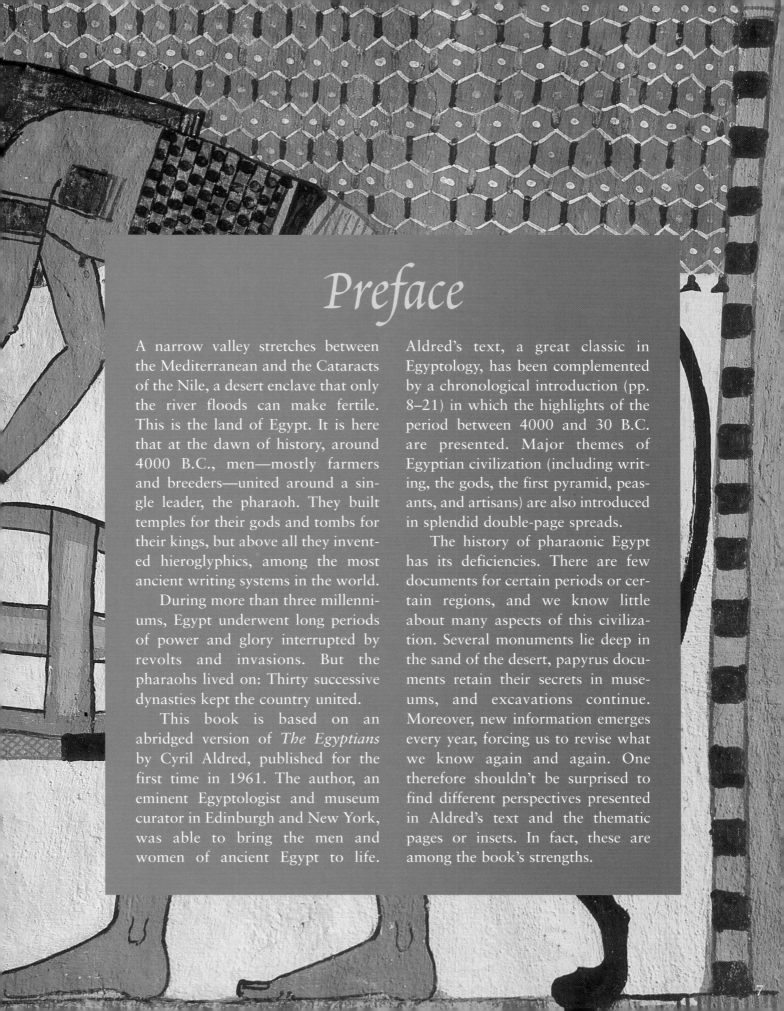

Preface

A narrow valley stretches between the Mediterranean and the Cataracts of the Nile, a desert enclave that only the river floods can make fertile. This is the land of Egypt. It is here that at the dawn of history, around 4000 B.C., men—mostly farmers and breeders—united around a single leader, the pharaoh. They built temples for their gods and tombs for their kings, but above all they invented hieroglyphics, among the most ancient writing systems in the world.

During more than three millenniums, Egypt underwent long periods of power and glory interrupted by revolts and invasions. But the pharaohs lived on: Thirty successive dynasties kept the country united.

This book is based on an abridged version of *The Egyptians* by Cyril Aldred, published for the first time in 1961. The author, an eminent Egyptologist and museum curator in Edinburgh and New York, was able to bring the men and women of ancient Egypt to life.

Aldred's text, a great classic in Egyptology, has been complemented by a chronological introduction (pp. 8–21) in which the highlights of the period between 4000 and 30 B.C. are presented. Major themes of Egyptian civilization (including writing, the gods, the first pyramid, peasants, and artisans) are also introduced in splendid double-page spreads.

The history of pharaonic Egypt has its deficiencies. There are few documents for certain periods or certain regions, and we know little about many aspects of this civilization. Several monuments lie deep in the sand of the desert, papyrus documents retain their secrets in museums, and excavations continue. Moreover, new information emerges every year, forcing us to revise what we know again and again. One therefore shouldn't be surprised to find different perspectives presented in Aldred's text and the thematic pages or insets. In fact, these are among the book's strengths.

The kingdom of the pharaohs

A narrow valley in the middle of the desert, Egypt benefits from a warm, dry climate. This land has played a role in history since the fourth century B.C. due to the Nile's annual flooding, which fertilized the banks until the Aswan Dam was built in the twentieth century. Egypt has seen splendid periods as well as very difficult times and has had no less than 30 royal dynasties.

A MYTHIC LAND
The vestiges of the Egyptian civilization, dating back some 6,000 years, have long fascinated the rest of the world.

OUTSIDE OF EGYPT...

THE MITANNI KINGDOM

Around 1500 B.C., the inhabited by the Mitanni people extended from upper Mesopotamia to northern Syria. There is little information about this kingdom, which dominated the region for more than a century. Nevertheless, the heroic deeds of the Great King, as he was known, are available to us thanks to the battle logs written by his enemies and the letters the rulers exchanged.

BABYLONIA

Between the Tigris and the Euphrates, a new kingdom was built on the ruins of the former Sumerian State. Around 2000 B.C., Hammurabi named Babylon its capital. A fierce conqueror, an excellent administrator, and an effective diplomat, he established an empire that endured until 1550 B.C. After a long dark period following a raid by the Kassites, who had come from the north, and after Assyrian domination, Babylonia was revitalized by Nebuchadnezzar II, who came into power in 605 B.C. He seized Jerusalem, which he destroyed, but was unable to invade Egypt. Babylonia eventually succumbed to attacks led by the Persian Cyrus in 539 B.C.

THE ASSYRIAN EMPIRE

The Assyrians, who for a long time were subjugated by the Babylonians, took power around 1150 B.C. and stayed in power for 500 years. Their kings commanded an awesome army by mobilizing their infantry and by using chariot warfare and cavalry. From conquest to conquest, the empire reached its peak under the reigns of Sargon and Assurbanipal in the eighth and twelfth centuries B.C. Spoils from Mesopotamia, Syria, and Egypt were collected in the capital, Nineveh. However, around 610 B.C., revolts and power struggles precipitated the fall of the Assyrian Empire, which was then divided into four independent regions: Egypt, Syria-Palestinia, the Upper Tigris Valley, and Babylonia.

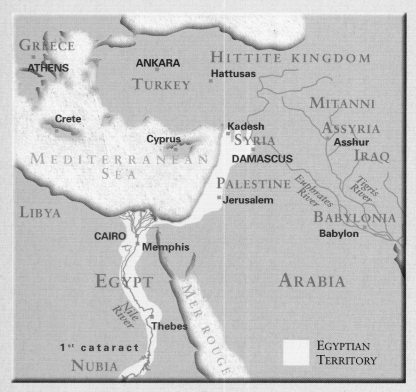

EGYPT UNDER THUTMOSE III
The kingdom of Egypt was at its greatest extent under the reign of Pharaoh Thutmose III (1482–1458 B.C.). This great builder was also an effective diplomat and a formidable warrior. He conquered the small kingdoms of the Near East and the southern regions extending to the 4th Cataract of the Nile.

THE TIME OF THE PYRAMIDS	THE CLASSICAL PERIOD OF THE MIDDLE KINGDOM
4000–2700 B.C. Predynastic and Thinite periods	**2200–2060 B.C.** First Intermediate Period
2700–2200 B.C. Old Kingdom	**2060–1785 B.C.** Middle Kingdom
Pages 10–11	*Pages 12–13*

4500 B.C.   **4000** B.C.   **2200** B.C.

- Ancient Predynastic Period in Egypt
- Bronze Age in Europe

- Around 3200 B.C.
  Unification of Egypt
  Hieroglyphic writing is developed

- Around 2600 B.C.
  Great pyramids of Cheops, Chepren, and Mycerinus

- Around 2070 B.C.
  The Mentuhotep rulers (11th Dynasty) reunite Egypt and take the title of kings of Upper and Lower Egypt

EGYPTIAN C

MEDITERRANEAN SEA

Rosetta
Alexandria
Sais
Tanis

Wadi Natrun

DELTA

LOWER EGYPT

Bubastis
Heliopolis
Giza **Bulag**
Abusir **CAIRO**
Saqqara
Dahshur **Memphis**
Lisht
Maidum
Faiyum **El-Lahun**
Crocodilopolis
Heracleopolis

Libyan Desert

MIDDLE EGYPT

Bahr Yusuf

El-Hibeh

Youna *Beni Hasan*

Hermopolis *Bersha*
Amarna
Meir
Assyat

Arabian Desert

SINAI

RED SEA

THE HITTITE KINGDOM

Around 1900 B.C., an Indo-European population settled in Anatolia, a region surrounded by the sea on three sides and by high mountains on its eastern border. The Hittite Kingdom, which was built around its capital, Hattusas, enjoyed four centuries of glory between 1600 and 1200 B.C. It expanded towards the east and southeast under the reigns of Hattusilis and Mursilis, who conquered northern Syria, progressed into Mesopotamia, and fought the Egyptians. The Hittite Kingdom disappeared as quickly as it emerged. Invaded by a great migration of Sea Peoples, it disintegrated into many small states that survived until 700 B.C.

SYRIA-PALESTINIA

In the third century B.C., the splendorous city-states of Ebla and Mari quickly vanished under successive attacks led by the Amorites, the Hurrites, and the Aramaens in this region. The land was ruled by Sumerians, Akkadians, Babylonians, Egyptians, Assyrians, and Hittites, and it often became the battleground of choice for all these empires. Forever being used and abused by those in power, the small states of Syria-Palestinia were eventually absorbed by Alexander the Great in 301 B.C. At this point, they joined the Seleucide Empire. In 64 B.C., when they were annexed by Pompey, they became Roman territory.

THE UPPER REGIONS OF ANCIENT EGYPT
The most impressive ruins of pharaonic civilization —the pyramids—are concentrated around Memphis, the capital of Lower Egypt. Around Thebes, capital of Upper Egypt, are colossal temples and the royal tombs of the Valley of the Kings and Valley of the Queens.

Deir el-Bahari

VALLEY OF THE KINGS
Temple of Hatshepsut
VALLEY OF THE NOBLES

Deir el-Medina

Temple of Thutmose III
Temple of Ramses II

VALLEY OF THE QUEENS

Médinet Habou

Colossi of Memnon

Palace of Amenhotep III

Nile River

Temple of Montu

Karnak

Great Temple of Amon

Temple of Mut

Thebes

Temple of Luxor

UPPER EGYPT

Abydos **Dendera**
Wadi Hammamat

Nagada **Koptos**
Karnak
Thebes
Luxor

Esna Tod

Hieraonpolis Elkab

Edfou

Kharga Oasis

Kom Ombo

Elephantine I. Aswan
1st Cataract
Philae I.

Dungul Oasis

Nile R.

Abu Simbel

Wadi Halfa
2nd Cataract

A PROSPEROUS AND UNITED KINGDOM

1785–1552 B.C.
Second Intermediate Period

1552–1069 B.C.
New Kingdom

Pages 14–15

A COVETED LAND

1069–330 B.C.
Third Intermediate Period and Late Period

Pages 16–17

EGYPT MEETS GREECE

330 B.C.
Alexander's conquest

323–30 B.C.
Lagid Dynasty

Pages 18–19

1785 B.C.   **1069** B.C.   **330** B.C.   **30** B.C.   **200** A.D.   **400** A.D.

- Around 1550 B.C. Necropolis of the Valley of the Kings
- Around 1500 to 1200 B.C. Massive building in Karnak, Luxor, and Abu Simbel

- Around 600 B.C. Canal from the Nile to the Red Sea
- Around 500 B.C. Camels appear

- Alexandria, key city of the Greek world

- 14 A.D. Roman Empire
- 25 A.D. Han Dynasties in China
- 70 A.D. Destruction of Jerusalem

- Barbarians invade Roman Empire
- 330 A.D. Founding of Constantinople

- 476 A.D. End of Roman Empire, end of antiquity

ILIZATION

The time of the pyramids
4000–2200 B.C.

At the beginning of the Old Kingdom, around 2700 B.C., Egypt emerged as a well-organized kingdom. It was ruled by a powerful king who lived in Memphis, the capital, surrounded by his family and carefully appointed senior officials. In his fields, his marshes, and his construction sites, his people worked hard and were supervised by numerous scribes who recorded reports in hieroglyphics, one of the oldest writing systems in the world.

A TRADITION OF BREEDING
Since time immemorial, the Egyptians had been breeding geese, ducks, donkeys, cattle, and sheep. They even attempted to raise hyenas and hoopoes, but never horses or camels. Cats and dogs were still wild animals. At the foot of the pyramid of Maidum, the first pyramid built by King Snefrou, the Nefermaat mastaba was decorated with splendid agricultural scenes. Being the extraordinary naturalists that they were, the artists of the Old Kingdom did not ignore any details, and in this way immortalized living animals.

PHARAOH DIDOUFRI
All that remains of Didoufri, Pharaoh of the 4th Dynasty, is this moving portrait, which was found in his Abu-Roach pyramid. It was made from bright-colored quartzite. In contrast to the statues immortalizing some of the kings of the Old Kingdom, Didoufri's portrait seems alive; his cheekbones protrude and he smiles a bit. On his neme, the traditional royal headwear, the uraeus cobra rears its head, ready to destroy all the enemies of the king— and therefore, of the country.

4000–3150 B.C.	Predynastic Period	3150–2700 B.C.	Thinite, or Archaic, Period		
	End of prehistory	1st Dynasty	Narmer (Menes), Hor-Aha, Djer	2nd Dynasty	Hotepsekhemuy, Nebre, Khasekhem
			• *Foundation of Memphis (The White Wall)*		
			• *Calendar fixed at 365 days*		

THE ART OF THE BAS-RELIEF

Coming from her mortuary temple in Giza, near the royal pyramid, this stele of Nefertiabet, sister or daughter of Cheops, shows the skill of sculptors from 4,600 years ago. Wearing a wig and a leopard-skin dress, the princess reaches her hand toward loaves of bread on a table. Hieroglyphics depict eternal offerings: ducks, oxen, wine, beer, fruit, ointments, and more. Nefertiabet could die in peace, with all she would need in the afterlife.

THE JOY OF FAMILY LIFE

Immortalized in limestone, which retains the brilliant paint, lady Sentiotes tenderly embraces her husband, Seneb, the dwarf. Their son and daughter stand in the classical childhood position, fingers in mouth. This group of sculptures (just over 11 inches in height), which was found intact in the dwarf's tomb near Cheops's pyramid, dates back to the 6th Dynasty. It points to the importance of family life for the ancient Egyptians.

THE GREAT PYRAMIDS

(background photograph) The great pyramids were built during the Old Kingdom. Constructed with local stone, the largest one, which belonged to Cheops (Giza), rises to over 480 feet in height. The thin limestone that covered it is now almost entirely gone. The pyramid for his son, Chepren, which is smaller, is at its side, forever guarded by a stone sphinx.

BOATS OF ALL KINDS

The Egyptians were fascinated by boats. Extremely useful in a country where the Nile was used for transportation, boats were often depicted in Predynastic pottery, which was also adorned with men, animals, and geometric designs. The schematic renderings do not accurately convey what the vessels were like. Some vases show ships with more than 50 oars, while others show tiny papyrus boats—but sails and masts are never represented.

2700–2200 B.C. Old Kingdom

2700–2625 B.C.	3rd Dynasty	2625–2510 B.C.	4th Dynasty	2510–2460 B.C.	5th Dynasty	2460–2200 B.C.	6th Dynasty
	Djoser, Huny		Cheops, Chepren, Mycerinus		Unis		Teti, Pepy
	• Permanent establishment of government in Memphis		• Great pyramids of Giza		• Texts of the pyramids		
	• First ties with Byblos						

The classical period of the Middle Kingdom 2200–1785 B.C.

Around 2200 B.C., the Egyptian State seemed to be disintegrating: 70 kings in 70 days, they say! The kingdom fragmented into principalities, famine struck, havoc and violence erupted. It was the First Intermediate Period. When the Prince of Thebes, Mentuhotep, reconquered the country, Egypt calmed and stabilized. This was the Middle Kingdom, which is considered the country's Classical period. Artists created masterpieces, writers inscribed wonders.

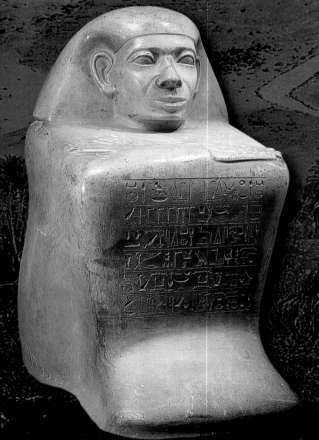

A NAÏVE AND POIGNANT ART
Sculpted and painted, this stele found in the south of Egypt tells us about Egyptian funeral practices and about the decline of art in the tumultuous period preceding the Middle Kingdom. Rendered awkwardly but movingly, Iry and his wife, sitting on a bench, receive offerings from their children. Charming details, like the seam in the girl's basket, take our attention away from the fact that the figures' arms are too long and their legs too thick.

THE DYNASTY OFFICIALS OF BENI HASAN
(background photograph) During the Middle Kingdom, "the great lords of the nome of Oryx" —these were administrators, the pharaoh's local representatives who exercised power in provinces known as nomes—built rock-cut tombs into the mountain of Beni Hasan. The necropolis consists of 39 underground tombs with modest facades. They overlook the river and are arranged in two parallel rows. The most beautiful has a courtyard with portico, a pillar room with a niche for a statue, and a passage leading to the tomb.

OSIRIS CULT
The priest Ser folds his arms and legs to sit in the cult position adopted by the Abydos pilgrims. Only his head emerges from his coat—hence the name "block statues" for these sculptures from the Middle Kingdom. Noticeable are the priest's panther skin on the back of the statue and, on the front, a prayer to Osiris, the god of the dead. In the temple to this god, Ser used his statue to practice daily rituals so that he would receive divine protection and eternal life.

2200–2060 B.C.   First Intermediate Period

- *Turbulent period (Bedouin invasions in the Delta)*
- *Sarcophagus texts*

2200–around 2140 B.C.	7th and 8th Memphis Dynasties
after 2160 B.C.	9th and 10th (2130 B.C.) Heracleopolis Dynasties in the north
after 2133 B.C.	beginning of the 11th Thebes Dynasty in the south

THE PHARAOH'S TREASURES

The founding of a temple was an occasion to collect precious objects. A depository from the Middle Kingdom in the name of King Amenemhat was found in 1936 near Luxor, in the ruins of the Temple of Tod, dedicated to the god Montu. Seven feet below the ground, four cases contained lapis lazuli, pendants, pearls, cylinders, amulets, lead, and gold and silver objects. At the time, silver was more expensive and rarer than gold. Forty-five silver bowls and cups are distinguished by their shape and relief decoration, which was hammered.

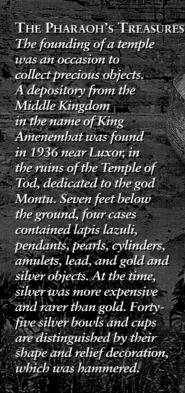

ROCK-CUT TOMBS

In Beni Hasan, after entering through the portico façade into Khnoumhotep III's tomb—he was "the hereditary lord, unique friend, known by the king, governor of the eastern desert"—visitors find themselves in a large room that was dug into the mountain. It is luxuriously decorated with offerings, hunting and fishing scenes, and more. In the rear, two vertical passages plunge towards the tomb, where the lord's sarcophagus rests.

A WEALTH OF FUNERARY FURNISHINGS

So that he would live well in the afterlife, a rich person was buried with an abundance and variety of furnishings. Women, representing his agricultural holdings, were painted or inscribed on the tomb walls; they bring offerings. Starting in the Middle Kingdom, these women took the form of amazing wooden statuettes that were painted and layered with stucco. Thanks to the statuettes, the deceased would have all he needed and also be overjoyed to see such pretty women gracing his eternal home.

2060–1785 B.C.   Middle Kingdom

2060–1991 (or 2130 in the south)	**11th Dynasty** **Mentuhotep** • *Great Mentuhotep monument in Deir el-Bahari*	

1991–1785 B.C.   12th Dynasty
Amenemhet, Sesostris
• *Founding of the Lisht residence*
• *Nubia at peace*
• *Satire of the Trades texts*

A prosperous and united kingdom 1785–1069 B.C.

A round 1785 B.C., domestic affairs in Egypt worsened while the Hyksos, from Asia, settled in the north of the country. It was the Second Intermediate Period. Once again, the Theban princes reunited the kingdom, and the New Kingdom began. This was a period of expansion and prosperity, as can be seen in the magnificent paintings, statues, and monuments that have survived from the era.

HATSHEPSUT'S MARK
(background photo) Known for her expedition to the country of Punt and for the buildings she erected, Hatshepsut truly reigned. Here, the temple of Deir el-Bahri, across from Thebes, was a mortuary temple for both her double] and the double of her father, Thutmose I. The temple was adorned with trees and flowers, bas-reliefs, and statues. At the end of an alley lined with sphinxes and three tiers of terraces, stood a great door of pink granite that opened onto an inner courtyard and sanctuary.

AN AFTERLIFE FOR ARTISTS
The artisans who built the royal tombs lived in Deir el-Medina, a New Kingdom village near the Valley of the Kings. When not working, they prepared their own tombs and funerary materials, notably boxes filled with chauabtis—small statues of the artisans. The statues' mission was to substitute for the artisans at work in the afterlife.

VICTORIOUS PHARAOHS
In the palace of Ramses III in Medînet Habû, these war prisoners painted on earthenware slabs are curious décor. Such representations were traditional and were similar to a spell. To appear as a victorious warrior imprisoning his bound enemies was the pharaoh's way of keeping them at bay. It was also a way to conquer them.

1785–1552 B.C. Second Intermediate Period
Turbulent times
1674–1633 B.C. 13th and 14th Dynasty
1674–1567 B.C. 15th- 16th Dynasty : The Hyksos in the north *Capital : Avaris*
1640 (?)–1550 (?) B.C. 17th Dynasty : The Thebian princes in the south *Capital : Thebes*

1552–1069 B.C. New Kingdom
1552–1295 B.C. 18th Dynasty
Ahmose I, Amenotep I, Thutmose I,
Hatshepsut, Amenophis IV- Akhenaton,
Tutankhamen

THE POWER OF QUEEN TIYE
Daughter of an Egyptian dignitary and wife of Amenhotep III (18th Dynasty), with whom she had six children, this queen had a strong personality and played an important political role, first at the side of her husband and later of her son, Amenhotep IV. She accompanied the latter to the new capital, Amarna. Promoting her role as the king's great spouse, she participated in cultural celebrations and even had herself represented as a sphinx.

FROM GALENA TO KHOL
The pharaohs mined the site of Gebel Zeit, on the coast of the Red Sea, for galena (lead sulfide), from which they could obtain a medicine (khol) that protected the eyes and served as makeup. The sanctuary at this site is home to figurines that date back to the Second Intermediate Period. The miners modeled them in clay and then offered them to Hathor, the goddess of (among other things) love and fertility. This explains the curves.

FROM VINE TO WINE
The wine harvesters picked grapes from the vines, filled the baskets, emptied them in round vats, and stomped on them. The juice drizzled into jars, where it fermented. Soon, the wine was ready. This New Kingdom painting points to the importance of vineyards in ancient Egypt. Every garden had a few feet of vine. And because every tomb, like the one belonging to Nakht in the Valley of the Nobles, had grapes, wine could be offered to its owner.

* Capitalslkj : Thebes and Amarna
* The Book of the Dead
* Expansion towards Sudan
* Thutmose I crosses the Euphrates

1295–1188 B.C.   19th Dynasty
Ramses, Seti, Mineptah
* Capital : Thebes then Pi-Ramses
* Battle of Kadesh (1275–1274 B.C.)

1188–1069 B.C.   20th Dynasty
Sethnakht, Ramses III to X
* Temple of Medinet Habû (Ramses VII)
* The pharaohs lose Asia

15

A coveted land 1069–330 B.C.

Starting in 950 B.C., the Libyans, Ethiopians, and Assyrians invaded Egypt in a successive wave of attacks. Psamtik, an Egyptian prince from the city of Sais, was able to drive them out; during the 50 years of his reign, he restored royal power and reestablished order. His successor, Necho, was almost as powerful as Ramses II. Necho hired more than 100,000 men to rebuild the canal that ran from the Nile to the Red Sea.

HYMNS TO GOD RE
On this wooden stele, which was stuccoed and painted around 900 B.C., a priest-musician, his head shaved, honors Re with his hymns. The god's falcon head is crowned by a solar disk. The priest plays the harp, an instrument that was already in existence in the early years of the pharaonic period. The god seems charmed. Unfortunately, the chants are lost, since the Egyptian scribes never recorded melodies.

FOR THE LOVE OF THE GAME
The Egyptians were so fond of playing—with both family and friends—that they brought games to their tombs for eternity. This hippopotamus board with 58 holes dates back to the Saite period. An earthenware piece with glass incrustations, it is unique. The game was played with dice and dog- or jackal-shaped pawns. Historians are uncertain about the rules of the game, but most likely, players had to finish a course as quickly as possible, with victory determined by a throw of the dice.

AN OASIS IN THE DESERT (background photo)
It was under the first Persian rule that Darius built the Temple of Ibis, in the Kharga Oasis. Like all the Egyptian pharaohs, he had his name engraved in cartouches (tablets). Dedicated to the god Amon of Thebes, the temple is a remarkable monument from the Persian period. There are other very ancient ruins in the western dDesert; for example, in the Dakhla Oasis, an Old Kingdom town is found.

1069–330 B.C. Third Intermediate Period and the Late Period

1069–945 B.C.	21st Dynasty at Tanis in the north	945–715 B.C.	Libyan epoch : 22nd to 24th Dynasties
	• Capital : Tanis		Sheshonk, Osorkon
1098–945 B.C.	Priest-kings in the south	747–656 B.C.	Ethiopian period : 25th Dynasty
	• Capital : Thebes		Taharka, Piankhi

THE ART OF THE SARCOPHAGUS

The sarcophagus was key to a proper burial. The first examples were rectangular and were decorated with architectural motifs reminiscent of a palace façade. Later, they conformed to the shape of the bodies they protected. Their decorations combined religious vignettes and funereal texts. In the Saite period, princes preferred sarcophagi made of rare materials and bursting with figures and inscriptions. The one belonging to Psusennes I, who reigned at Tanis 3,000 years ago, was golden.

MAGIC MEDICINE

Egypt teemed with serpents and scorpions, which explains the Egyptians' healing statues engraved with magic formulas. Directions were simple: Pour water on the head of the statue and let it dribble down the body over the hieroglyphics; collect the water, now infused with the power, in a bowl, and simply drink it for protection.

ANUBIS, GOD OF THE NECROPOLISES

Whether he was fending off a jackal-god feeding on the bodies or a wild dog wandering through a cemetery, Anubis protected the dead in their tombs. Finding himself before the decomposed cadaver of the god Osiris (killed by his brother, the god Set), Anubis reconstituted him and wrapped him in strips of cloth. Osiris was revived, and Anubis had created the first mummy. So it was that this god of the necropolises became the burial authority and the patron of embalming.

672–525 B.C. **Saite period : 26th Dynasty** **Psamtik** • *Capital : Memphis* • *Naucratis, first Greek establishment*	**525–359 B.C.** **First Persian period : 27th Dynasty** **404–343 B.C.** **Last Egyptian pharaohs : 28th and 30th Dynasties** **Second Persian period**

Egypt meets Greece
330–30 B.C.

After years of upheaval and surrender to invaders, Egypt was conquered by Alexander the Great. He went on to found cities, the most important being Alexandria. During the Ptolemaic era, Alexandria became a great commercial hub; its famous library and museum made it the largest intellectual center of antiquity. Hellenistic civilization was born.

COLOSSAL ARCHITECTURE
(background photo) During the Ptolemaic era, sanctuaries were restored or built to honor the Egyptian gods. To the south of Thebes, construction of the temple of Edfu for the falcon-god Horus began in 327 B.C. and was finally completed 195 years later, after several interruptions. It's a classic structure—a pylon (entrance façade made of two rectangular pillars), a large courtyard, two hypostyle rooms, two vestibules, and a sanctuary surrounded by many chapels. Its size was impressive — more than 400 feet long, with a pylon almost 110 feet high.

TO THE GLORY OF HATHOR
To the north of Thebes, the temple of Dendera, built under the last Ptolemaic kings and completed during the Roman era, is the dwelling place of the goddess Hathor. Its sandstone columns are impressive. Several of the capitals represent the face of the goddess, a smiling woman with cow ears. Other capitals depict a sistrum (a musical rattle), one of the belongings of this goddess of love, fertility, joy, and music.

THE CONSUMMATE ARTISTRY OF EARTHENWARE
Dating back to the third century B.C., this original bottle reflects the perfect technique of this Egyptian earthenware artisan. Pure quartz is covered with a glaze made of siliceous glass, then colored with cuprous compounds, yielding many shades of blue. This is how the artisan could imitate expensive and rare lapis lazuli and turquoise at a lower cost. He drew on his skill and knowledge of the kiln to make vases, jewelry, or amulets.

332—330 B.C. Conquest of Alexander the Great
- *Death of Alexander the Great (323 B.C.)*

323–30 B.C. Dagid Dynasty
- *Temple of Philae, Dendera, Edfu, Esna*

305–145 B.C. from Ptolemy I Soter to Ptolemy VI
- *Construction of the beacon of Alexandria*
- *Export of papyrus forbidden (260 B.C.); invention of parchment in Pergamum*
- *Decree de Ptolemy V engraved on the Rosetta Stone*
- *Antiochus IV in Egypt (176 B.C.)*

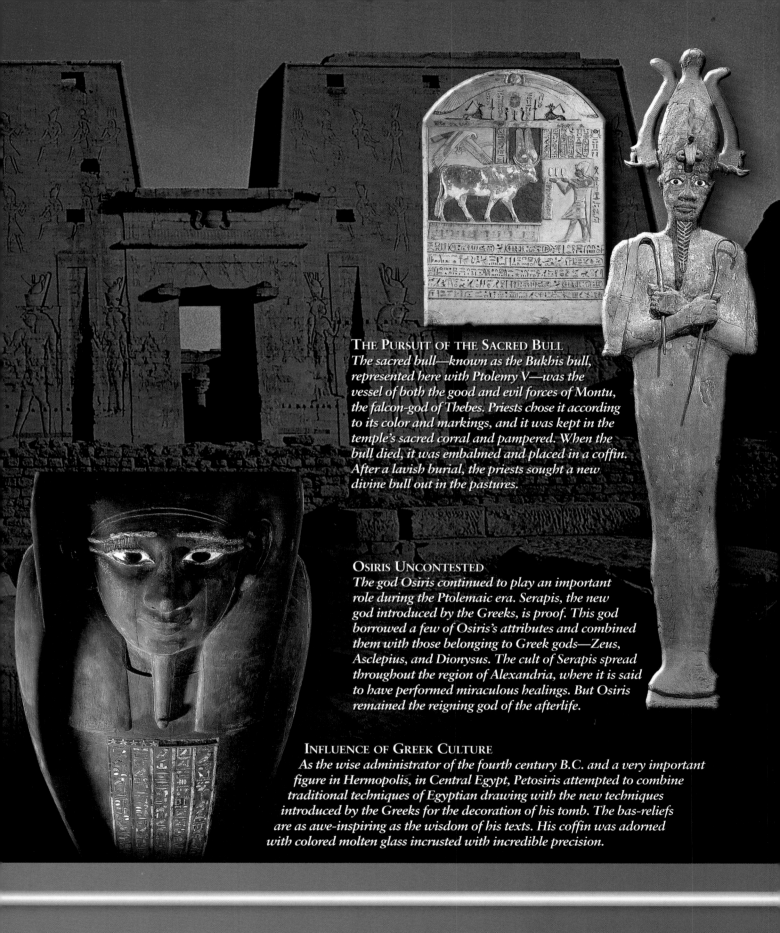

THE PURSUIT OF THE SACRED BULL

The sacred bull—known as the Bukhis bull, represented here with Ptolemy V—was the vessel of both the good and evil forces of Montu, the falcon-god of Thebes. Priests chose it according to its color and markings, and it was kept in the temple's sacred corral and pampered. When the bull died, it was embalmed and placed in a coffin. After a lavish burial, the priests sought a new divine bull out in the pastures.

OSIRIS UNCONTESTED

The god Osiris continued to play an important role during the Ptolemaic era. Serapis, the new god introduced by the Greeks, is proof. This god borrowed a few of Osiris's attributes and combined them with those belonging to Greek gods—Zeus, Asclepius, and Dionysus. The cult of Serapis spread throughout the region of Alexandria, where it is said to have performed miraculous healings. But Osiris remained the reigning god of the afterlife.

INFLUENCE OF GREEK CULTURE

As the wise administrator of the fourth century B.C. and a very important figure in Hermopolis, in Central Egypt, Petosiris attempted to combine traditional techniques of Egyptian drawing with the new techniques introduced by the Greeks for the decoration of his tomb. The bas-reliefs are as awe-inspiring as the wisdom of his texts. His coffin was adorned with colored molten glass incrusted with incredible precision.

145–30 B.C.   Ptolemy VII to XII, Cleopatra VII, Ptolemy XIII to XV

- *Troubles at the royal palace (145–80 B.C.)*
- *Assassination of Pompey in Alexandria (49 B.C.)*
- *Alexandria library burns down (47 B.C.)*

3 August 30 B.C.   Octavian seizes Alexandria

- *Egypt becomes a Roman province*
- *Cleopatra commits suicide*

19

The Egyptians

BY CYRIL ALDRED

CHAPTER 1

The loss and recovery of pagan Egypt

Decline and coma

In 130 A.D., during the golden summer of the Roman Empire, Hadrian, with his empress Sabina and a numerous retinue, toured his domains in Egypt. The visit was notable for a number of events, apart from the great singularity that an emperor in Rome had chosen to explore his personal estate. Hadrian disputed in Greek with professors at the Museum of Alexandria, and building work on towns and temples was initiated or reinvigorated throughout the land. A tragic incident occurred when his catamite, the handsome Bithynian youth Antinous, drowned himself in the Nile to avert from the emperor some mysterious calamity forecast by an oracle. At the site of this disaster, near modern Sheikh Abada in Middle Egypt, Hadrian founded the city of Antinoë in his honor, and its ruins were still extensive at the beginning of the last century.

The emperor and his suite camped for several days in the plain at Western Thebes before the two monolithic quartzite colossi, which were all that remained visible of the gigantic mortuary temple of Amenhotep III, built some 15 centuries earlier. In classical times, the northern statue was held to represent the Homeric Memnon slain at the siege of Troy, since occasionally, as its fissured stone warmed up in the rays of the rising sun, it emitted a low moaning note, as though the dead hero were greeting his mother, Eos, the dawn. She in turn responded by shedding tears, which fell as the morning dew. Memnon did not fail to salute Hadrian, even

STONE GIANTS
One has to get close to the colossi of Memnon, standing alone in the landscape, to comprehend their size. A single foot is more than 9 feet long.

HATHOR AND SETI
(opposite page)
On this painted bas-relief from the tomb of Pharaoh Seti I (Valley of the Kings), Hathor, goddess of the sky and protectress of the dead, offers her necklace as a sign of protection (19th Dynasty, Louvre Museum).

21

THE COLOSSI OF MEMNON

Today these famous colossi stand alone, rising up in the middle of the landscape facing east, looking toward the desert. They are so enormous that they can be seen from the desert mountain where the Valleys of the Kings, Queens, and Nobles lie. These huge statues once framed the entrance to the mortuary temple of Amenhotep II. It was a gigantic monument—but, unfortunately, almost nothing has survived except a broken statue, a stele, and scattered rocks.

The monument was destroyed during the terrible earthquake of 27 A.D. Only the colossi remain, damaged and cracked. Built on a base that is about 7 feet high, the royal statues rise up almost 50 feet. A person could lie down in the hand of the sandstone colossus that represents Amenhotep III. He is rendered with traditional headwear and is seated with his hand on his knees, a traditional position. The mother of the king, Queen Tiye, is depicted on the side of the thrones and is tiny in comparison to her son.

Known as the "colossi of Memnon," these royal statues are in no way related to Memnon the Greek (son of Tithonus and Eos, goddess of dawn), hero of the Trojan War. The Egyptians called all religious foundations *mennu,* and the ancient Greeks, combining this name with that of a man, identified it with their Memnon.

before the sun rose, and with a clearer note like the sound of a gong at the second hour, and yet a third time later, showing how beloved was the emperor among the gods. The court poetess, Balbilla, commemorated the occasion in Greek verses which are inscribed on the left leg of the colossus.

These are the last pictures we receive of a pharaoh exercising his governance in the land of Egypt. Half a century later, an earth tremor demolished the upper half of the statue of Memnon; and although it was crudely repaired, it never spoke again. During the same period, despite persecution, Christianity had established itself in the fifth century. In the second century, Christianity spread throughout the Delta and from there to the rest of Egypt, steadily ousting the old pagan religion and its cultural manifestations, including the writing of the native language in hieroglyphic and hieratic scripts, although demotic writing continued in use for the business of everyday life until the fifth century A.D. Such learning had by this late period become little more than the secret lore of a few priestly adepts, but with their displacement by the new activist presbyters, their pagan learning expired with them.

In the previous century the practice had arisen of writing the contemporary spoken Egyptian in the letters of the Greek alphabet, supplemented by seven characters derived from the demotic script to indicate sounds not represented in Greek speech. This script is called Coptic, after the Copts, the Christian descendants of the ancient Egyptians, and was chiefly employed in the writing of biblical and ecclesiastical literature. Indeed, the ancient language is still used for chanting and praying in the Coptic Church, though it has not been generally spoken or understood since the sixteenth century, when it died out in favor of Arabic.

The adoption of Christianity by the Egyptians was as much political as religious in its motivation. The imperial prefects from the time of Augustus onwards had ruthlessly exploited Egypt as a source of cheap grain for feeding the unruly mob at Rome. The xenophobia and resistance that such oppression provoked found the simple doctrines of the early Church particularly congenial. Moreover, Coptic religious thought embraced a concept which had been cherished in Egypt since earliest pagan times—that the Son of God was wholly divine, and every human element had been absorbed by his divinity. The Egyptian Church adhered fervently to this belief, even when the Council of Chalcedon in 451 A.D. promoted the rival doctrine that Christ combined a human with a divine nature.

The Monophysite dogma of the Copts was regarded as a heresy by the Eastern Orthodox Christians and alienated the Egyptians from their Byzantine rulers. In 641 A.D., they welcomed the armies of the Caliph Omar as their deliverers from an intolerable torment.

The Copts had desecrated the monuments of their pagan past, hammering out the figures of gods from the walls or covering them with plaster and whitewash in order to convert ancient shrines into Christian churches. The Mohammedans no less eyed askance the monuments of their ancient past with new-found revulsion as the work of the Devil and abandoned them to encroaching sands when they did not quarry them for convenient stone or eviscerate them in search of the treasures they were popularly thought to conceal. In the face of this indifference and even hostility, the study of Egypt's pagan past had to await a change of mind elsewhere, and this arose in Europe at the end of the Middle Ages when scholars returned to the inspiration of the literature of Greece and especially Rome. The revival of classical learning, however, meant that the Egyptian past was known only as it was reflected in the writings of Greek and Roman authors, many of whose manuscripts became available with the fall of Constantinople in 1453 A.D. and the dispersal of Byzantine scholars to the West.

Students of ancient Egypt were not well served by the writings of Classical authors. The first Greek visitors to Egypt in the seventh century B.C. were overawed

AMAZING EXCAVATIONS
Secrets lie underneath Alexandria, like this huge necropolis that dates back to the beginning of the common era.

23

by a wealthy and unified power in contrast to their own warring congeries of rival city-states. In seeking their own antecedents in a civilization that seemed to have existed since the beginning of time, they clutched gratefully at any straw that appeared familiar in a turbulent flood of novelties. Thus they heard the name of modern Luxor pronounced as something like *ta'ipe* (the Sanctuary) and thought it must be the original of their Thebes. They also tried to identify the gods of their pantheon with equivalents among the deities of Egypt, but they never really understood Egyptian religion and were inclined to see in inexplicable acts and beliefs a more profound significance than actually existed.

For Herodotus in the fifth century B.C., Egypt was remarkable for the number of marvels which it contained. Yet the inhabitants in their manners and customs seemed to have inverted the general practices of mankind. In his observations, he often goes sadly astray, but his remarks suffice to paint a picture of a nation apart, talented but perverse.

Other classical travelers, such as Diodorus Siculus and Strabo, found it difficult to reconcile what seemed to them childish beliefs with stupendous technical achievements, and they thought that an esoteric wisdom must lie behind the appearance of foolishness. Thus originated the myth of the superior and mysterious wisdom of the ancient Egyptians, which has persisted until very recently.

It is unfortunate that as Renaissance scholars became familiar with the works of Classical authors, they should also have fallen under the spell of the Neoplatonists who, in Alexandria in the third century A.D., developed Platonic ideas with oriental mysticism. An obsession with the meaning of symbols is characteristic of the Renaissance Neoplatonists. Horapollo's *Hieroglyphica* of the later fifth century A.D. was intensively studied, since his exposition of Egyptian hieroglyphs was particularly concerned with a mystical interpretation of these picture-signs. The works of other Classical commentators were also combed for further elucidation and only confirmed the view that Egyptian hieroglyphs conveyed abstract moral and philosophical ideas of profound significance, despite the extreme paucity of actual specimens of the script. The few examples that were available were almost exclusively

ALEXANDRIA: THRESHOLD OF HELLENISTIC CIVILIZATION

In 332 B.C., Alexander the Great chose to found a new city on a rocky isthmus located between the Mediterranean Sea and Lake Mariut, near the western branch of the Nile Delta. A long bay protected by Pharos Island became the site for a port that could harbor a sizable fleet. A sea wall was soon built to connect the island to the mainland. It was more than a half-mile long and formed a port with two basins. Alexander himself would have decided where the main urban sites were to be situated, but he had the city laid out by the Rhodian architect Deinocrates.

When Ptolemy, Alexander's former general and founder of the Lagid Dynasty, took control of the country, he left Memphis (the former Egyptian capital just south of the Nile Delta) and established his government in Alexandria. The city quickly became a rich commercial hub and an important cultural center.

Today, the ancient city, a masterpiece of antique urbanism, has almost disappeared. Modern buildings have replaced ancient ones, and the coastal area has been swallowed by the sea. Only the Serapeum, with its column said to be from Pompeii (although dedicated to Diocletian), underground areas, and tombs can be visited.

Ancient Alexandria, divided into five districts, was crossed from east to west and north to south by two large streets. A gigantic tower with a light at the top led seamen toward Pharos Island; this beacon was one of the Seven Wonders of the World.

The neighborhood of palaces was near the port and included official buildings, the theater, gardens, the zoo, tombs, the museum, and the library, the most famous one of antiquity. The largest city of ancient Egypt unfurled around this center, where Alexander was placed in a golden coffin upon his death.

carved upon obelisks carried off to Rome in imperial days. Some of these were still standing, while others were brought to light during building operations throughout the sixteenth and subsequent centuries.

The history of Egyptology in Europe over the next two centuries is an attempt to interpret hieroglyphic writing according to the esoteric Neoplatonist ideas. During the Age of Reason, skeptics with a more rational attitude towards the subject gradually emerged. In this long progression from mysticism to intellectual comprehension many scholars made small but significant contributions, notably Warburton and Young in Britain; Zoëga and Niebuhr in Denmark; Montfaucon, Barthelemy, and Silvestre de Sacy in France; and Åkerblad in Sweden. By the end of the eighteenth century, Egyptian studies were ready to take a new direction.

Reawakening

In 1798, this new course was set by a sudden and dramatic coup. Napoleon Bonaparte, at the head of a French army, dusted off a plan of campaign which the German philosopher Gottfried Leibniz had earlier urged upon Louis XIV. This embraced the mounting of an expedition to Egypt, with the construction of a canal across the isthmus of Suez as one of its objectives. But Napoleon decided also upon the study of the Egyptian past in the process. His exhortation to his troops at the Battle of the Pyramids—"Soldiers, forty centuries look down upon you"—rang up the curtain on the Romantic discovery of Egypt. The baggage train of his army included nearly 200 savants whose business it was to explore, describe, and

NAPOLEON'S SCHOLARS
The engineers, writers, and artists of the Egypt Commission discuss their plans in a garden. Europeans can thank them for unearthing the splendors of both ancient and modern Egypt, starting at the beginning of the 19th century.

25

even to excavate. No such scientific expedition had till then visited any ancient site, and it set a pattern for several such missions in the new century. While Napoleon's adventure was militarily ill-fated, it firmly established French ascendancy in the cultural affairs of Egypt. The 36 illustrated volumes of the *Description of Egypt*, in which Vivant Denon (1747–1825) and his collaborators described the monuments that they found in Egypt, appeared between 1809 and 1823 (2nd edition) and created the liveliest stir. For almost the first time, scholars in the seclusion of their libraries could study copies of ancient monuments and texts existing in the land of Egypt itself and were no longer dependent upon the meager trickle of miscellaneous antiquities that had come into the cabinets of dilettanti during the eighteenth century as a result of visits to Alexandria and Grand Cairo.

By the Capitulations of Alexandria, the British seized possession of the Rosetta Stone, a large fragment of basalt inscribed with a text in Greek, demotic, and hieroglyphic scripts, which a French officer had unearthed while digging a trench at Rosetta in the Western Delta. This antiquity, now in the British Museum, carried the trilingual text which scholars sought as a means of discovering the key to the hieroglyphic system of writing. Various students now took halting steps along the path of decipherment, but the credit for the first valid decipherment of hieroglyphs goes to the Frenchman Jean François Champollion (1790-1832), the virtual founder of Egyptology as a serious discipline. To his many natural gifts, Champollion added an extensive knowledge of Coptic as well as other oriental languages, and from his eventual recognition that hieroglyphs were merely a means of expressing in picture-signs a language which also survived in a greatly modified form written in Greek characters, his progress was rapid. In September 1822, his celebrated *Letter to M. Dacier,* read at a meeting of the Academie des Inscriptions et Belles Lettres in Paris, first gave the world the correct system for deciphering Egyptian hieroglyphs. The phenomenal progress that his studies had made in the short space of ten years, before his death in 1832 at the early age of 41, is seen in his *Precis* (1824) and in the grammar and materials for a dictionary that he left for posthumous publication.

THE ROSETTA STONE
Dated 196 B.C., this trilingual stele was unearthed in 1799 by Captain Bouchard while building a military fort near Rosetta, the small Egyptian port along the Mediterranean Sea.

Almost at a blow the scientific study of the ancient Egyptians had begun: for the first time since Theodosius I, they could speak for themselves.

Champollion's successors carried the study of the ancient language to ever greater degrees of refinement, so that today philology is a vast and separate study within the Egyptological ambit. The researches of Lepsius, Birch, Goodwin, Brugsch, Chabas, de Rougé, Maspero, Stern, Erman, and others in the nineteenth century consolidated the ground won and embraced also the intensive study of the hieratic and demotic scripts, as well as Coptic. In the twentieth century, the work of many philologists, but notably that of Möller, Griffith, Sethe, Gunn, and Gardiner, resulted in an ability to read most Egyptian texts with grammatical precision, even when the meaning is not entirely clear to our modern understanding. The greatest lack is in the documents themselves, the texts that have survived being but a fortuitous sampling of the ancient literature. Official inscriptions with historical implications carved in hieroglyphs on temples, stelae, and other monuments are not uncommon for some periods but are almost entirely lacking for others. Funerary and religious texts, often of baffling obscurity, are found written in hieroglyphic and hieratic scripts on temple walls, tomb chambers, coffins, and papyrus rolls. A meager selection of poems and stories has survived from a restricted period, largely because they were set as exercises for schoolboys to copy. Wisdom texts, satires, meditations, lamentations, and prophecies also exist. Works of a semi-scientific nature throw light on the ancient understanding of surgery, medicine, and mathematics. A single papyrus roll (the Wilbour Papyrus), giving a cadastral survey of Middle Egypt in the twelfth century B.C., has provided some insight into topography, taxation, the raising of summer crops, land-owning and ancillary matters. Opinions vary whether an incomplete account of a mission to the Lebanon in the eleventh century B.C. to buy cedar wood—the *Report of Wenamun*—is an official report or a work of fiction. The duties and responsibilities of a vizier are set out in a number of texts inscribed in some tombs of the earlier Eighteenth Dynasty. Other documents record contracts, lawsuits, the findings of royal commissions set up to investigate allegations of tomb-robbing, and a conspiracy in a royal harem. Correspondence, unfortunately all too rare, has also been recovered.

Further great finds of secular papyri, similar to those from the Theban area during the first half of the last century, seem unlikely, and future studies will have to focus upon a more accurate and intensive study of the documents already to hand. More meticulous translations of the ancient records have led to new evaluations and interpretations, and the pace of change in our knowledge of ancient Egypt is still brisk.

Explorations and discoveries

From the first, Champollion had realized that the crying need in his time was for more and accurate copies of inscriptions on the monuments still visible in Egypt, and in 1828, with the Italian scholar Ippolito Rosellini (1800–43), he embarked on a year-long survey. He was followed by others, notably the great Prussian expedition of Richard Lepsius (1810–84) in 1842–45. A vast store of inscriptional material from Egypt, Nubia, and the Sudan was published between 1849 and 1859 in the 12 massive volumes of Lepsius's *Monuments of Egypt and Ethiopia,* consisting of plates only; the text appeared posthumously (1897–1913). This remains a fundamental work and will never be entirely superseded, as some of the monuments it records have since been destroyed or mutilated. Its accuracy, unhappily, like that of its predecessors, is of a limited kind.

A ROOM WITH
24 COLUMNS
In Esna, the temple of Khnum, built during the Ptolemaic era, was already below the modern city when Lepsius, the scholar, made this engraving.

Later in the century, several expeditions shared in the work of recording surface monuments with a progressive degree of accuracy. In particular, the Egypt Exploration Fund (later Society), founded in 1882 by a band of amateurs in Britain who were deeply disturbed at the continuing destruction of the antiquities of Egypt, set itself the task of recording the more important of the extant monuments. The careful copying of monuments is still among the most valuable work undertaken by foreign missions in Egypt, notably by the Oriental Institute of the University of Chicago and the German and French Institutes in Cairo, in addition to the Egypt Exploration Society, and employs all the resources of photography and other modern techniques for securing and publishing a faithful record. Much, however, remains to be done in this particular field.

The French expedition of 1798 had set a fashion for visiting Egypt, and this burst into more feverish life at the end of the Napoleonic Wars, which had interrupted the tradition of the educational Grand Tour. By 1815, vistas had widened to include the Near East. The spirit of inquiry was also stimulated by a resurgence of piety on the part of European Christendom, with its reformed doctrines, evangelical fervor, and missionary zeal. Visits to the Biblical Lands became not only an object of idle curiosity but also an act of faith.

At the same time, the Albanian coffee-merchant-turned-soldier, Mohammed Ali (1769–1849), by a combination of ruthless cunning and sheer ability had made himself master of Egypt; suppressed the Mameluke beys, already defeated by Napoleon; and won a virtual independence from his Turkish overlord in Istanbul. His rule was marked by the creation of an effective army, the expansion of Egypt into Asia and the Sudan, and improvements in irrigation-works and agriculture. As he and his successors became more Westernized, many European doctors, engineers, bankers, merchants, missionaries, and the like were assisting in the travail of Egypt as a modern power.

But some of these Europeans were also interested in the antiquities that, since the French expedition and the discovery of the Rosetta Stone, had awakened Europe to the importance of actual objects as well as the inscriptions upon them. Even before Champollion had discovered how hieroglyphs should be read, the consuls of the various powers, particularly Henry Salt (1780-1827) of Britain and Bernardino Drovetti (1775-1852) of France, together with their agents, were vying with each other in amassing bigger and better *antikas*. It was this rivalry that filled the museums of London, Leyden, Paris, Turin, and other cities of Europe with huge monuments, which even today give the layman almost his only acquaintance with Egyptian antiquity. During this period of "unbridled pillage," almost as much was destroyed as was preserved. Tombs were opened with battering-rams or gunpowder, precious written records were reduced to disjointed scraps, and hardly anything was secured with its pedigree intact. Into this spoiling of the ancient Egyptians their descendants entered with as much zest as anyone, being only too eager to sell chance finds that they neither understood nor cherished.

In 1854, an event occurred which was to have far-reaching effects on the rediscovery of the Egyptian past. A young French official of the Louvre, Auguste Mariette (1821–81), was commissioned to go to Egypt and collect Coptic manuscripts, but while on a visit to Saqqara, thinking that he recognized half-buried in the sands

THE TEMPLE OF LUXOR
Around 1840, when D. Roberts made this engraving, the temple of Luxor was disappearing under rubble and modern buildings. Work to clear the area began in 1883 and lasted many years.

29

monuments which seemed to mark an ancient site described by Strabo, coolly renounced his mission and "almost furtively" began to dig. This enterprise, which took him four years to complete, uncovered the vast Serapeum (the tomb of the sacred Apis bulls) and greatly enriched the Louvre with antiquities of different periods. It also sealed his destiny, for in 1858 the Khedive Said appointed him conservator of monuments, and thereafter his life was dedicated to the excavation and preservation of the antiquities of Egypt on her own soil. The creation and development of an antiquities service to promote and regulate proper archaeological exploration and the establishment of a national museum to display, conserve, and facilitate the study of Egyptian antiquities were the life-work of Mariette, who relentlessly carried out his mission in the face of obstacles from all sides—the intrigues of dealers and officials who were doing well out of the unregulated sale of *antikas,* the jealousies of other scholars who thought they could do better, and the indifference and treachery of the Khedive himself.

While Mariette's labors cannot be underestimated, much of what he achieved would have been lost if his immediate successor, another Frenchman, Gaston Maspero (1846–1916), had not followed him as director-general in 1881. Maspero's long and diplomatic, though interrupted, tenure of office saw the firm consolidation of the shaky foundations of the antiquities service and the training of Egyptians to play an increasing part in its concerns. The building of a worthy museum and the proper publishing of results were also actively pursued.

By the eighties of the century, the exertions of such scholars, and their works of popularization, had created new patrons of Egyptology—the educated middle classes of Europe and America, many of whom had visited the Nile Valley, and who, banded together in learned societies, were prepared to give the financial support that hitherto had been provided only by wealthy individuals or state coffers.

In 1884, the Egypt Explorations Fund commissioned for their explorations at Tanis a comparatively unknown surveyor, Flinders Petrie (1853–1942), who was destined to revolutionize the technique of excavation in Egypt. Petrie was a man of no systematic education but with the most remarkable natural gifts, which he dedicated entirely during his long lifetime to the pursuit of Egyptian and Palestinian archaeology. Applying the principles of excavation first invented in Britain by General Pitt-Rivers, and developing them in an Egyptian milieu, he broke entirely with the traditions of the old déblayeurs, who were concerned only with uncovering substantial buildings from encroaching sands or moving colossal monuments into museums. He paid attention to the many unconsidered trifles that had previously been overlooked or despised,

AUGUSTE MARIETTE
In this portrait dated 1861, the French scholar is dressed in the oriental style, in clothes well-suited to the Egyptian climate.

MARIETTE AND THE FIRST EGYPTIAN MUSEUM

Viceroy of Egypt between 1854 and 1863, Saïd Pacha strove to modernize his country. He developed the railway, supported Ferdinand de Lesseps's plan to build the Suez Canal, and understood the advantages of excavations that revealed Egypt's glorious past. In 1857, he called back Auguste Mariette, who had returned to France a few years earlier. He financed the French Egyptologist to do excavation work and to found a museum in Boulaq, near Cairo, in which the objects found could be displayed. In 1858, Mariette was appointed director of the Service of Antiquities of Egypt and was made responsible for protecting everything.

Despite his respect for Mariette, Pacha considered the museum to be his, a kind of store where he chose gifts to offer to his distinguished guests. Mariette convinced him to stop such behavior. In the four rooms on the ground floor, the Egyptologist set up display cases in which more than 22,000 objects were soon piled—and very quickly ran out of space.

In 1863, Ismaïl Pacha, Said Pacha's successor, gave Mariette the money needed to expand the Boulaq museum. This is where the scholar was buried, in a marble sarcophagus topped by a bronze statue. The museum, still too small, would later be moved to Cairo.

the scribbles on potsherds, the broken bits of amulets and rings, fragments of crude domestic pottery, loose beads, discarded drill cores—all the dross and rubbish of antiquity—and he showed that in their context they had a story to tell. Many of his innovations are now so much the accepted practice of field archaeology that it is difficult to believe that they were once revolutionary, such as the use of melted wax to secure fragile objects *in situ,* or the study of the stylistic development and degeneration of artifacts as a means of dating. For half a century, he followed the routine of excavating a site in the winter months and publishing the results in the following summer. His publications are an almost inexhaustible mine of information and are indispensable despite the faults occasioned by haste and often the exercise of a too-imaginative leap to conclusions. In his time he trained two generations of excavators, and his methods were adopted and developed by others.

The techniques followed by Petrie and his pupils revolutionized fieldwork in Egypt and have resulted in considerable refinement in excavation methods, requiring the collaboration of several specialists and the incorporation of statistical analyses in the marshaling of data.

In recent years, a much greater emphasis has been placed upon survey methods, in which the maximum information is gained from an area without the destruction inherent to excavation, although this of course remains a fundamental means of recovering an ancient site. A means of penetrating below the surface without even lifting a trowel exists in various remote-sensing techniques, such as resistivity measurement. These detect anomalies below the ground that can indicate the presence of buildings, tombs, and other features. They have been successfully applied in the Valley of the Kings, Saqqara, and a number of other locations.

Yet more "new" approaches include ethnoarchaeology and experimental archaeology. These harness the observation of modern handling of archaic problems and practical attempts to reproduce ancient results. The British expedition to Tell el-Amarna under Barry J. Kemp has seen much work in these directions, including the brewing of ancient Egyptian beer, following the excavation of a brewery sponsored by a modern British equivalent.

ALREADY TOURISTS
Seated on a broken statue or standing with a triumphant air, these tourists from the 1900s are resting for a few moments during their visit. Inexhaustible, their guide is admiring the hieroglyphics.

AN ARTISAN'S TOMB
*The ruins of a village of
artisans at the foot of the
Theban mountain, in
Deir el-Medina, and its
New Kingdom necropolis
has amazed excavators.
Before World War I, first
the Italians, then the French
began to dig at this site. In
1925, workers carefully
removed one of the tombs.*

Changes in the Egyptian antiquities service's regulations in 1936 led to a reduction in the number of foreign missions working in the country, with their activities effectively stopped by the outbreak of war three years later. Egyptian archaeologists, on the other hand, made some important discoveries between 1939 and 1945 and in subsequent years. Foreign work was, however, slow in recommencing owing to post-war economic difficulties, the political problems that followed the Egyptian revolution, and the Suez Crisis of 1956.

In 1960, however, the threat to the ancient sites in Nubia and the Sudan that arose through the proposed creation of a vast lake behind the High Dam at Aswan in 1971 induced the authorities to relax their conditions, and foreign missions were cordially invited to take part in a crash program to rescue the doomed monuments. Much of the old fruitful cooperation between the foreign expeditions and the native antiquities services was restored. International experts collaborated in recording and moving the threatened temples and other monuments to places of safety. Other missions excavated sites threatened by total immersion, uncovering new information in the process and publishing their results. In return, they received a proportion of the finds not retained by the national museums in Cairo and Khartoum. Important antiquities from other sites in Egypt, and some of the dismantled temples from the threatened riverine area, were offered in return for the services rendered. In this way, for example, the shrine of Pedesi and Pihor from Dendur has been re-erected in New York, and a colossal sandstone head of Akhenaten from Karnak is now proudly displayed in the Louvre.

Such cooperation has happily continued since this huge rescue operation, and it continues to be welcomed in view of fresh threats to the ancient sites in Egypt itself, with the rapid encroachment of agriculture and industrialization, not to mention the general rise in subsoil water as a result of perennial irrigation.

There are still aspects of the Egyptian heritage, however, both ancient and medieval, that arouse concern. It is not sufficient to excavate with skill and record with accuracy. Publication and conservation are also important, and the antiquities rescued from oblivion must be made readily available for exhibition and study. Such obligations, which Egypt shares with other advanced nations, are a drain upon resources. The Egyptian Museum is now badly crowded, and its material in store is not easily accessible. The same conditions prevail at the many local magazines scattered on the important sites, despite the building of a fine new museum at Luxor. The monuments themselves are suffering from the constant attentions of thousands of visitors and a rise in industrial pollution.

A number of earthquakes have also undermined the structures of certain monuments, and flash floods caused further damage to Theban tombs. Yet another threat is posed by the astronomical prices commanded by Egyptian artifacts on the international art market. High-level corruption has seen scenes cut from the walls of sealed and protected monuments, to reemerge shorn of all identifying features in the salerooms of Europe, America, and Japan.

Only with the full cooperation and goodwill of the international community can projects to safeguard Egypt's heritage come to full fruition—cooperation which is owed to a land that possesses so much of mankind's cultural patrimony.

Magic writing

BEWITCHMENT

On this 9th Dynasty statuette, depicting a nude man with his arms bound, the following inscription can be read: "The death of Henoury, son of Antef." This is about a dangerous dead man wandering across the land, whom they want to stop from causing harm by representing him and naming him. The fact that the statuette was "inscribed" made him real and also subjugated him. The magic could work.

The Egyptians called their writing "divine words." The ancient Greeks named it *hieroglyphoi*, which translates as "sacred carving."

Archives dating back to ancient times inform us about when, how, and why writing was born. (Writing is considered to exist when signs are not isolated but are integrated into a whole.) As early as 3150 B.C. in Egypt, royal proper names were being inscribed in hieroglyphics on monuments. The words in this case had a magical function to prolong the life of the king and to manifest his presence.

Hieroglyphics had a sacred character, which is not the case with cursive (hieratic) writing, which seems as ancient as the hieroglyphic monumental writing. In addition, both ideas and sounds were represented in hieroglyphic symbols, written horizontally or vertically in either direction. The earliest hieroglyphs were annotations to the scenes cut in relief on slabs of slate in chapels or tombs; the writings were donated as votive offerings.

Considered to be the language of the creator, hieroglyphics were alone in being able to correctly say things. In certain circumstances, they also created and gave a reality to named things. Representations like drawings and paintings, or the objects in tombs or temples, were there for their utility and not for their beauty. They were not even meant to be seen.

The effectiveness of the writing was based on the fact that it both named things and was itself made up of things. Each hieroglyph was believed to possess authentic power, and each word was the authentic representation of the object named. These drawings and images were found everywhere—not only on papyrus but on walls, statues, and everyday items.

The great majority of Egyptians were illiterate. Only high-ranking figure—civil servants, servicemen, priests, and the many scribes who worked under their orders—knew how to write. Present throughout the country, these scribes noted what was to be known by the king and his envoys: grain production, river levels, the number of residents, and so forth. Every day, the premier Egyptian scribes passed on the orders from their superiors and applied the decisions that had been made. Other scribes were responsible for religious texts, wrote amulets, or recounted royal exploits.

HIEROGLYPHICS IN MOLTEN GLASS *(4th century B.C.) Religious phrases and protective mythological scenes are combined on Petosiris's sarcophagus in superb alignment.*

A SCRIBE AT WORK *(New Kingdom) The scribe oversaw the work of artisans and peasants. He calculated and collected the tax. If necessary, his helpers would fight bad payers.*

SCHOOLBOY'S TABLET *(New Kingdom) On this wooden tablet, the student scribe systematically noted his work dates. His exercises in copying hieratics were staggered over 17 days; accordingly, he wrote two lines per session!*

HIERATIC WRITING *(papyrus, New Kingdom) For daily messages, the scribes simplified hieroglyphics, which were too long to copy. This was hieratic writing. The signs no longer had any resemblance to drawing.*

URGENT ORDER *(19th Dynasty) On this piece of broken pottery, a Theban scribe reminds Nakhtamon, the carpenter, that he has to make four 12 x 16-inch barred windows "by tomorrow."*

THE TOOLS OF THE SCRIBE

"My profession is the most important of all," brags the Egyptian scribe, proud of being one of the rare people who could read, write, and count. He chewed on the end of his calamus, a simple reed, or sharpened it to a point to make a brush. He dipped it in water to dilute his inks. He prepared black ink with black from smoke and red ink with ochre, the iron oxide drawn from the ground. The scribe wrote dates, chapter titles, or important points in red. He placed his ink tablets in his palette's cup, which also served as a box for his calamus. While there were six or eight cups in the palette of the painter-draftsman, whose job was to decorate the papyrus vignettes, the palette of the scribe-writer had only two. The palettes were fitted with ties so that the owners could hang them from their belts when traveling.

CHAPTER 2

The ancient places

Sudan and Nubia

The heavy monsoon rains that fall on the Abyssinian tableland each year from May to September swell the waters of the Blue Nile and change it into an immense mountain torrent, rising in spate and sweeping all before it. The raging flood grinds the boulders in its bed and carries the finer red-brown silt in suspension for thousands of miles. At the modern town of Khartoum, the Blue Nile is joined by the White Nile, which flows from the natural reservoir of the great lakes of central Africa and provides a steady flow of clear water throughout the summer months. Almost 200 miles north of Khartoum, the last great tributary, the Atbara, rising in the Abyssinian plateau, pours its flood into the Nile during the rainy season. At other times, it shrinks into a number of pools within its sandy bed. By the middle of June, the inundation formerly reached Aswan and continued to rise in Egypt until the beginning of September, when it slowly fell and disappeared by the following spring. This is the river system which the Egyptians since prehistoric times have tried to control and which they only succeeded in taming with the building of the Aswan High Dam.

From the Atbara northwards, the main stream flows in a vast sweep between tawny hills of Nubian sandstone. Its passage through this hot, flybitten region is

IN THE HEART OF AFRICA
The Nile, the longest river in the world at over 4,000 miles, was born at the equator. The waters of the White Nile, the Blue Nile, and the Atbara mix before entering Egypt. Running over hard terrain in a steep bed, the Blue Nile breaks into impressive waterfalls.

impeded at five major points by reefs of hard igneous stone, polished black by the action of sun and spray and forming the cataracts or turbulent rapids amid craggy islands. Between the Fourth and Third Cataracts stands Gebel Barkal, the southernmost boundary of Egypt at the time of its greatest expansion in the New Kingdom, when the dependencies of Wawat (Nubia) and Kush (the lower Sudan) were under the charge of an Egyptian "prince" or viceroy, appointed by the pharaoh. From here northward lie the sand-engulfed ruins of the outposts of empire which the Egyptians built at this period at Sesebi, Sulb, and Amara.

About 15 miles north of this point, the traveler reaches the southernmost shore of Lake Nasser, the great artificial lake that has been formed by damming the Nile near Aswan, 300 miles to the north. Lake Nasser has drowned all the ancient sites on the banks of the Nile and effectively expunged Nubia from the map of Africa. Many of the visible monuments, such as the two great *speos* (rock-cut) temples at Abu Simbel, have been removed to higher ground in various enclaves or to the museum precincts at Khartoum and elsewhere.

SAVED FROM THE WATERS
Ramses II undertook an enormous construction project when he built the temples of Abu Simbel. The men of the 20th century matched it by moving them a few miles so that they wouldn't be swallowed up by the waters of Lake Nasser. The four colossi at the façade, representing Ramses II seated, were not damaged in the move.

Upper Egypt

About 4 miles south of Aswan, the northern extremity of Lake Nasser is marked by the High Dam opened in 1971. From this giant reservoir the Nile, now carefully controlled, flows into the channel that it has worn throughout the ages in a great still of granite, which interrupts the broad mass of Nubian sandstone. The action of the water has eroded the granite barrier into a string of rocky islands, of which Elephantine is the most northerly. In this frontier region of granite outcrops and rocks sculptured by the swirl of the rapids into fanciful abstract shapes, inscriptions cut into the stone mark the passage of ancient viceroys and other officials to and from their seats of government farther south.

Many of the graffiti were carved with propitiatory prayers to the gods of the cataract by travelers anxiously preparing to undertake the hazardous passage of the rapids. Other graffiti commemorate the successful completion of great works in the quarries of the vicinity, such as the extraction of obelisks and colossi.

The granites, basalts, and quartzites of the Aswan region have always been the main sources of hard stone in Egypt. Impressive evidence of the ancient workings is found in the northern quarry on the east bank, where an unfinished obelisk still lies undetached in its giant trench. It is over 130 feet long and weighs some 1,170 tons—i.e., six times as much as the "Cleopatra's Needle" on the Thames embankment in London. A series of fissures in the granite matrix, which were only revealed as the work reached a late state, obliged the engineers to abandon their project. Massive monuments that were even heavier, such as the colossus of Ramesses II in his mortuary temple, or another at Tanis, were successfully extracted and moved hundreds of miles to the north.

The quarrying operations were important to the east bank, which also had the function, like so many frontier settlements, of acting as an entrepot and customs house for imports from the south. The name of Aswan derives from the Egyptian word for "trade" or "market."

The natural political and defensive boundary was on the island of Elephantine, in the middle of the river just below the cataract. This was the southernmost extent of Egypt proper, and it was proverbial that a native from the island would be unintelligible to the Delta-dwellers, probably because he would speak the Nubian language, which still persists, along with the Nubian race, to the north.

Elephantine maintained a frontier fortress and a garrison from early times. A Jewish cohort was stationed there during Persian times in the sixth century B.C. and got on bad terms with the local populace through religious disputes, as we learn from Aramaic papyri found on the site. In the later Old Kingdom (ca. 2663–2195 B.C.), the pharaoh's peace was kept by the local barons who bore the title of Keeper of

THE UNFINISHED OBELISK
Several obelisks come from the granite quarries in Aswan. Some unfinished ones are still there. They weigh several tons and therefore the removing, transporting, and erecting of them was difficult.

QUARRIES: THE WEALTH OF EGYPT

The deserts of Egypt provided fine stone for sculptors and architects, who could use each kind for its best qualities. Each kind of stone required its own technique. In the limestone quarries near Memphis, workers cut levels, while along the Aswan they exploded granite out in the open. In Wadi Hammamat, they gathered the schist which had cracked and fallen. They also extracted red quartz, diorite, alabaster, and other minerals.

Their work methods were simple: They chose what they needed from among the blocks that had fallen on the landing or, after climbing the mountain, rolled other blocks so that they would break when they fell. Finally, if necessary, they attacked the rock. To make holes, quarry workers struck the contours of the blocks to be extracted. They then inserted pieces of wood in the holes and saturated them with water. The wood would swell and the stone would split, break

apart, and fall from the rock. Placed on sleds, the rocks were dragged to the river and transported.

Mining the quarries was neither permanent nor regular. The pharaoh would organize an expedition as needed, sometimes with several thousand men. A large, efficient management crew consisted of managers, army scribes, officers of the central government, police officers, artist foremen, quarry foremen, head draftsmen, and head engravers. Soldiers supervised the quarry workers and stone masons who formed the majority of the company. Mostly prisoners of war or common law criminals, the workers provided the wealth of the country: It was because of them that the land was covered with luxurious temples. Meanwhile, the important figures, who were accustomed to luxury, were the ones who spent eternity in magnificent tombs decorated with superb funerary objects.

the Gateway of the South. These marcher lords are among the earliest African explorers who have left any account of their adventures. They led trading caravans and punitive expeditions far into the southern hinterland and recorded some of their experiences in the tombs, which they built for themselves along a hill terrace on the western bank. Thus we read of the exploits of Harkhuf, who brought back a dancing pygmy to the delight of his young king.

Elephantine was always renowned for its religious significance. The Nile was believed to well up every year from a cavern beneath the island to produce the inundation, and this miracle was accomplished by a ram-head aspect of the Creator, the god Khnum, who ruled the entire cataract region. He was accompanied by two goddesses to form a triad—his consort Satis and his daughter Anukis. A restored Nilometer with its calibrated steps leading down from the high bank to the low water-level still bears witness to the importance of Elephantine in the use of the Nile flood.

It was customary in the Eighteenth Dynasty, at least, for kings to celebrate their second jubilees by

NILOMETER MEASURES

The Nile regularly floods, and its water levels were essential elements in the daily life of ancient Egyptians. Each temple had its Nilometer, a steep stone staircase that descended into the river. A priest in charge of the Nilometer would read the water level regularly.

At certain times of year, the Egyptians would gather around these wells to sing hymns and make offerings to Hâpî, the spirit of the Nile. In the course of the ceremony they threw into the river things as varied as cakes, fruit, amulets, female figurines, and animals that had been sacrificed. In this way they fed the force of the flood, which they considered the source of all wealth. The person in charge of the Nilometer had to watch for the beginnings of the flood so that the ceremonies would take place at the right time.

Furthermore, the Nilometer readings were sent to the pharaoh. If the flood was adequate, the harvest would be good, and therefore taxes would be raised. A flood of 16 cubits (more than 24 feet) was considered satisfactory.

The most famous Nilometer at Elephantine Island looks something like a winding stairwell with a wide landing. Its 90 steps dive into the Nile, and the graduated scale on the walls measures the river's water level.

erecting little peripteral temples on Elephantine in honor of the Khnum triad. Pillars from shrines with the names of Amenhotep II and Thutmose IV can be seen in the foundations of the temple at the southern end of the island, where various kings have added their constructions over several centuries—the most recent being that of the Emperor Trajan. By this time, however, Elephantine had lost its primacy as the seat of the inundation to the island of Bigga, 8 miles to the south, where tradition affirmed that the left leg of the god Osiris had been buried, and where his tomb was situated. The drowned Osiris was believed to float in the Nile at each flood time, when he became the "Lord of the Inundation." The legend was fostered by the presence of the cult of Isis, the wife of Osiris, on the adjacent island of Philae, which became the center of the cult of Isis and the Horus-child and a place of pilgrimage for her worshippers throughout the Roman world.

The temples on Philae, now rebuilt on the adjacent island of Agilkia, are the first of a series of magnificent stone buildings that arose on ancient foundations at Kom Ombo, Edfu, and Esna in Ptolemaic and Roman times as far as Dendera 115 miles to the north. These vast edifices, in their huge proportions, their unstinted use of sandstone and granite, their elaborate floriated capitals, their astronomical ceilings, and their scrupulous detail and technical triumphs, have a solemn grandeur. They were built according to an architectural plan which was supposed to have been revealed in a codex that fell from heaven at Saqqara in the days of Imhotep. The most complete of them is the temple of the falcon god Horus at Edfu, built between

PHILAE
The Temple of Isis, with its impressive pylons, was located to the south of Aswan on a tiny island. Nearby, the Roman Kiosk of Trajan (a kind of embarcadero), offered easier access to the goddess's processions.

237 and 57 B.C., the most perfectly preserved monument of the ancient world. Its many inscriptions have bequeathed a wealth of information about the founding of such temples, their construction and use, and the daily ritual.

Its companion temple of the goddess Hathor at Dendera was linked to Edfu by a new-year festival. Amid scenes of wild rejoicing on both banks of the river, the image of Hathor was brought in her gilded barge, like Cleopatra in her meeting with Antony on the Cydnus, to repose in the birth-temple at Edfu. As a result of this union, a divine child, Horus, Uniter of Upper and Lower Egypt, was engendered. The temple of Dendera deeply impressed the French expedition, and through the engravings in their *Description of Egypt* influenced the design of contemporary architecture and the applied arts.

At Edfu, the yellow Nubian sandstone gives way to the pinkish nummulitic limestone from which the Nile has scoured its ancient bed, and for the next 350 miles the river flows between verges of rich alluvial soil hemmed in on both sides by arid desolation. On the west lies the Western or Libyan Desert, an immense eroded tableland broken by lines of shifting sand-hills and by a string of fertile depressions which run almost parallel to the Nile. These oases are watered by subterranean wells supplied from the Nile water-table, and their inhabitants have traded their produce with Egypt from earliest times.

The Arabian desert on the east presents an awe-inspiring landscape as it thrusts a protective range of barren mountains rising to over 6,500 feet between the Nile Valley and the Red Sea. It is scored by deep wadis, or dry water-courses, which on occasions can become raging torrents as sudden and violent storms break out over the desert hills, especially in winter. Protected by these inhospitable deserts, Egypt exists for most of its length as a narrow strip of cultivated land, seldom more than 7 miles in width and often much less.

A dozen miles north of Edfu, at Kom el-Ahmar and Elkab, lie the ruins of the twin cities Nekhen and Nekheb, on opposite banks of the Nile, which together probably formed the capital of Upper Egypt in prehistoric times. The former site was first dug at the end of the nineteenth century and revealed antiquities of the highest importance in the study of the Predynastic and Archaic Periods. A long-term program of work has greatly expanded our knowledge of the growth of what was one of the very earliest of Egyptian cities. Named Hierakonpolis by the Greeks, the town had a falcon god as its local deity and may have been the natal town of the kings who were ultimately to unite Egypt. Elkab, on the other hand, was presided over by a vulture, Nekhebet ("she-of-Nekheb"), who came to be regarded as the patron genius of the whole of Upper Egypt. She is frequently associated with her counterpart, the cobra goddess Edjo of Buto and Lower Egypt, in heraldic devices.

Elkab is notable for its stout walls of mud brick still standing, though the considerable space that they enclose, larger than the town site, is something of an enigma. Here too in the eastern hills are tombs of worthies who during the sixteenth century B.C. played an important part in the wars of their Theban overlords against the Hyksos power in the far north. Texts inscribed on their chapel walls and two of their statues are valuable records of the early Eighteenth Dynasty. The most impressive of the tombs, however, despite some ancient and modern damage, is that of Paheri, dating to the early reign of Thutmose III. Its carefully sculptured low reliefs give interesting scenes from Paheri's life as governor of the locality but are more remarkable for the amusing, even punning, captions to the various incidents represented, including a jingle, first identified by Champollion, that the herdsmen sing as they drive the cattle around the threshing-floor: "Thresh away, oxen tread the grain faster; straw for yourselves, corn for your master."

THE CAPITALS OF DENDERA
To the north of Luxor, the temple of the goddess Hathor is topped by capitals that depict her. She has the face of a woman and ears of a cow.

Thebes, center of resistance

From Elkab, the Nile describes a huge S-bend as far as Koptos, about 120 miles farther north, and almost midway between these two points on the east bank stands the modern town of Luxor, which with the adjoining village of Karnak

SYMBOLS OF THE MONARCHY

Far from being only symbolic attributes, the emblems of the monarchy were filled with very real power and enlivened by a supernatural life. They were considered "great by their spells."

Before the country was unified, the prince of the South Kingdom wore the white crown belonging to the vulture-goddess Nekhbet. The prince of the North Kingdom wore the red crown belonging to the goddess Neith, which was adorned with Ouadjet's cobra. Attached to the ruler's forehead, this cobra protected the monarchy from its enemies by spitting burning venom. These emblems survived throughout all of Egyptian history, while others were added.

Under the first pharaohs, the two crowns— the red and the black—were combined to form the *pschent*, the symbol of the kingdom. The royal headwear then diversified: The pharaoh wore the *khepresh* (a blue crown) or the *neme,* (striped fabric wrapping the head). Other symbols were added to such headwear: a very short fake beard; the *héka* scepter, which was hooked; and the *flagellum*, nicknamed "the flycatcher."

On the pharaoh's throne, two gods of the Nile were represented facing each other and intertwining lotus and papyrus around the hieroglyphic *sma* ("to unite"). These gods were the symbols of Upper Egypt and Lower Egypt.

and other localities forms the site of Thebes, the southern capital at the period of Egypt's greatest development during the New Kingdom. To Belzoni, the Italian adventurer who acted as the agent of the British Consul Henry Salt early in the nineteenth century, the remains of Karnak and Luxor were like those of "a city of giants, who after long conflict were all destroyed, leaving the ruins of their various temples as the only proofs of their former existence." After more than a century of clearances and excavations, the picture is still true.

It is, however, on the west bank, with its many ruined temples and cemeteries, that the most intensive exploration has been made during the past century. It is from these realms of the dead that the bulk of the antiquities have come that grace the collections of Europe, America, and Egypt itself.

Perhaps it was the luminous quality of the atmosphere in this locality that induced the Thebans to conceive of Amun, their city god, as having sovereignty over air and light.

Thebes rose to prominence only in the Middle Kingdom when its local princes fought their way to supreme power and ruled as pharaohs over a reunited Egypt. Throughout its history, Thebes remained a center of resistance to alien rule from the north. After the expulsion of the Hyksos by its princes, it won great prestige and wealth as the birthplace of the new dynasts. It was here that the pharaohs now had their tombs hewn in the rock of a lonely wadi on the west bank, the Valley of the Kings, dominated by a pyramidal hill, "The Peak." The wadi was used for the burials of kings from Thutmost I down to the end of the Twentieth Dynasty, when Rameses XI left his tomb unfinished there. In addition, during the Eighteenth Dynasty, a number of very favored private individuals were granted burial chambers there, although their mortuary chapels remained amongst those of their peers, on hillsides facing the Nile. These chapels, which honeycomb the hills, together with many burial chambers, are of great importance, as their painted walls have bequeathed us many lively scenes of contemporary life and aspirations.

All the pharaohs' tombs in the Valley of the Kings were pillaged at various times during the New Kingdom itself, with one exception: That of Tutankhamun escaped anything more than superficial robbery and survived to be discovered in 1922. The despoiled bodies of other royalties were hidden away by officials in two mass burials, two of which were only discovered in the nineteenth century; interestingly, it appears that these very same officials were responsible for relieving the tombs of what precious material remained in them before transferring their occupants to places of safety.

The mortuary temples which complemented the royal tombs stood in a row a mile away, facing the Nile and overlooked by the tomb-chapels of the nobility. They stretch from Gurna in the north to Medinet Habu in the south and include those of almost all pharaohs from the early Eighteenth Dynasty to the latter part of the Twentieth, by which time the king was permanently resident in the Delta.

THE VALLEY
OF THE KINGS
During the 18th Dynasty, Thutmose I was the first pharaoh to have his tomb built into the Theban mountain, on the Nile's west bank. More than 60 other pharaohs would do the same.

ROYAL STATUES
*The stone pharaohs at
the Temple of Luxor
wear the traditional
double crown and
fake beard. They are
accompanied by the
queens, who barely
come to the height
of their knees.*

The rise of Thebes naturally increased the influence and wealth of Amun, whose great temple at Karnak became a sort of national shrine to which kings of all subsequent periods added their chapels and endowments. The brief but momentous reign of the so-called heretic pharaoh Akhenaten in the fourteenth century B.C. encouraged the eclipse of the many local gods of Egypt in favor of his sole god, the Aten. But none suffered more grievously than the wealthy Amun, whose images were smashed, whose shrines were desecrated, and whose priests were dispersed. Amun, however, recovered, though slowly, under subsequent kings.

Even early in the Eighteenth Dynasty, Thebes had ceased to be the pharaoh's chief residence, and thereafter it gradually became the holy city of Amun, the king of the gods, and therefore a focus for pilgrimages. In the ancient world, the feasts of the gods were momentous affairs of which the modern Christian Easter and Christmas are but echoes. The celebrations of the festivals of Amun were sufficiently important to bring rulers to Thebes to take part in these joyous events. Thus the feast of Opet—during which the Amun triad were towed in their resplendent barges, amid rejoicings on both canal banks, from Karnak to Luxor during the second month of inundation—was an occasion when the god gave oracular judgments on human affairs not capable of resolution by normal means. Several kings found it expedient to attend these events when their assumption of power, or nomination to the throne, received divine approval.

ROYAL STATUES
The stone pharaohs at the Temple of Luxor wear the traditional double crown and fake beard. They are accompanied by the queens, who barely come to the height of their knees.

The west bank at Thebes was also within the domain of Amun, who had first manifested himself at the creation of the world in the form of the primeval snake, Kneph, residing in an underground cavern at Medinet Habu. The barque of Amun, containing his veiled image, or fetish, was taken across the river in the second month of summer for a festival. Thus Amun of Thebes united the world of the living on the east bank and the realms of the dead on the west. But in the latter region, he also shared his power with the goddess

Hathor, the patroness of the deserts in which the necropolises were situated. She was manifest as a wild cow, or a comely queen wearing cow's horns on her crown, and her image is encountered frequently in the temples and tombs of Western Thebes.

The sunset of Thebes was long and blood red. In the seventh century B.C. it was sacked by the Assyrians. The Persians under Cambyses assailed it a century and a half later. Under the Ptolemies, the rival center of Ptolemais eclipsed it in power and privilege, though it recovered some self-esteem for a time during the rebellion against Ptolemy V. It again revolted under Ptolemy X and was recaptured after a lengthy siege which wrought great damage. Undeterred by its unlucky fate, it opposed the oppressive rule of the Romans in 30 B.C. and was thoroughly devastated for its pains. Of the "hundred gated Thebes" mentioned by Homer, only a dozen damaged pylons among the temple ruins now remain.

HATHOR, GODDESS OF MANY FACES

At the time of the first pharaohs, Hathor was the goddess of the sky as well as wife or mother of Horus, the sun god. Her name means "House of Horus." She gradually lost this characteristic but continued to be represented as a cow, a sun disk between her horns. Hathor was alternately represented as a pretty woman with either the ears or head of a cow.

In time, Hathor became the nurturer *par excellence*, the goddess of motherhood, women, love, joy, music, and festivity. She was able to make young people fall in love, and maternity was a natural consequence. In the temples dedicated to Hathor, women celebrated her with dances and songs accompanied by the sounds of their sistrums (metal rattles with handles), tambourines, and necklaces.

From Upper Egypt, Hathor's worship spread far and wide. Consequently, she was identified with several local goddesses, as at Deir al-Bahri. Because of the city's nearness to the necropolises of Thebes, she became "Lady of the West" and patroness of the region of the dead. Hathor greeted the newly deceased on the day of the burial ceremonies. Rising from the side of the desert mountain, she would watch the funeral procession go by, allowing the sun and the dead enter into the afterlife.

Abydos, home of Osiris

Some 100 miles north of Thebes as the Nile flows lies Abydos, the next ancient site of importance, near the modern village of el-Araba in an area which is rich in prehistoric cemeteries. Somewhere within its bounds, probably near Girga, was This, the seat of the immediate ancestors of the first pharaohs. The kings of the First Dynasty built their tombs and associated funerary enclosures at This, surrounded by the graves of their retainers.

The local god was originally a black dog-like animal known as the "Chief of the Westerners" — i.e., the Lord of the Dead. But by the Eleventh Dynasty, his position and titles had been entirely absorbed by another god, Osiris, who was probably a human manifestation of the same chthonic power. Osiris is represented as a king in his mummy wrappings, wearing the characteristic conical White Crown of Upper Egypt. As a death god of Upper Egypt, he was identified with similar deities in Lower Egypt, such as the falcon-headed Sokar, who gave his name to the necropolis of Memphis at Saqqara, where he existed in a cavernous underworld. As a prehistoric king, Osiris also assimilated the similar god Andjeti of Busiris in the Delta, usurping his herdsman's crook and "flail" and the two tall plumes of his headgear. Andjeti was evidently in origin a deified pastoral chieftain who had been ritually slain by drowning and whose dismembered corpse was buried in various parts of the country for its greater fertility. By the middle of the Fifth Dynasty, a song sung by peasants refers to the Herdsman of the West drowned in the Nile flood.

Abydos rapidly rose to fame in the Middle Kingdom as Osiris's principal cult-center and the place where his mythical tomb was located. The Egyptian antiquarians of the Thirteenth Dynasty, seeking tangible proofs of the ancient myth, mistook the contaph of Djer, the third king of the united Egypt, for the tomb of the god, and so directed to it the votive offerings of generations of pious pilgrims.

The pilgrimage to the holy city of Abydos became an essential funerary ceremony, and those who could not make their tombs near the burial-place of Osiris had their mummies taken there by boat before entombment and participated in the water festivals that formed part of the Osirian mysteries. Or they made the journey by proxy. Other devotees contented themselves with setting up memorial tablets or statuettes in the precincts of the temple of Osiris, thereby assisting in the rituals or religious dramas. Their very modesty has preserved many of these private monuments intact.

THE KING'S OFFERINGS
In the temple of Abydos, the pharaoh Seti I, from the 19th Dynasty, makes an offering to Osiris, the god of the dead.

The royal monuments have suffered more severely, perhaps through iconoclasm in the region of Akhenaten. The best preserved is the celebrated temple of the Osirian triad and the state gods of Egypt built by Sethos I in fine hard limestone, which allowed the sculptors of the reliefs full scope for delicate and detailed work of great technical excellence.

Immediately behind the rear wall of the temple was a curious subterranean complex within a natural tree-girt mound, to which the name of the Osireion has been given in recent times. It has as its nucleus a central hall of massive granite monoliths on an island surrounded by a water channel, with emplacements for a sarcophagus and a canopic chest which were probably still lacking on the death of Sethos I. The Osireion is the cenotaph of the king at Abydos and was evidently made in the form of the mythical tomb of Osiris, with whom he would have been identified on death. Although the completed monument is certainly the work of Sethos and certain Nineteenth Dynasty successors, the resemblance of the basic structure to Old Kingdom work has been much remarked. Some scholars are now reverting to an old view that it was indeed an Old Kingdom foundation, rediscovered and rebuilt by Sethos I as his own. Sethos I promoted a restoration of ancient traditions after the collapse of Akhenaten's religious innovations and associated with the god Osiris in the main temple a number of deified ancestors from Menes, the first pharaoh. Not the least valuable feature of these reliefs is the famous Abydos list of 76 predecessors whom Sethos considered important or legitimate enough to commemorate.

THE MYSTERIES OF OSIRIS

Every year, great festivities in honor of Osiris were celebrated in the city of Abydos, which guards the relics of the head of the dismembered god. The entire city, including the many who made a pilgrimage to it, joined in. The purpose was to retrace the different episodes of the terrible story of Osiris, the god of the dead.

A special envoy from the pharaoh was charged with overseeing the preparations for the celebration by confirming the good condition of the "material": portable chapels made of gold and silver-plated wood and encrusted with lapis lazuli, divine statues, the sacred boat, clothing, jewels, and offerings with which to honor the god. The preparations for the procession were complex, since the mysteries were broken down into three episodes.

To begin, Osiris's cadaver had to be torn away from the hands of the god Seth. The enemy had to be fought, and Osiris's victory over his assassins had to be reenacted. Divided into two groups, the participants confronted each other before coming together to escort the god to his tomb. At this point, amid mourning and funerary hymns, Osiris was buried in the ground. Then the mystery of his resurrection was repeated and the living god was escorted, with exaltation and honors, to his palace, the temple of Abydos.

Middle Egypt and the Faiyum

There could be no greater contrast to this stronghold of orthodoxy than the next great site some 100 miles downstream, the modern Tell el-Amarna, the ancient capital of heresy. At this point the flanking cliffs on the eastern bank recede to leave a semi-circular sandy plain about 8 miles in diameter. It was in this amphitheatre that one of the great dramas of ancient Egypt was played out when, for scarcely more than a decade, it became the residence of King Akhenaten (ca. 1360–1343 B.C.), visionary and religious reformer. Here it was that he was directed by divine guidance in his fifth regnal year to found a great city to his sole god, Re-Herakhty, immanent in the sunlight that streamed from the Aten, or disk of the sun. Akhetaten, or Horizon of the Aten, was built, occupied, and dedicated to the Aten all within the space of the remaining 12 years of his reign. Here the palaces, temples, and official buildings, the mansions of the wealthy and the hovels of the poor, were hastily constructed of mud brick, wood, and stone, only to be abandoned by his successor, the young Tutankhamun.

Half a century later, when Akhenaten and all his works were execrated as heretical by the kings of the next dynasty, iconoclasts were sent to the desolate site to smash statues of the king and his family and to obliterate his features and names—and sometimes the name of his god—on the temple and tomb reliefs. In the reign of Rameses II. demolition groups squatted among the ruins while they removed the stonework right down to its foundations for use elsewhere.

Despite this brutal destruction in antiquity and even more inexcusable vandalism in modern times, much of the township has survived, even to the ancient chariot roads and the paths tramped into the desert sands by long-dead feet in their walk between residence and place of work. But far less vestigial are the 14 great stelae hewn into the cliffs that enclose the site on the east and west banks and define its boundaries. On them, beneath scenes of the king and queen worshipping the rayed symbol of the Aten, are carved texts, now much damaged and weathered, recounting how Akhenaten came to choose and demarcate the bounds of Akhetaten and

DIPLOMATIC ARCHIVES
A storage area filled with cuneiform tablets was discovered in Amarna. The tablets revealed diplomatic secrets from the time of Akhenaton, pharaoh of the 18th Dynasty.

ROYAL COUPLE
Queen Nefertiti, famous for her beauty, holds hands with her royal spouse, Akhenaten, who can be identified by his sickly face and bloated stomach.

listing the various buildings that he proposed to erect there, such as palaces, temples, a family tomb in the eastern hills, and tombs nearby for his followers.

The other surface monuments at Akhetaten are these same tombs on the eastern bank. Their rock-hewn chapels with their scenes in relief are nearly all incomplete, but still give vivid pictures of the daily life of the royal family at Akhetaten; they are almost our only means of learning of events that happened at this critical and turbulent moment in Egyptian history. In them we catch glimpses of the passing royal pageant; the private and state functions within the palaces; the daily worship in the temples, with lavish offerings made to the Aten under an open sky; and the royal family mourning the early death of an elder daughter.

The buried evidence has proved no less eloquent. Atketaten (now Amarna), built and abandoned to the desert after a mere 12 years, is an archaeologist's paradise with its simple stratigraphy. The most dramatic discovery was made not by a professional excavator but, as is so often the case, by a casual cultivator. In 1887 a local peasant woman digging for *sebakh*, the nitrous fertilizer into which ancient mud brick so often decays, uncovered a cache of some 300 sun-dried clay tablets impressed with cuneiform signs. The hoard had evidently been hidden under the floor of the Bureau for the Correspondence of Pharaoh at the time of the abandoning of Akhenaten, and were part of the discarded dispatches sent to the pharaoh from the great kings and vassal princes of Asia during the time the court was in residence at this place.

A most vivid and scarcely suspected picture has since emerged from the study of these sadly damaged lumps of clay. We see that in the civilized world of the fourteenth century B.C., privileged officials traveled from one court to another bearing dispatches by which marriage treaties were arranged, trade-goods exchanged, extradition requested, diplomatic alliances negotiated, protests submitted, demands made, aid requested, warnings administered—in fact all the features of a sophisticated system of international relations, with its own protocol, which differs little in essence from that of Europe in modern times and suggests an already long development.

The chance discovery of the Amarna Letters, or Tablets, as they came to be known, brought other investigators to the scene. First Petrie, then the Germans, then the British again have dug over the site and laid a great part of it bare. In the process, much has been learned about town planning and domestic architecture in Egypt, but little definite about the course of events during the reign of Akhenaten.

A most spectacular find was made by the Germans in 1911–12 when they excavated the ruins of sculptors' studios in the central city and found a number of statuettes, plaster casts, sketches, and studies which have given us a new appreciation of the scope of Egyptian sculpture and its techniques. Among them was the painted bust of Queen Nefertiti, which has since become the most publicized portrait from the ancient world.

Opposite Amarna, on the west bank, lie the remains of Khmunu ("Eight-Town"), so called from the eight primeval gods present in the waters of Chaos. But by historic times, their worship had been largely displaced by the cult of the moon god, Thoth: inventor of the lunar calendars of Egypt; god of learning, writing, and calculation; and the divine messenger whom the Greeks equated with their Hermes—

hence the name of Hermopolis, which they gave to the place. Rameses II erected a temple here built of stone largely pillaged from Akhetaten, the remains of which were excavated by the Germans from 1929 to 1939. A British expedition investigated earlier foundations in the area, including a shrine of Amenhotep III which housed colossal quartzite statues of a squatting baboon, the familiar animal of Thoth.

Khmunu, however, is very much older. In the Middle Kingdom, it was the capital city of the "Hare" province (or *nome,* to use the later Greek word for a province), whose powerful princes held the balance between the Thebaid in the south and the metropolitan power in the north. They made their rock tombs at Deir el-Bersha across the river on the east bank. The Bahr Yusuf ("River of Joseph"), which is a branch of the Nile that leaves the main stream on the western bank near Asyut, separates Hermopolis from its necropolis at Tuna el-Gebel. This place is a veritable city of the dead dating from the time of the Rameses but is particularly notable for a free-standing tomb-chapel of Petosiris, a much-traveled high priest of Thoth in the fourth century B.C., who evidently called in a Greek to assist in the design of the reliefs on the exterior vestibule.

THE SCULPTORS

The Egyptian sculptor used very simple tools to make statuettes, life-size statues, colossi, and bas-reliefs. He cut the blocks with a saw and then rough-hewed the reliefs by striking them with a hard stone. He then engraved the stone with wooden-handled copper scissors and a heavy mallet. He polished with his rounded flints and an abrasive paste of sand.

The sculptor's work required great patience and skill. He also worked with other artisans. The draftsman used his calamus and palette to trace the contours of the hieroglyphics, which the sculptor then engraved. Then, once the wooden or limestone statues were polished, the painter would do his part. These artists used transportable scaffolding to work the upper parts of the sculpture, but they also felt free to climb up a sphinx's paw, a statue's knee, or a bull's back, if necessary.

A "fashioner of life," the sculptor created statues that were meant to exist eternally once they were given life by the Opening of the Mouth ritual. In the tombs, these statues acted as the body of the deceased when offerings were made or when the mummy became "inhabitable." So it was that through the sculptors, the deceased in the temple could take part in the divine cult for eternity.

Nearby is a chapel built also as a house for visitors to the tomb of Isadora, a young woman who was drowned in the Nile in the reign of Antoninus Pius in the second century A.D. and given a splendid burial at the expense of the local community in conformity with a very ancient tradition mentioned by Herodotus.

In following the Nile northwards from Hermopolis, the traveler also journeys back further in time as the predominantly New Kingdom sites of Upper Egypt give way to the Middle and Old Kingdom centers. This reign was full of thriving provincial towns during the early Middle Kingdom, until a decline following the reign of Sesostris III (ca. 1881–1840 B.C.). At Deir Rifa, Asyut, and Meir southwards, and at Beni Hasan northwards, are important quarries, rock tombs, and cemeteries of the period which have contributed greatly to our knowledge of Middle Kingdom culture and politics. But a district closely associated with this particular period of Egyptian history lies farther downstream at the Faiyum depression, which is really the easternmost of a string of oases, The Faiyum, with its lake, the Birket Qarun (now very much smaller than it was in ancient days), is irrigated by the Bahr Yusuf, which enters the depression through a gap in the chain of Libyan hills at el-Lahun and divides into innumerable channels to water the whole region.

The Faiyum has been noted from early days for its wonderful fertility and pleasant climate, its vines, olives, wheat, and legumes. The earliest Neolithic settlements in Egypt have been found here. The vigorous kings of the Twelfth Dynasty increased its prosperity by improving its irrigation and colonizing the area with new settlements. Here, at el-Lahun and Hawara in the Faiyum and farther north at Dahshur, they erected their stone and rubble pyramids, which have ill resisted the hand of time and the despoiler. Nevertheless, treasures belonging to royal ladies of this dynasty and the next have been recovered from these sites and have bequeathed us a most impressive testimony of the fine taste and superb technical skill of the ancient court jewelers. The Faiyum enjoyed a second period of prosperity during Ptolemaic and Roman times, when it was recolonized by Greek settlers from the officials and soldiery of the Greek and Roman pharaohs. The rubbish mounds and cemeteries of their townships such as Arsinoë, Karanis, Bacchias, Dionysias, Tebtunis, and Dime have yielded a great hoard of Greek literary works previously unknown or incomplete, as well as many other documents. These discoveries have rejuvenated Classical studies and instituted the science of papyrology.

Near the pyramid of Sesostris II at el-Lahun have been found the remains of the walled village that was built, largely of mud brick, for the workmen and officials servicing his pyramid-tomb. Its excavation by Petrie in 1889 brought to light a wealth of domestic equipment and household fittings of the workers and their families who lived there.

THE WORKERS' VILLAGE OF EL-LAHUN

During the Twelfth Dynasty, Sesostris II ordered that a village for workers and senior officials who were building his pyramid be constructed in the middle of the desert. Today, only a desolate stretch of jumbled stones, bricks, broken pottery, and sand remain on this site where men lived for almost a century.

The plan of this artificial, rectilinear, monotonous city is astounding. Straight streets separated houses that were oddly similar looking—desolate streets with no palm trees or acacias and without water. The city was crammed within brick ramparts without foundations. There were two neighborhoods separated by the ramparts; each had its own door. For the workers, there were more than 200 tiny houses pressed against each other. For the officials, there were large homes (25 times the size of a worker's house) that included private apartments, several auxiliary buildings, basins, and gardens. The door to the officials' neighborhood was guarded day and night.

The constricted nature of this 1,200-foot-long city is surprising. Did the pharaoh fear that his workers would escape? Was he protecting them against the dangers of the desert—bandits, wild animals, and the dead who escaped their tombs? It remains a mystery.

The winter migration of birds to the reed banks of the Faiyum is still an impressive event, but in antiquity the wealth of pond fowl and fish in the area was even more prodigious. Hunting birds with the throw-stick and spearing fish with the bident were not only recreations but were also of religious significance—the sport of the marsh goddess.

Mysterious Memphis

The ruined pyramids at the very lower margin of Middle Egypt form the southernmost end of a chain of such monuments that lie on the west bank of the Nile and mark the sites of the ancient residence-cities of the Pyramid Age (ca. 2663–2195 B.C.) all the way to Cairo, and north of it as far as Abu Rawash. At Dahshur, near the crumbling mud-brick and rubble ruins of pyramids of the Twelfth Dynasty, and to the south of it at Maidum, are the earliest stone pyramids of the Old Kingdom. In the neighborhood of each pyramid are clustered the mastaba tombs of the relatives and officials of their king (the mastaba is the bench-like superstructure built over the tombs). The stone walls of the chapels, or offering-chambers, of these private mastaba tombs were invariably sculptured in low relief and painted with scenes which are the chief source for our knowledge of everyday life and funerary

ritual and belief during the Pyramid Age. In a *serdab,* or separate chamber—usually sealed off but connected by a spy-hole to the chapel—were stored statues of the owner and his family in painted wood or limestone, rarely in granite. Some of these tombs in their sculpture and statuary have preserved the artistic masterpieces of their day, though hardly one is now in its pristine condition. The majority of these mastabas lie buried in the stands at Saqqara, where kings of the Third, Fifth, and Sixth Dynasties built their funerary monuments; others are at Dahshur, and yet others are at Giza near the most celebrated of all ancient tombs, the three stone-built pyramids of Cheops, Chephren, and Mycerinus of the Fourth Dynasty.

These various cemeteries were near the northern capital of Memphis, of which scarcely any other record survives. Memphis was the premier city of Egypt, a vast metropolis, the "white walls" of which were traditionally thought to have been raised by Menes, the first pharaoh, on reclaimed ground at the junction of Upper and Lower Egypt. It was a great religious and administrative capital throughout its long history. As a trading center, all manner of crafts were carried on there, from shipbuilding to metalwork, under the auspices of the city god, the artificer Ptah,

PYRAMID OF MAIDUM
South of Memphis, the pyramid of Maidum was the first of three pyramids built by King Snefrou. Built from limestone blocks that have turned yellow over time, it is still 75 feet high.

51

whose high priest proudly bore the title of "Greatest of Craftsmen." Even in Roman times, it was still prosperous and only suffered decline and extinction when the Arab conquerors pillaged its stone for building Cairo 10 miles to the north on the opposite bank of the Nile.

The modern village of Mitrahina is the site of the temple of Ptah, and near its palm groves the colossal statues which Rameses II raised there have lain for centuries in fallen grandeur. Votive statues and other monuments from the temple site have come to light as a result of sporadic digging, but the greater part of Memphis lies under the Nile silt and must have been irretrievably lost. Various expeditions have dug selected portions of the vast site from time to time during the past century, but the high water-table necessitated expensive pumping operations and specialized excavation skills. The Egypt Exploration Society began explorations in the area on a regular basis with promising results. Until this capital city is properly excavated, our knowledge of ancient Egypt cannot be but lop-sided.

Lower Egypt

A few miles below Memphis in ancient times, the Nile divided into several branches as it wandered across the broad alluvium of its Delta, eventually entering the sea through seven principal and five secondary mouths. It was a region of potentially great fertility, but in antiquity it was only very gradually developed, its pools and marshes being progressively drained, so eliminating their thickets of reeds and papyrus rush. It was flanked on its eastern and western borders by wide pastures where large herds of goats, sheep, and cattle could be raised. The flowery meadows produced both milk and honey. Along the "Western River," presumably the Canopic branch of the Nile, lay the large estates from which the pharaohs obtained their choicest wines. Wine labels in the form of dockets written in ink upon the jars themselves defined the particular clos, the vintage year, the name of the vintner, and the quality of the wine, suggesting that the pharaohs or their butlers enjoyed a cultivated palate. Surrounded by their domains among the water-courses stood the

THE GOD PTAH

In appearance, the god was a handsome man with a thin fake beard and shaved head. He wore a heavy necklace and bracelets around his wrist. He was always dressed in a tight-fitting shroud, from which only his arms emerged, holding a scepter. This was Ptah ("He who opens"), god of Memphis, the ancient Egyptian capital. He was the master of craftsmen, founder of the trades, patron of silversmiths and goldsmiths, inventor of techniques, the greatest of sculptures, but above all, a demiurge (creator).

According to the legend of Memphis, Ptah was the supreme creator who came from man. Through his intelligence and utterance, he created the universe and formed the earth. He also brought forth the sky and the primordial gods of Ogdoad—eight male-female pairs. Nun and Naunet were god and goddess of primordial waters; Ket and Keket, of darkness; Heh and Hehet, of the infinity of space; and Amun and Amaunet of hiddenness. Gods, goddesses, and spirits born one after the other included Horus the Powerful, with his falcon head, and Thoth the Wise Man.

Ptah then created Egypt, the life force, humans, animals, and the plants and rocks of Egypt. But he was not yet ready to rest. He melted the metal that made the flesh of the kings and colored their bodies with the colors of life. He ordered Nun's waters to flood the barley and wheat fields. He invented working hands, walking, labor, and bread, on which all humans depend.

Creating both from his heart (spirit and will) and his tongue (words), Ptah had an original personality among the Egyptian demiurges. This intellectual god created through thought, by pronouncing the essential words. He had both all the intelligence that lay in the heart and the will that emerged through language.

famous towns of Lower Egypt—Heliopolis, Sais, Buto, Mendes, Bubastis, and Tanis, each centered around a shrine of ancient foundation.

Heliopolis, the On of the Bible, was the center of the influential sun cult. The temple of Re-Herakhty, the active form of the supreme god, was the largest outside Thebes, and its high priests were the traditional wise men of Egypt, even in the Late Period when the solar faith was in eclipse. The preoccupation of these sages with the movement of the sun and other celestial bodies encouraged the development of astronomy and the mensuration of time as well as space. An early high priest of the sun god at Heliopolis was Imhotep, later deified as Imuthes, a god of healing and wisdom, who was celebrated throughout the history of Egypt as the virtual founder of its culture. One of the last of these intellectuals was Manetho.

The temple of Re-Herakhty has also vanished, but its appearance can be surmised from reconstructions of the sun temples that have been excavated near the pyramids of some kings of the Fifth Dynasty. Worship focused upon a cult object, the *ben-ben,* a stone of pyramidal or conical shape, probably a meteorite, elevated upon a podium or tall pillar (from which On gets its name) to form an obelisk. One such monument, the earliest now surviving from a pair erected by Sesostris I, still stands amid the fields, in a small park surrounded by a suburb of modern Cairo to mark the site of the vanished temple entrance. The pair raised here by Thutmose III now adorn London and New York under the incongruous name of "Cleopatra's Needles."

The cattle economy of the Delta was evident in the cult of the sacred Mnevis bull at Heliopolis, as it was in the Apis bull of Memphis. A ram cult was observed at Mendes, the ruins of which at Tell el Qasr, near the northeast corner of the Delta, have been excavated by American and Canadian expeditions. Mendes was the seat of the fighting pharaohs of the Twenty-Ninth Dynasty, who with their Greek mercenaries successfully resisted the onslaughts of the Persians in the fourth century B.C.

South of Mendes, near modern Zagazig, lie the ruins of Bubastis—the Pibeseth of Ezekiel, a city with an ancient foundation that goes back at least to the reign of Cheops and may well be earlier. It was, however, greatly developed during the first millennium B.C., when immigrant Libyans settled in different areas of the Delta. Their kings, ruling as the Twenty-Second Dynasty, embellished Bubastis as their chief residence, enlarging its ancient tree-girt temple. The city deity was Bastet, an aspect

FIELD WORK
Since ancient times, the Egyptians have been cultivating their valley with courage: Rain is so rare that they have had to constantly water their land by drawing from the Nile.

of the universal mother goddess, incarnate in the Egyptian domestic cat. On the occasion of her joyous festivals, pilgrimages were made to her shrine by boat with fluting and castanet playing.

To the northeast of Bubastis, near the shores of Lake Manzala, are the ruins of Tanis, the Biblical Zoan, which has been explored by Mariette, Petrie, and most recently by the French, who are still investigating the place. Tanis was a prosperous entrepot for trade with the Levantine states during the late New Kingdom. It grew to greater importance as the chief city of the kings of the Twenty-First and Twenty-Second Dynasties, who in their stirring times found it expedient to have their seat of power nearer to their Mediterranean frontier. They adorned it with the monuments of earlier kings moved from elsewhere and as far afield as the Faiyum.

FACE OF ETERNITY
According to Egyptian legend, gold was the flesh of the gods. This mask was found in Tanis. It dates back to the 21st Dynasty.

In 1939, the French Egyptologist Pierre Montet made a brilliant discovery within the temple precincts of a group of tombs containing the remains of six kings of this period and their relatives. Most of the burials had been violated at one time and rearranged, but despite certain depredations, Montet was able to recover extremely rich funerary equipment containing much gold- and silver-work and throwing new light upon the history, art, beliefs, and resources of an age which was contemporary with that of Solomon in all his glory. Tanis was not far from the great fortress of Tjel, the last outpost on the northeastern frontier, and was always subject to influences from Asia. In the vicinity is Tell ed Dab`a, where the Austrians uncovered the huge site, which was founded in the Middle Kingdom and rapidly became a center of Palestinian immigrants into Egypt. A number of Canaanite temples and other materials show without doubt that this was Avaris, the capital city of the Hyksos. Even more exciting have been the discoveries of the remains of Cretan Minoan frescoes, considerably earlier than those known on Crete itself. The paintings' significance, and their relationship to others found over recent years in the Levant, remain the subject of much debate.

A mile to the north at Qantir is the site of Pi-Ramesse, the great treasure-city and residence-town of the Ramesside kings, which a poet of the day describes as "beauteous with balconies and dazzling halls of lapis lazuli and turquoise, the place where the chariotry is marshalled and the infantry assembles and where the warships come to anchorage when tribute is brought." The mooring posts for these ships was found on a dried-up branch of the Pelusian arm of the Nile by an expedition from Hildesheim which was re-excavating this area. Pi-Ramesse was bereft of its statues and monuments to adorn Tanis, and the crumbling brick ruins of houses and a palace are all that are left of its glory, with the exception perhaps of a great number of blue and polychrome faience tiles, which are dispersed among different collections and which are doubtless the (artificial) lapis lazuli and turquoise referred to by the poet.

Of Sais, the wealthy residence of the powerful kings of the Twenty-Sixth Dynasty, only "inconsiderable" ruins exist near the modern Sa el-Hagar. Herodotus visited it soon after its apogee and describes the remarkable temple of the presiding archer goddess Neith, with its gigantic monolithic shrines and obelisks and its sacred lakes. Of all this nothing now remains.

Sais shared with Buto the distinction of being a place of pilgrimage, particularly in the Old Kingdom, when the blessed dead were taken to these holy cities, if not for burial, then for consecration at the shrines of ancient kings, a ritual later usurped for the cult of Osiris at Abydos. Buto was the Place of the Throne, the old capital of the prehistoric kings of the Western Delta, and the legendary birthplace of the demiurge who manifested himself here upon the primeval hill in the form of a heron, just as a falcon had appeared at Hierakonpolis, the counterpart of Buto in Upper Egypt. Buto now survives only as a few mounds near Tell el-Farain, which have been partly explored by the British with disappointing results.

But in Herodotus's day, Buto was a flourishing city with a noted oracle in the temple of Edjo, the cobra goddess of the city and the presiding genius of Lower Egypt. From the top of the temple pylon on a clear day, it would have been possible to glimpse on the far horizon the flash of light upon what our Egyptian guide would have called the Great Green, which we today call the Mediterranean.

NEITH: GODDESS OF MANY GIFTS

Goddess of the cities of Sais to the north and Esna to the south, Neith was very much in good graces at the beginning of Egyptian history. Temporarily losing renown, she regained her former prestige when the princes of Sais became pharaohs. But the goddess always appeared in various roles in Egyptian mythology.

As a warrior goddess, Neith struck the enemies of the country with fear when she flexed her bow. She also flattened the way before Pharaoh when he moved along his war path and then accompanied him in battle.

According to the priests of Esna, the goddess Neith came into existence alone, appearing as a cow. She wandered through the primordial ocean and illuminated her gaze to create light. Everything her heart imagined immediately came into being. Neith created the primordial mound and the 30 initial gods, one after the other, by naming them. She then placed excrement from her flesh in an egg. When the shell cracked, the sun-god Re appeared. Thereafter, gods and goddesses were born from his rays and humans from his tears. Neith breast-fed the young Re, placed him between her horns, and swam in the primordial waters to Sais.

But Neith was also the goddess of floods, and as such owned the banks of the river invaded by the crocodile in times of flooding. The goddess's son is Sobek, the crocodile.

Dressed in a tight-fitting dress and wearing the red crown of the North, Neith was also very wise; she understood the secrets of the writings and used the power of words. At times Neith became the vault of the skies and merged with the goddess Nut, protectress of sleep, creator of weaving, one of the four goddesses watching over the sarcophaguses and urns of the Egyptians.

Living with the gods

～～

PHARAOH AND THE GODDESS MAAT
To please the gods and maintain the world's balance, this young king from the 19th Dynasty— his name has unfortunately been obliterated —made of gold-plated silver, is making an offering of a statuette of Maat, the goddess of justice and truth.

Magnificent stone temples, gigantic tombs covered in superb paintings, luxurious funerary objects: These all point to the importance of religion in the life of the ancient Egyptians. The fearful world of the deities, which included more than ten gods and goddesses, was not seen as separate from the world of humans; even the smallest acts of nature were thought to be governed by a god whose power to create or destroy was to be forever feared.

Egyptian religion was an astonishing mix of myths that evolved through the centuries and varied from one region to the next, except for the creation myths.

In the beginning there was liquid Chaos, the Nun—a vast icy ocean in which lay infinite possibilities. This is where the demiurge (creator) created himself. He became conscious of his existence and emerged from this Chaos into the primordial mound on the Day of the First Time. So he created the universe, gods and men, animals and plants. Of course, every Egyptian thought that his hometown was built on this mound and that the local god was the demiurge. But the balance of the world created by the gods was precarious, and its harmony was constantly threatened. Men have had to do everything possible to maintain it.

Several gods represent the elements of the universe, among them Re, the sun; his children Shu, the atmosphere, and Tefnut, humidity; his grandchildren, Geb, the earth, and Nut, the sky. Other divinities watch over human activities: Tait, the goddess of weaving; Neheb the incarnation of bushes teeming with game; Baba, the spirit of fertility; and Shesmu, the god of wine. On earth, the gods lived in temples, which were closed to the people, but many priests were devoted to their well-being. It was believed that upsetting the gods would threaten the harmony of the earth, which could then go back to Chaos.

The Egyptians built temples for their gods and devoted certain days or weeks to celebrate them. They lived in close contact with the gods and with the afterlife. They respected sacred animals, wore amulets, embalmed the dead and offered them impressive burials, and sometimes picnicked in the cemeteries.

Whenever Egyptians had small daily problems, they chose to address the minor gods because these gods were more accessible than the greater ones.

GRIMACING SPIRIT

Watching over women, children, and sleep, Bes entertains with his dancing and music. He keeps away the demons with his knife. Protecting daily activities, he adorns common objects like this earthenware kohl pot from the 18th Dynasty.

CAT MUMMY

As the hunter of mice, scorpions, or snakes, the cat was the divine animal of Bastet, the cat goddess who protected homes and children. This mummy, with a cloth mask on its head, shows the importance of cats in the Late Period.

CHAOUABTIS CASE

Chaouabtis were statuettes meant to do work for the deceased in the afterlife. Placing cases filled with them in a tomb quickly became tradition. On this New Kingdom case, the deceased stands before Ptah, the god of Memphis.

DIVINE PROCESSION

These priests carrying Amun, god of Thebes, were drawn on a piece of limestone during the New Kingdom. When the god comes out of his temple, he is well protected in a chapel that stands on a boat decorated with ram heads. Pilgrims and spectators gather to watch his passage.

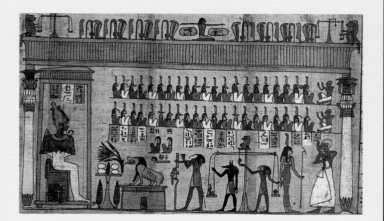

THE WEIGHING OF THE HEART

The *Book of the Dead* is composed of papyrus scrolls that collect the magic formulas for conquering the dangers of the afterlife, for receiving offerings, and for entering and exiting one's tomb. Their very presence assured a peaceful existence for eternity. The scroll fragment pictured above represents the weighing of the heart. Osiris, god of the dead, presides over the assembly of 42 gods. His sisters, Isis and Nephthys, surround him. The heart of the deceased is weighed on a huge balance scale, with Maat, goddess of truth and justice, in the second pan. The deceased begs the heart to be favorable to him. The pans of the scale swing. Will he end up in the jaws of the animal that is part crocodile, part hippopotamus, part lion? Or will he take his place among the gods?

THE TEARS OF ISIS

With this wooden statue from the Ptolemaic era, Isis can eternally mourn the death of Osiris, her brother and husband. Soon she will give him the breath of life again through the power of her magic and the wind from her wings.

CHAPTER 3

The natural resources

Egyptian foodstuffs

Within these boundaries ancient Egypt enjoyed many resources. When the inundation was neither too copious nor too meager, the tremendous fertility of the soil, rich in phosphates, brought forth produce of all kinds. The main grain crops were summer and winter wheat and six-row barley, providing the staples of the national diet, bread and beer for both king and peasant. In the Late Period, the rations of the soldiery contained about 5 pounds of bread per day for each man, a regimen that induced the Greeks to dub them *artophagoi* (the bread-eaters).

This fare, however, was supplemented by such vegetables as leeks, onions, lettuces, melons, cucumbers, and beans and other pulses. Vegetable oils used in cooking, lighting, cosmetics, and medicine were expressed mostly from the fruits of the balanos and moringa trees and from sesame and castor oil plants. The olive was not extensively planted, but its oil was imported from Palestine in large quantities and probably also from Libya.

Fruits were provided by such trees as the jujube (*Zizyphus spina Christi*), sycamore fig, and date palm. The *dom* palm, with its nuts encased in a hard carapace resembling gingerbread, could be raised only in latitudes south of Asyut. The caprification, or pollination, of figs was practiced, and doubtless also the hand pollination of date palms.

THE SACRED TREE

On the day of his enthronement, the new king, surrounded by princes, nobles, and priests, participated in religious ceremonies. Hymns and long, complicated rituals were offered in the depths of the temple. The king was presented to the gods and men. From the hands of Horus and Seth (roles played by priests), he received the crowns of Upper and Lower Egypt. He "walked around the walls" to symbolically take possession of his domain.

In general, these ceremonies took place in Memphis. But the king also had to go into the sacred courtyard of the temple of Heliopolis, where there grew a persea, an evergreen tree that was carefully tended by the gardener-priests. It was the *ished*, the tree of the sun-god Re, in which the soul of Osiris, the god of the dead, dwelled. Once the "chancellery of the gods" established its protocol, the king received his new names (official protocol required five), which had to be written on the leaves or fruit of the sacred tree.

This occasion was serious enough to call on the gods. Seated on his throne before the persea, the young king watched as the goddess Sechat ("mistress of writings, ruler of divine books") and Thoth (the wise god), wrote his names on the sacred tree in their best hand.

Grapes in abundance were grown from predynastic times, and vineyards in historic times were planted in new ground in the Delta and the oases.

Pomegranates and possibly the carob, yielding the sweet fleshy bean, St. John's bread, were not introduced until the New Kingdom. Apart from the groves of palm trees around villages, most fruit trees were cultivated in gardens, that characteristic oriental pleasance with its pool of water open to the evening breeze. Trees, in fact, were valued as much for their shade as for their fruit and flowers. Several trees were

regarded as sacred, such as the persea *(Mimusops schimperi),* the *ished* tree of Heliopolis, and the sycamore, inhabited by a goddess, sometimes Nut but usually Hathor, who is represented as leaning out of the trunk to pour a cooling draught of water for the deceased in paradise.

Individual trees growing in isolation were often venerated as sacred, their shade sought by a particular god. Hathor was worshipped at Memphis as the "Mistress of the Southern Sycamore." At the site of Heliopolis today, both Moslems and Copts revere a centuries-old sycamore as the Virgin's Tree, under which the Holy Family is believed to have sheltered on the flight into Egypt. Nearby is a spring of sweet water originally called into being by the Christ Child.

The papyrus plant abounded in the Delta and the undrained areas of Upper Egypt and supplied a host of needs, including a food prepared from its roasted rhizome. Herbs and aromatic plants provided flavorings, medicines, and perfumes. Together with such plants as the woody nightshade, the mandrake, and wild celery, and with cornflowers and the petals of blue and white water-lilies, they could be made into formal bouquets or wreaths and garlands by sewing them onto sheets

DANGEROUS CROSSING
Fearing crocodiles, which were habitually hungry, herdsmen led their animals from a papyrus boat. Crocodiles are immortalized in the bas-reliefs of the Mastaba of Ti, dating back to the Old Kingdom.

MILKING
On this relief from the sarcophagus of Queen Kawit, from the 11th Dynasty, a young man is milking a cow after tying the calf to one of its legs.

of papyrus or strips of palm fiber. Such gay and sweet-smelling but ephemeral decorations were used at feasts, not only for adorning the person but also for decking animals destined for sacrifice and for offerings to the gods.

In addition to its vegetable products, Egypt supported a vast population of domestic animals. The chief ceremonial meat offerings were usually beef in the form of head, legs, ribs, and offal. Religious traditions prescribed the creatures of the wild as the preferred victims for sacrifice, and domestic animals, apart from the ox, do not therefore appear among the offerings.

Nevertheless, pigs, sheep, goats, and asses were also raised. The pig was an important article of diet among the peasantry, though representations of the animal, and references to it, are rare. Even if fabrics made from goat's hair and sheep's wool have not been found until the Classical Period, clips of sheep's wool have been excavated at Amarna and Deir el-Medina. There is no doubt that certain garments, such as shawls, were woven from these animal fibers from earliest times, though evidently they were not deposited with the dead, probably because they were considered as ceremonially impure.

Cattle from Nubia, and hump-backed bulls introduced from Asia in the New Kingdom for breeding purposes, were imported to replace losses caused by the diseases that periodically have devastated herds in Egypt until very recent times. Milk was an important farm product, and cheese and butter were prepared from it. The same flowery meadows that fattened the prize cattle so that their legs became bowed under the weight of their bodies, also produced honey, which was used as a main source of sugar. Beehives were made of hollow cones of dried mud similar to those found in rural Egypt today. A jug of ancient honey in the Rhind Collection in Edinburgh plainly shows the hexagonal construction of the wax comb.

The Nile and its pools abounded in fish, and although fish, like pork, was regarded as ritually impure, it is shown among the water produce offered by the personified figures of the Nile. Fish was an important article of food for the working population, and the artisans concerned with hewing and decorating the royal tombs at Thebes were entitled to share in the 40 pounds of fish provided every ten days by the fishermen attached to each gang.

The enormous flocks of migratory birds that visited Egypt in the winter could be trapped with a clap-net and supplemented the herds of geese and duck that were raised on the Egyptian farms and supplied eggs, flesh, and fat. The domestic barnyard fowl does not make an appearance until the reign of Tuthmose III, and then only in isolated instances. Cranes caught in the wild were artificially fattened with prepared pellets and are often depicted with geese among the offerings. Swans and pelicans also appear, but very rarely, and are not represented among the sacrifices. Pigeons are depicted at all periods. The northern palace at Amarna had an extensive aviary with nesting boxes cut as niches into the walls; the birds painted on its decorated dado are of different species. All such birds, like fish and various cuts of meat, could be preserved by jerking in the dry Egyptian climate and storing with salt in sealed pottery jars.

Besides Nile water, which was supposed to have special life-giving virtues, and could be kept cool in porous jars, beer was brewed; this used to be thought of as a thick substance not unlike modern Nubian *bouza*, but it has now been shown to be a far more palatable brew, although rather unlike modern confections. Wine made from palm sap was occasionally fermented. The annual grape harvest in various parts of the country, chiefly the border areas and the oases of the Libyan desert, was the most usual source of wine.

Except for certain interludes when the inundation failed, Egypt was a land of plenty, its surplus grain succoring the Hittites during a famine in the reign of Merenptah (around 1211 B.C.), as well as the city mob at Rome well over a millennium later, in the days of the emperors. The residence-city Pi-Ramesse, on the building of which the Israelites were alleged to have toiled in the thirteenth century B.C., is celebrated by the poet Paibes as being...

"...full of good things and provisions every day. Its channels abound in fish and its lakes in birds. Its fields are green with herbage and its banks bear dates. Its tall granaries are overflowing with barley and wheat. Garlic, leeks, lettuces and fruits are there for sustenance and wine surpassing honey...He who dwells there is happy, for there the humble are like the mighty elsewhere."

A GOOD CATCH
Found in Deir el-Bahri in Meketre's tomb (11th Dynasty), these wooden models offer a faithful reproduction of a fishing scene. In boats made of papyrus stems, fishermen are bringing back their nets filled with fish.

SHADE AND WATER
Represented on the walls of
his tomb in Deir el-Medina
—on the west bank in front
of Thebes—the artisan
Pachedu quenches his thirst,
protected from the sun by
a large palm tree.

Well might the Israelites in the wilderness of Zin bewail the loss of the fleshpots which they enjoyed even as a subject people.

Plant products

Only in one thing was Egypt notably deficient, and that was good constructional timber, which had to be imported from the Lebanon, a traffic which is probably as old as the seagoing ship. The native trees, mostly acacia, sycamore, and tamarisk, were too knotty, contorted, or unresilient to provide good-quality timber, though they were used for simple domestic furniture, boxes, and coffins and were often veneered with ivory, ebony, and other fine woods to make a better appearance. The palm tree, however, served a multitude of purposes—its trunk for ceiling rafters and staircase supports, the fronds for cladding brick piers and for roofing, its ribs for cages and frails for holding produce. The Egyptian from earliest days was skillful in using various rushes and reeds for making all sorts of articles in wickerwork, such as tables, stands, tools, and boxes.

Above all, the remarkable Egyptian discovery of how to prepare a flexible paper from the pitch of the papyrus rush, on which it was possible to write rapidly with a pen and ink, made the highly organized Egyptian state possible. Portable records of all kinds could be kept by this method. By the first millennium B.C. at the latest, Egypt was exporting rolls of papyrus to other civilized states in a trade which reveals that writing with pen and ink was ousting the old cumbersome system used in Asia of impressing lumps of clay with cuneiform signs.

Another valuable vegetable crop was flax, which was grown during the winter. The bundles of stems were rippled through a large fixed comb to remove the bolls containing linseed, from which the oil was extracted. The bast fibers were separated by retting the stems in convenient pools, then spun by the spindle-whorl into thread of all weights. Linen was woven on a simple horizontal loom in various grades. It formed the essential material for all clothing and bedding. On death, a person's sheets were torn into strips for use in bandaging his mummy. A fine material, royal linen, was evidently of a gossamer-like texture and was celebrated in erotic poetry as being semi-transparent. It was highly prized abroad. The thieves who plundered the royal tombs were in search of linen garments as much as gold and silver.

Minerals

While the cultivation yielded produce in ample quantities, the deserts that bordered the Nile Valley were not totally sterile. The wadis had not yet been overgrazed by goats and camels, and they supported game, particularly various species of antelope, ibex, ostriches, and hares, and their predators, the lion and his relations.

Occasional native trees and low, thorny shrubs provided kindling and charcoal for fuel. The inhabitants of the oases in the Western Desert had carried on a trade with Egypt in such products as wine, aromatic woods, grain, fruits, hides, salt, natron, and minerals since early times. Similarly, the inhabitants of Nubia and the Lower Sudan exchanged their goods for the industrial products of Egypt—weapons, furniture, textiles, and faience, or glazed earthenware. By this commerce Egypt became the great center for the export to the rest of the Eastern Mediterranean of the tropical products of Africa: ebony, ivory, ostrich feathers and eggs, gold, amethysts and other semi-precious stones, and exotic pelts.

The main products of the Eastern Desert were minerals, gemstones, and metals, particularly gold and silver and their naturally occurring alloy, electrum. The mining of the gold-bearing rocks and the transport of their crushed fragments by donkey-back to washing stations on the Nile were energetically pursued during the New Kingdom when it became proverbial among the nations of Asia that gold was as dust in the land of Egypt.

For most of its ancient history, Egypt lived in the Bronze Age, or rather the Copper Age, bronze not coming into use until the later Middle Kingdom. Copper ore

FASHIONABLE LINEN
This dress made of pleated linen was found carefully rolled up next to a mummy. It clearly shows the skill of Middle Kingdom weavers.

was mined in Sinai and the Eastern Desert, and copper ingots were imported in later times from Cyprus and Syria. The smelting of iron, however, lagged behind the craft as practiced in other countries of the Near East, such as Philistia. In many crafts, such as the working of hard stones, the techniques and equipment of the late Stone Age were retained to the end.

Other products of the deserts were the large deposits of sodium salts in the form of natron, brine, and soda. These were necessary for all kinds of industries, providing the salt required for preserving, flavoring, and tanning as well as a host of medical uses. Natron was employed in the manufacture of faience, or glazed earthenware, and glass and as a flux for the soldering of metals. It was also used with salt for preserving fish and fowl and was essential in the similar mummifying processes. Used with oils, it produced a kind of soap; alone, it acted as a mouthwash.

Quartz sand was an important ingredient in glass- and faience-making, and when used with copper saws and drills it enabled hard stones to be cut, worked, and polished. The great industry of the desert regions, however, was the supplying of the various stones in which Egypt was remarkably abundant. Apart from its semi-precious stones, it had inexhaustible deposits of limestone and sandstone of varying qualities flanking both banks of the Nile. These were easily worked and transported and provided the bulk of the materials for the monumental buildings. At the cataracts were vast intrusions of igneous rocks, granites, basalts, diorites, and dolerites, which the Egyptians early learned to work supremely well. Quartzite sandstone, graywacke, alabaster (calcite), indurated limestone, and gray-green diorite had to be sought out in desert places. In the case of the gray-green diorite, used particularly in the Fourth and Twelfth Dynasties for statuary and cosmetic vessels, a remote quarry in the Nubian desert some 40 miles west of Abu Simbel was the source of supply. Deposits of serpentine, steatite, and similar rocks were also prospected and used for small and delicate articles, from scarabs to statuettes.

The consummate stone-working skills of the Egyptians were recognized widely abroad, and their stonemasons were employed by Persian kings, not only to carve their granite statues but also to cut the reliefs on palace walls at Persepolis.

ROYAL HUNTING IN THE DESERT

With its mines and quarries, the desert, called the Red Earth, was distinguished from the Black Earth of the valley. The fearsome god Seth reigned over this country of all dangers, the domain of wild animals and the necropolises of the dead. It was a risky venture to enter here. Thirst, famine, and bad encounters would lead to death quickly, and the Egyptians knew it. Grass was thicker than today, and it was teeming with game—antelopes, hyenas, wild bulls, ibexes, gazelles, oryxes, and lions.

These were the pharaoh's hunting grounds. He would hunt frequently, alone or with important Egyptian figures, as a game of skill or for pleasure. But, above all, it was a ritual of power. In this hostile environment, the game symbolized the feared enemy, the forces of evil, demons, threatening foreigners, and the wandering dead. By killing them in defensive combat, the king protected his kingdom, proving his strength and reassuring his people. For him, hunting was an affirmation of force and eternal youth.

During the New Empire, the pharaoh penetrated the desert on his chariot pulled by superb horses and accompanied by tall greyhounds. He was equipped as he would be for a military campaign, with arrows, javelins, nets, arcs, lances, two-edged swords, and shields. A few beaters would chase the game, which fell into the artfully stretched nets. The pharaoh threw his arrows, and his helpers prepared the lassos.

Good warriors and hunters, the pharaohs took advantage of the hunting even while on military campaigns. According to accounts, Amenhotep III massacred 102 lions in 10 years and recounted the victories he won over elephants from the banks of the Orontes River and rhinoceroses from the Sudan.

The people

The people of ancient Egypt were very much like those of today, ranging in skin tone from olive-skinned Mediterranean types to the dark brown of the inhabitants of the south and Nubia. Movements within the country and immigration from abroad led to wide varieties being present in the major population centers.

These human resources, despite a steady infiltration of contiguous peoples, remained fairly constant throughout their ancient history and reveal an ability to assimilate the immigrant. This was doubtless because the vast majority of the ancient population was concerned with agriculture and committed to the cultivation of the land as much by predilection as by necessity. The peasant was deeply attached to the soil and unhappy away from his valley. His successful methods in contending with the peculiar agrarian conditions in Egypt were more in the nature of gardening than of farming. Nevertheless, his was a technique that was followed for many generations, like the mystique of other crafts. The racial type of the Egyptian peasant, like his physical environment, remained remarkably constant throughout historic times and is still apparent in some of the more remote areas of Upper Egypt.

MODEL OF A GRANARY
While peasants gathered heavy bags of grain, a scribe, seated comfortably above them, would note their number and capacity.

The ruling class which directed the toiling mass of peasants was often of foreign origin, but nationalistic ideas played a very subordinate role in the ancient world. It is not until the New Kingdom, when Theban princes challenged the northern kingdom conscious of its Asiatic ties, that any awareness of a racial and national identity becomes dominant. Just as the peasantry assimilated other cultivators settled on the land, so the strong traditions of the divine kingship and its institutions ensured that the pharaoh and his entourage, whether native, Hyksos, Semitic, Libyan, Kushite, or Greek, would always act as the government of the Egyptian people.

The amalgam of Asiatic and African elements in the ancient population is reflected in the language they spoke, which is related to the Semitic tongue in grammar and some of its vocabulary and yet has affinities with Hamitic languages—particularly Berber dialects suggesting a fusion of two tongues. Egyptian is characterized by its conciseness, concrete realism, and keen observation. It has, as Sir Alan Gardiner pointed out, a preference for the static over dynamic expression and—apart from some rare surviving words—has no genuine active tense.

Herodotus regarded the inhabitants of Upper Egypt in his day as among the healthiest in the world, and certainly the region, with its sunshine and dry winter climate, has always attracted invalids from the days of the Romans. But pathologist who have examined Egyptian mummies have claimed to identify some of the lesions of several ailments that trouble the modern fellahin, or farm worker—notably rheumatism and water-borne diseases. Moreover, owing to the Egyptians' practice of using fine quartz sand in the milling of grain, their bread contained enough grit to wear down to the pulp the grinding surfaces of their teeth over the years. Both Amenhotep III and his father-in-law Yuya, for instance, must have suffered miserably from alveolar, or tooth socket, abscesses in middle age.

Most Egyptians, however, escaped this fate, for while they prayed for a good old age and set the ideal life span at a hundred and ten years, the average expectation of life for the wealthier settlers in Greco-Roman times has been estimated at about thirty-six years, and there is no reason to believe that it was any higher in pharaonic days. While the birthrate was doubtless high, the infant mortality rate was far from low, and it has been computed on somewhat insecure foundations that the population in the Eleventh Dynasty did not greatly exceed a million.

In common with so many of the nations of antiquity in the Mediterranean, the Egyptians matured early, puberty being attained at the age of twelve and official manhood at not more than sixteen. Heavy responsibilities were undertaken by people whom we should now regard as children.

A certain nomarch of Asyut relates how the king appointed him governor of a province when he was only a cubit high (the royal cubit was 21 inches) and made him learn swimming with the royal children. The high priest of Amun, Bakenkhons, who entered the priesthood on reaching the age of sixteen, had already spent some years as chief of the training stable of Sethos I. Of course, such statistics can be as misleading as any average, and the short and youthful reign of Tutankhamun or Siptah, for instance, can be offset by that of Pepy II, who is generally believed to have had the longest recorded reign in history (ninety-four years), or Ramses II, who ruled for sixty-seven years, celebrated thirteen jubilees, and was succeeded by his thirteenth son. Nevertheless, there is sufficient evidence to show that much of the Egyptian achievement was secured by an extremely youthful population schooled by strong traditions rather than by personal experience.

MAGIC MEDICINE

The Egyptians were very familiar with the workings of the skeleton, heart, and stomach. They knew that the body's vessels ferried all liquids (blood, tears, urine) to the body's extremities. They protected themselves from the sun's dangerous rays by putting kohl around their eyes and wigs on their heads. They made excellent medicines, they filled dental cavities with a mineral cement, and when abscesses occured they drilled into the jawbone.

The Egyptians believed that diseases were caused by hostile powers—discontented spirits returning from the dead or genies acting under the orders of the goddess Sekhmet. The priest-scribe-physician-magician checked his patient's vital signs, recited magic formulas, and created amulets to expel the dangerous spirits from the diseased body. He also prescribed remedies. It was a curious blend of real medical knowledge, magic, and religious beliefs.

To enhance the power of his words, the physician pronounced them four times. For immediate results, he added the word "today." As a remedy for snake or scorpion bites, he advised patients to drink the water trickling over statues blessed with healing properties and covered with magic formulas.

He often resorted to the power of amulets, which symbolized abstract notions such as life, strength, and prosperity. Or else he relied on statuettes of deities, which possessed part of the power of the god depicted. A magic formula, for example, written on a folded fragment of papyrus and hung from the neck by a thong with seven knots, was an effective amulet.

In this way, the Egyptian physician countered all poisons, healed all wounds, cured all diseases, and triumphed over the menacing beings who inflicted such evils upon people.

CHAPTER 4

The settlement of Egypt

From nomad to colonist

Recent studies tend to show that the end of the fourth interglacial period in Europe, ca. 30,000 B.C., coincides with the last of the pluvial, or rainy, epochs in North Africa, which then alternated rainy interludes with drier conditions down to the end of the Neolithic we phase ca. 2350 B.C. During the earlier part of this epoch, a warm and humid climate favored the growth of lush savannahs and forests in what are now the desert regions of North Africa and made it possible for early Paleolithic people to lead a hunting and food-gathering existence, living in the open under light shelters, probably of reed and thatch.

In the Nile Valley, when the river was cutting its channel deeper and narrower into the accumulations of gravels and other waterborne detritus, the floodplain was covered in winter and spring with luxuriant herbage that provided rich grazing for such large game as elephant, rhinoceros, wild cattle, and asses. The wadi beds were also carpeted with vegetation that supported a population of antelope, gazelle, ibex, and barbary sheep, while the Nile and its creeks teemed with fish, hippopotamus, and the ever-lurking crocodile. The reedy swamps gave cover to resident and migratory birds in profusion. This favorable environment allowed humans to find ample sustenance while staying in one tribal settlement, by fishing, trapping, hunting, and gathering seasonal foods. The hunting part of this economy persisted with diminishing importance well into historic times, though by then it had become more of a recreation than a way of life.

The Paleolithic world left its faint imprint upon the later civilization of Egypt in other ways. That empathy that develops between the hunter and his quarry ensured that the Egyptian never lost his awe of the animals of the wild as repositories of numinous force. Their periodic migrations, particularly of birds and fish, seemed to him divinely inspired, purposeful, and effective. The magic-working rock drawings of Paleolithic times, near the ancient water-holes in what is now desert, are early examples of that veneration shown to certain animals in historic times which never wholly lost its power. Similarly, the keen observation of animal forms evident in the ivory carvings of predynastic times anticipates the precision of the later hieroglyphic designs of mammals, birds, and reptiles.

The nomad camping out under clear night skies was especially conscious of the brilliance and proximity of the moon and stars. He imagined a destiny among the stars or a future existence as a star, beliefs which survive in the later eschatology of the historic Egyptians.

The later phases of the Paleolithic age (ca. 15,000–10,000 B.C.) were characterized by erratic climatic conditions as the ice-cap over Europe retreated. Increased rainfall allowed vegetation to revive in parched savannah-lands in North Africa,

THE FIRST FIGURES
This prehistoric female statuette has arms that are hardly defined, but her eyes are quite expressive.

**IN THE SHADE
OF PALM TREES**

*The Egyptians and their
livestock always looked
for shade under the palm
trees that grew along the
roads or dotted the fields—
much as in this photograph.*

while intervals of drought encouraged migrations of men and animals to more fertile tracts. With a general aridity creeping over the upland plains, the wandering tribes became ever more dependent upon their rainmakers, who, like their equivalents in the Sudan in recent times, were believed to exercise a magic control over the weather. Increasing desiccation steadily drove men and animals into the more fertile regions of the oases in the Libyan desert and the verges of the Nile itself, where they found themselves in competition for food resources with earlier groups of squatters.

As the Nile Valley was gradually settled, the first colonists encountered an entirely new set of conditions, for the land of Egypt exhibited an environment absolutely unique in the ancient world. It was not dependent upon the caprices of the local weather for its prosperity, but straggled—a long oasis in the increasing wastes of North Africa, favored by a circumstance that rendered it potentially the most fertile of all the countries of the Near East. The inundation of the Nile, which began to rise each year in July, was predictable in its yearly appearance, soon after the heliacal, or first, rising of the bright star Sirius; only its volume was uncertain. While a succession of low Niles could spell privation, even disaster, pharaonic Egypt remained for most of its existence an agricultural paradise.

This sanctuary, however, was a later development. While early squatters near the Nile in Paleolithic times may have found an environment extremely congenial to their hunting and fishing way of life, later immigrants experienced difficulty in adapting the conditions to a farming economy. The annual inundation reduced the entire area to a long narrow lake which, while it may have flushed rubbish and vermin in the Mediterranean, also swept away dwellings and landmarks and made use of the land impossible for several months. But this destructive flood also deposited the heavier sands and gravels into turtle-back mounds, or levees, along the verges of the river, eventually building them up into banks that only an exceptional rise of the Nile could cover. Such hillocks formed suitable sites for settlements; in their lee, flooded land could be developed into basin cultivation. From these physical features, the characteristic husbandry of Egypt developed, for the natural gaps between the levees could be filled by raising dikes, and the water trapped in the basins beyond could be slowly released by breaching embankments as the Nile began to fall. Growth was rapid and lush in the well-soaked virgin soil left behind.

The organization of the land of Egypt as a rich agricultural state was, however, a gradual process and was still incomplete by the end of the pharaonic period. New land was won from the deserts and swamps in most years of prosperity and brought into the fiscal system.

While the wayward force of the inundation could level, irrigate, and fertilize tracts of sterile land, it could also shift the cultivation by altering to a minor extent the former course of the river. Land could also go out of production some years through excessive flood, or drought, or fallowing, or neglect in times of political upheaval. The chief concern, however, of good government was to maintain agricultural prosperity.

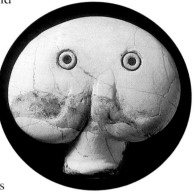

NICE EYES
Sculpted in a serpentine marble that was rare in Egypt, this bull's head with encrusted eyes dates back to the Predyanstic Period.

The Nile and the Cosmos

The change from hunting and food-gathering to crop cultivation affected profoundly the outlook of the dwellers on the banks of the Nile, and their view of the universe and how it functioned The exploitation of the land to sustain a farming economy was wholly dependent upon hydraulic engineering, on the raising of dikes and embankments, the draining of swamps, the cutting of channels and sluices, and the transporting of water. Furthermore, most of this work had to be done rapidly. In the absence of any machinery apart from primitive picks, hoes, baskets, and water jars carried on yokes, such projects required the conscription of labor under skilled organizers and inevitably involved the peasantry thrown out of work by the drowning of their fields annually under the flood.

The Egyptian thus early became inured to a disciplined way of life in which he docilely accepted direction from a corps of specialists—the ancestors of the hydraulic and civil engineers of pharaonic days. Above all, such irrigation works could not be confined to narrow sectors of the river banks but inevitably spread ever farther involving neighboring tracts together with their denizens and governors. The outcome was a political system to ensure the success and persistence of the methods of controlling and exploiting the Nile flood. Since, in order to do this, decisions often had to be taken at short notice and in conditions of stress, it was inevitable that the form of government would be authoritarian.

The magic powers of the rainmaker were irrelevant in the Nile Valley, where the life-giving water came from the inundation and not from the heavens. Nevertheless, it is almost certain that magic was still exercised by the tribal leaders to ensure that the Nile flood would arise at the proper time and in sufficient quantity. Eventually such power was vested in the national leader, the pharaoh who was thought to have command over the Nile in a virtually rainless land. Each year he performed ceremonies which were designed to bring about the rise of the Nile at the proper season with a bountiful flood.

Of even more importance, however, than these magico-political implications was the effect of this oasis culture upon the beliefs and speculative thought of the ancient Egyptians. Looking across the Nile, for most of its length they could see the

THE LANDSCAPE OF EGYPT
*The Nile rolls lazily in the
middle of a narrow valley.
Beyond lie only sand, rocks,
and arid mountains.*

boundaries of their world in the rich red-brown mud that was deposited each year. Beyond this narrow fertile belt was tawny desert, mostly sterile, inhospitable, and dangerous. The division between cultivation and wilderness, fecundity and barrenness, life and death, good and evil, was therefore clear and complete and gave the Egyptian his characteristic awareness of the essential duality of his universe.

The phenomenon of the yearly rising of the waters, with its cycle of destruction and rebirth, entered deeply into the consciousness of the Egyptian and determined his ideas of the world, his cosmology as much as his system of agriculture and his political institutions. Each year he saw his world dissolve into a waste of water, followed by its reappearance, first as a narrow spit or mound of new land as the flood subsided. Perversely, he interpreted this emergence as caused not by the subsidence of the waters but by the raising of the land. In a short time, what had been a barren hillock showing above the watery waste was a flourishing thicket of plants with its attendant insect and bird life. The Egyptian came to believe that this was a model of how the world began. Out of the waters of Chaos, containing all the germs of things in inchoate form, had arisen a primeval mound on which the work of creation began in the First Time, as he phrased it.

This idea of creation is fundamental to a number of different beliefs which existed in Egypt and make up the fabric of the ancient religion. In the course of its prehistory, the Egyptian state was slowly formed from various human settlers: pastoralists and hunters from the savannahs and deserts, herdsmen of the marshlands and coastal pastures, primitive farmers, and fowlers and fishermen from the creeks and marshes. As these people were obliged to cultivate the Nile Valley, they brought their different beliefs and myths with them, which were modified by the gradual welding of these isolated groups into larger communities until, by the end of the fourth millennium B.C., a unified state had been created. Throughout Egyptian history attempts were made at different religious centers, particularly at Heliopolis and Memphis, to reflect a unity in theological thought that had been achieved in the sphere of politics and to reconcile the various regional beliefs without entirely discarding any of them.

All had in common the concept of the primeval mound on which the Creator first appeared to fashion the universe out of elemental chaos. We shall find that this idea influences profoundly many of the institutions of Egypt—its ideas of kingship, of death and burial, and even of its architecture.

CHAPTER 5

Predynastic Egypt

The earlier phases (ca. 5000-3500 B.C.)

Some recent stages in the long march of the Egyptians from the savagery of food-gathering and hunting to the civilization of King Scorpion have been recognized as a result of excavations on various sites, but the earlier horizons still lie hidden under the Nile silt. Five blank millennia separate the Sebilian remains of the most recent Paleolithic hunters at Kom Ombo from the earliest traces of Neolithic farmers in the Faiyum. During this interlude, a momentous revolution occurred in the production of food. Meat ceased to be the chief article of diet and was replaced by plants grown intensively as crops and not gathered at random in the wild. Superior strains of wheat, barley, and flax were introduced into the Nile Valley, and there became the lifetime concern of countless generations of Egyptians to cultivate for food and clothing. The cereals required special processes in their preparation and cooking to make them palatable and digestible, and with their introduction came the widespread adoption not only of milling stones but also of that other index of a sedentary culture—receptacles of baked clay that could hold liquids as well as solids and withstand the heat of fire. Thereafter, man's progress during several millennia is mapped in the infinite forms and differing qualities of his almost indestructible pottery.

In step with his cultivation of selected plants came his domestication and breeding of certain animals, notably sheep, goats, and pigs, which were also developed in southwest Asia. Later, cattle were raised on the pastures of the Nile Delta, and the wild asses of the wadis were tamed and bent to man's will. By the time the Neolithic Age begins to reveal its vestiges in Egypt, the agrarian revolution is gathering momentum.

The later prehistoric age, or Predynastic Period, as Egyptologists are apt to term it, is most conveniently divided into two broad phases—the earlier, from ca. 5000 to ca. 3500 B.C., and the later, from ca. 3500 to ca. 3050 B.C. The first has been identified on Neolithic sites at Merimda on the southwest verges of the Delta, in the Faiyum depression (the Faiyum A culture) and at Deir Tasa in Upper Egypt. It

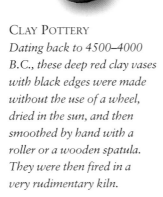

CLAY POTTERY
Dating back to 4500–4000 B.C., these deep red clay vases with black edges were made without the use of a wheel, dried in the sun, and then smoothed by hand with a roller or a wooden spatula. They were then fired in a very rudimentary kiln.

extends through the distinctive Chalcolithic cultures of el Badari and of el Amra near Abydos in Upper Egypt. The later manifestations of this earlier phase are referred to by continental prehistorians as the Naqada I culture, from the extensive sites at Naqada and Ballas near Koptos.

From a survey of the material remains found on these sites, it is evident that the early Egyptians gradually adapted themselves to a farming economy which, by the end of the period, differed little from that surviving among the tribes of the Upper Nile in recent times. Both wheat and barley were grown and stored in pits lined with mats. Basketry was practiced, and the techniques of weaving linen improved steadily. Garments were also made of animal skins which could be tanned and softened. Needles were of bone. Bracelets of shell and ivory, and perforated stone beads and disks made from shell, are common as personal ornaments. Eye-paint ground from green malachite on schist palettes and cleansing oils expressed from the wild castor plant show that the cosmetic arts, always important in the hot, dry, flybitten Egyptian summer, with its eye and skin disorders, were surely developing. Combs made from bone or ivory are decorated with figures of animals in Amratian times. Tools and weapons were almost exclusively of stone or flint, arrows being tipped with chert points or bone barbs. The throw-stick, probably used in fowling, was known in a form that differed little from that used in pharaonic times. A mace with a pear-shaped stone head replaces earlier disk and bi-conal patterns by the end of the Amratian Period, but the narrow perforation suggests that the haft was still of some resilient material such as horn or hippopotamus hide.

During this early phase, food was apparently plentiful. Dogs, goats, sheep, cattle, pigs, and geese had been domesticated, and wild game still abounded. Grain was probably boiled for porridge as well as ground for bread. Cooking and storage vessels were of pottery made by the coiling method, and the ceramic arts show a steady advance from the coarse clay cups and bowls of Faiyum A. Vases hollowed out of stone also appear near the end of the phase, the precursors of one of the most characteristic and cherished products of ancient Egypt.

The earlier cultures of Faiyum A, Merimda, and Deir Tasa reveal no evidence of the use of metals. Copper appears a little later among the Upper Egyptian sites of Badari, as at Mostagedda and Matmar, in the form of pins, ornaments, and a few modest tools. This suggests that the first employment of the metal was in the form of native copper found at sites in the Eastern Desert.

The true nature of the spiritual life of these early Nile dwellers in the periods before the invention of writing can never be known to us. They evidently believed in a hereafter for some members of the community at least, since in the burials of this period in Upper Egypt, the body is usually crouched on its left side as though awaiting rebirth, wrapped in skins or matting, and accompanied by a garniture, or adornment, of pots, cosmetic palettes, weapons, and personal ornaments. Sometimes rudimentary clay or bone figurines of women are found in the later examples, and these tend to resemble the so-called concubine figures of historic times, though their exact purpose is somewhat obscure. A statuette in the form of a cloaked and bearded figure, usually in bone and often reduced to a simple plaque, also appears occasionally in these deposits, and it has been hazarded that this object may represent a local chieftain worn as a protective amulet.

At the Faiyum A site no traces of any dwellings were found, but at Merimda and on Amratian sites post-holes have been found and remains of hearths; it is disputed whether these indicate the presence of true houses or mere shelters. At Mer-

THE WOMAN
WITH BIG EYES
In prehistoric times
(ca. 4500 to 4000 B.C.),
men were already making
sophisticated objects of bone,
wood, ivory, or stone. These
included amulets, jewelry,
and statuettes that were
astonishingly realistic.

THE FIRST ANIMALS, THE FIRST GODS

In the Valley of the Nile between 4000 and 3150 B.C. (Predynastic or Nagada Period), pottery techniques developed rapidly. Shapes changed and decorative styles diversified. Pottery was adorned with magnificent geometric patterns, stylized flowers and animals, characters, and people and boats flaunting emblems that were probably divine—perhaps the forerunners of provincial standards of the historic period. The fauna depicted is that of the desert (ostrich, ibex, and gazelle), of rivers and swamps (fish, hippopotamus, crocodiles, geese, ducks, frogs, and even turtles). Of all these animals, only the crocodile, frog, and hippopotamus were still revered in the time of the pharaohs.

In the historic period, animal gods also included Amun the ram, Anubis the jackal, Bastet the cat, Apis the bull, Sekhmet the lion, Hathor the cow, and Thueris the hippopotamus. Among the reptilian gods and goddesses were the Heket the frog, Wazet the cobra-goddess, and the Sobek the crocodile.

Bird gods included the Horus the falcon, Mut the vulture-goddess, and Thoth the ibis (also represented as a baboon). Fish, gazelles, and turtles were considered vehicles of malignant powers and were the object of ritual sacrifices. Religious figures, including the king and his priests, were forbidden the consumption of fish under any circumstances.

It is difficult to explain why so many animal gods fell from grace, given that we normally consider the religion of prehistory to be the ancestor of religion in the historic period. Were the animals on prehistoric pottery representation of deities, or simply animals that inspired the Egyptians' fear and admiration? Could beliefs have changed so radically in the time of the kings?

KNIFE FROM
GUEBEL EL-ARAK
Having a flint blade and an ivory handle made from hippopotamus tooth, this knife (3500 B.C.) is decorated with finely sculpted hunting and war scenes.

imda, the dead were buried usually in a crouching pose within the village area and even within the house precincts, a distinctly Lower Egyptian custom. The graves were often elaborately lined with reed-work. By contrast, at Badari and other Upper Egyptian sites, the dead were interred in cemeteries on the desert borders, separated from the settlements where they dwelt. The political system under which these people lived is quite obscure. Probably communities were small, self-supporting, and relatively isolated around village centers.

The later phases (ca. 3500-3050 B.C.)

Further cultural developments have in the past often been attributed to direct influences from western Asia, and it is certain that Delta sites show evidence of close links with contemporary Palestinian culture. However, the transitions in Upper Egypt certainly do not require direct intervention; the processes leading from the earlier predynastic phases to the Archaic Period are best explained with reference to the infiltration of concepts from, for instance, Mesopotamia. Good examples of the latter are the imprinting of clay with cylinder seals and certain artistic motifs, such as confronted figures and intertwined motifs; also derived from Mesopotamia may have been the idea of writing, a pictographic system being in place in the Jemdat Nasr culture by the end of the fourth millennium B.C.

Important sites for the study of the later phases of Egyptian prehistory have been identified at el Gerza, Haraga, and elsewhere in Middle Egypt. The first was nominated by Petrie as proving the type-specimen for the entire period; he therefore called it Gerzean. Nowadays, it is generally referred to as Naqada II, after the distinctive cemeteries on the extensive sites at Naqada in Upper Egypt, where it succeeds the Amratian cultures (Naqada I). The sequence of grave goods shows clear advances in technology and increases in population.

Copper working is more widespread and developed. The ceramics reveal better design and finish with the introduction of a characteristic pottery coated with a fine pinkish buff slip and painted with designs in red of animals, ships, plants, human beings, and religious emblems. The working of flint itself achieves an unrivaled perfection, thin knives being produced by pressure flaking. In this mastery over material the Egyptians were already displaying that superb technical skill that distinguishes their best work from that of other nations of antiquity.

The same skill is evident in the cosmetic, or decorative, palettes, which are a development of the greenish slate slabs and rhombs of the earlier Badarian and Amratian deposits. They are thinner, more finely worked, and often take the shape of animals, birds, and fish.

In the second half of the Late Gerzean Period (Naqada III), there is evidence of increased political activity, and the general opinion is that a struggle for predominance developed between Upper and Lower Egypt. In both regions the basic unit was now the local community clustered around a town or group of villages, under the protection of a local variant of one of the universal deities and looking for leadership to some powerful chieftain. These districts, or nomes, were the smallest fragments into which the country naturally splintered in times of anarchy. There has been much debate over the development and form of the earliest proto-states in Egypt. On the basis of later myth and legend, there is the implication that there was an Upper Egyptian confederation, centered at first at Naqada and presided over by the storm-god Seth, incarnate in a long-snouted animal. This was paralleled by a Lower Egyptian group that looked to Behdet as its leader, with the falcon-god Horus as its lord. Both these deities were looked upon in historic times as personifications of the Two Lands. However, it is unclear whether such northern and southern politics actually existed in the form apparently envisioned in later times.

In Naqada III times, one may trace the first emergence of a pattern that occurs again and again in Egyptian history—it is from the south that an ambitious prince arises who puts an end to a period of anarchy by combining the districts of Upper Egypt under his sway and swallowing piecemeal the local rulers of the north, so creating one state out of a collection of rival powers.

The evidence for the political ferment which produced dynastic Egypt is contained in a number of votive objects—chiefly palettes and maceheads, some of which have been excavated at Hierakonpolis, and others from Abydos or sites not specified. The palettes are concerned with the all-conquering might of the supreme ruler, who is shown on these greatly damaged monuments as a lion, wild bull, or jackal triumphing over foes who appear to be of northern type, wearing the penis-sheath, the characteristic male garb of Libyan tribes in historic times, and of Egyptians themselves in hunting rig.

THE "DANCER"
This footless woman with arms raised is painted terra cotta from the early Predynastic Period. Barely a foot tall, she undoubtedly played a magical role.

BEARDED MAN
This amazing male statuette shaped like a skittle was sculpted from hippopotamus tusk during the early Predynastic Period.

THE NARMER PALETTE
Wearing the red crown of the North, Narmer, first king of the 1st Dynasty, triumphs. Preceding him is a man who seems important (his vizier?) and bearers of emblems from the victorious provinces. In front, the dead are lined up, their severed heads between their legs.

The Battlefield Palette, shared among collections in London, Oxford, and Lucerne, shows corpses on a battlefield being savaged by the lion-king and attacked by crows and vultures, while an incomplete cloaked figure drives a personified captive district before him, and the standards of the Third Nome of the Delta similarly have other captives in their power. Another fragment, the Bull Palette in Paris, shows the presence of a confederacy of symbolic nomes from Upper and Lower Egypt, assisting to hold captive by a rope the Libyan foeman that the bull-king has subdued.

A third fragmentary palette from this group, now in Cairo, evidently represents operations in Libya. The high relief on one side shows tribute or booty marshaled in rows of cattle, asses, rams, and probably incense trees, together with two glyphs which later become important in the hieroglyphic group for "Libya." On the other side, beleaguered walled towns are being demolished by symbols of the king, or his confederates, wielding picks.

One of the spectacular finds made in Hierakonpolis is the great shield-shaped palette of King Narmer, which has often been interpreted as recording the very unification of Egypt. It can easily be regarded as the first complete antiquity of "pharaonic" Egypt to have survived, and in its almost immaculate condition, fine detail, and clear design, it worthily inaugurates three millennia of Egyptian artworks of all kinds.

Its reverse shows Narmer wearing the White Crown that is thereafter to become the emblematic headgear of the king as ruler of Upper Egypt. He is accompanied by his foot-washer and sandal-bearer and stands before a falcon with a human arm perched upon a symbolic tract of papyrus-land which the falcon holds by a leading-string, a rebus with the significance, "the god Horus offers the captive Delta to the King." Narmer raises his club to dispatch a foeman of Northern appearance; below lie two fallen men of Asiatic type, doubtless symbolizing fortified villages and kite-shaped gazelle traps characteristic of the Sinai peninsula. On the obverse, Narmer, now wearing the Red Crown of Sais and Buto, soon to distinguish the king as ruler of Lower Egypt, inspects a battlefield, evidently near Buto, the northern capital. Around the circular grinding depression are arranged two lionesses with serpentine necks in the charge of attendants, perhaps symbolizing the idea of union. Below them, Narmer as a wild bull breaks into a fortified place and tramples upon its fallen chieftain, probably an Asiatic.

The palette commemorates a series of victories by Narmer, evidently in Lower Egypt and on its eastern and western borders. Its virtually perfect condition shows

how carefully it had been prized over the centuries, despite the destruction of the temple in which it was found. Moreover, each figure is accompanied by hieroglyphs, which though for the most part were to remain in the repertory of such signs, are here difficult to interpret but seem to be the personal names of the protagonists in the scene. We have thus to do with the writing of a civilized state and the record of a historical event.

CHAPTER 6

The Archaic Period

Menes and the pharaonic state

According to Manetho and other Classical writers, seconded by some of the extant pharaonic lists, the first unification of Upper and Lower Egypt was achieved by Menes. However, his name has not yet been found securely on contemporary documents. Some scholars equate Narmer and Menes, while others make the latter Aha, or a conflation of Scorpion and Narmer. Narmer was, however, the first of the "historic" kings to build his tomb at Abydos, although a number of generations of earlier monarchs built their tombs near the site chosen for his.

It is from the plundered royal tombs at Abydos, and the less desecrated sepulchers of the senior nobility at Saqqara in the north, that the archaeological evidence has been recovered from which a tenuous history of the Archaic Period has been reconstructed. The kings mentioned in these tombs were identified by their Horus names (i.e., their names as incarnations of the god Horus), which differ from their personal names recorded in the king-lists. But no scholar believes that these kings are not the rulers of the first two dynasties, nor that acceptable equations between the two sets of names cannot be established. There is ample evidence that the Union of the Two Lands (ca. 3050 B.C.) by Menes, whoever he may have been, was regarded as the most important event in Egyptian history, a "First Time" similar to the establishing of the universe by the Creator. By uniting two opposed forces,

THE TRIAL OF SETH AND HORUS

Seth, of Upper Egypt, or Horus, of Lower Egypt—which would succeed to the throne now that Osiris dwelt in the world beyond?

This quarrel was the object of an 8-year trial conducted by the gods. Seth, the brother of Osiris, claimed that Horus (conceived and born after that god's death) was not Osiris's son but a usurper with no right to the throne, since he could not succeed the god who was not his father. He, Seth, was the one who must reign as the brother of Osiris (whom he himself had murdered!). As for Horus, he asserted that he was the legitimate son of Osiris and Isis.

It was left to the divine court to decide. Was Horus—who was conceived after his father's death—really the son and heir? The gods found themselves divided. The majority favored Horus. But Re, the sun god, fiercely supported Horus and so prolonged the discussions to benefit his protégé.

Requests for information followed, along with violent fights, flights, and pursuits. Unable to impose their will, however, the gods began to renegotiate. With a series of developments rife with trickery and lies, the hearings dragged on. When at last they consulted Osiris, he agreed to intervene. From the world of the dead, he confirmed that Horus was indeed his only son. The trial was at an end. Horus, crowned King of Egypt, ascended his father's throne. Isis, who had done all in her power to help him, was delighted.

Seth accepted the court's decision, and Re reluctantly acknowledged the verdict. When the god Ptah raised the question of Seth's fate, the court decided to give him the Red Lands (the deserts). They now came under the sway of Seth—he who must be feared, he whose voice must be heard in the heavens. And so it was that Seth became the dreaded god of the deserts and of thunder.

Horus and Seth, the gods of Lower and Upper Egypt, in his own person, Menes set a precedent for every pharaoh who followed him.

He did more: He created a new fulcrum between the two regions by building a residence-city on neutral ground that belonged to neither Upper nor Lower Egypt. Tradition ascribed the founding of "White Walls," later to be called Memphis, to Menes, and this capital was built on ground recovered from the Nile by diverting its course. Memphis was thereafter to be intimately associated with the pharaoh and the union for as long as the kingship lasted, being the primal place of the king's coronation and his jubilees.

The new land that was reclaimed by Menes also probably gave form to the concept of the demiurge Ptah, the god of the new town of Memphis. Ptah caused the primeval mound to arise from the waters of Chaos, in which he existed before the First Time, by taking thought and uttering a word. In the beginning was the Word. To the primitive mind, to name a thing is to create it from nothingness. So important was this utterance that in time it came to be represented as a separate deity, together with the magic thought that had created it. Thereafter the pharaoh, the incarnation of the Creator, was believed to rule by the same divine attributes of creative thought and authoritative utterance.

As the new-risen earth-mound, Ptah contained within himself all the seeds of vegetation, as well as the clay, earth, stones, metals, and minerals from which the works of men as well as nature were formed. As such, and with his intangible means of procreation through utterance, he represented a more sophisticated concept than earlier deities such as Atum. His late arrival in the pantheon is suggested by his human aspect as a man closely shrouded and inert upon his mound, carrying a scepter which incorporated the attributes of divine kingship—stability, power, and the ability to confer life.

The invention of Ptah as the god of the new land upon which White Walls was built thus reflected the same independence that had been secured by Menes in the political sphere.

The successors of Menes

The pattern of kingship set by Menes was followed by his successors as a divine formula for success. Each king in turn was crowned at Memphis, when he made a circuit of the (white) walls in a ceremony which signified his taking formal direction of his kingdom. He continued the policy of extending irrigation works and land reclamation as much by the power he was supposed to exercise over the flood as by the demands of a growing population. A steadily expanding prosperity is to be inferred from the progressive increase in the size of the tombs of the dynasty and in the magnificence of their furnishings, though all that remains of them is now mostly in random fragments. The large timber joists, roofing beams, and linings used in these constructions suggest that trade with Lebanon flourished. Articles in ivory, ebony, and lapis lazuli show that trading contacts had been made with tropical Africa and Hither Asia. Menes evidently engaged in operations against tribes in the Western Desert and in Sinai. His successor, Aha, was active in Nubia. Djer, the third king, is commemorated in a relief on the rocks near the former Second Cataract showing Nubian foes fallen in battle, others taken prisoner, and townships captured. The fifth king, Den, is shown on an ivory label from his tomb smiting the bedouin, or nomads, of the Eastern Desert or Sinai.

THE SERPENT-KING
From the dawn of the 1st Dynasty, the serpent-king —represented by a large falcon perched on top of a fortified palace and paired with a serpent—crowns this limestone stele. The stele stands 4.5 feet high.

79

The monuments of the Second Dynasty (ca. 2813–2663 B.C.) are even scantier than those of their predecessors. The substructures of two of their kings' tombs have been found at Abydos, while two more lie at Saqqara. Fire damage to the tombs of the First Dynasty has been attributed to hostility on the part of the new line but remains unproven.

Hotepsekhemwy, the name of the king of the Second Dynasty, means "The Two Powers are at Peace." However, the second part of the dynasty seems to have been riven with conflict. This may have begun when King Peribsen seems to have overturned the tradition that the pharaoh was the incarnation of the falcon-god Horus by surmounting his name in his *serekh* by the Seth-animal. King Khasekhem seems to have been forced to retreat to Hierakonpolis in the south before being finally victorious under the name Khasekhemwy— "Appearance of Two Powers." As self-proclaimed reconciliator, he prepared the way for a new dynasty, the Third, from the the Archaic Period.

A SCULPTED PALETTE
On this palette dating back to the Predynastic period, bulls, sheep, and rams march ahead on different levels.

The culture of the Archaic Period

Despite the evidence of religious contention, the achievement of the first two dynasties was considerable, resulting in the establishment of many of the institutions and traditions of the pharaonic state. In particular, the office of kingship evolved. From the first, the pharaoh wore the trappings of a pastoral chief, his loins protected by a *shemset* apron, his back guarded by a bull's tail hanging from his belt, the goat beard of his flocks attached to his chin, and he carried the crook and incense-gum collecting flail of a Mediterranean shepherd. When he officiated as King of Upper Egypt, he wore the tall conical White Crown. As King of Lower Egypt, he wore the Red Crown; but in the reign of Den a combination of both crowns appeared in a new headgear, the Double Crown. At the same time, a new title, He-who-belongs-to-the-Sedge-and-the-Bee (usually translated as "the King of Upper and Lower Egypt"), and an additional name to accompany it, were added to the name he had adopted as an incarnation of the god Horus.

THE CREATION OF THE WORLD AND THE DIVINE DYNASTY

On the day of the First Time, said the priests of Heliopolis, Re (the future sun god) assembled himself, floated, and awoke to life. Dreaming and imagining, he suddenly created a tiny island in the icy waters of the primordial ocean. There he took refuge, transforming himself into a phoenix with ashen wings before flying away.

Shu, god of the air, and Tefnut, goddess of moisture, were born from his saliva. Shu and Tefnut gave birth to Geb, god of the Earth, and Nut, goddess of the heavens. Re created the gigantic *Hehu,* four men and four women whose task was to hold up the world. He gave shape to the gods and goddesses, to Egypt and the Nile, to human beings, and to all feathered, fur-bearing, and scaly creatures.

Geb and Nut quarreled so constantly that their father, Shu, decided to separate them. He raised the goddess of the heavens high above his head, leaving the earth beneath his feet. But Geb and Nut continued to love in secret, giving birth to five children: Osiris, Seth, Horus the Old, Isis, and Nephthys.

Meanwhile, Re reigned as absolute master and slowly grew old. Weary of those who dared to plot against him, he sought refuge in the heavens with Nut. He bequeathed his throne to his son Shu, who, with the full backing of his sister-spouse, Isis, would much later pass it on to his son Osiris, a good and equitable god-king. It is written, "Osiris raised the Egyptians from their condition of wild beasts wanting for everything, acquainted them with the fruits of the earth, gave them laws, and taught them to respect the gods."

But jealousy drove his brother Seth to murder Osirus. At the end of a long trial, power was entrusted to his son Horus, the last god to reign on earth. After him came the pharaohs—"sons of Horus"—their successors to the throne of the Two Kingdoms.

The pharaoh also inherited all the magic virtue of a primitive medicine man. His power over the Nile and its life-giving waters accredited him with seminal influences, keeping drought and sterility from his peoples. He contended with evil which manifested itself in the form of human predators on the cultivators of the valley, or in the wild animals and birds that preyed upon the domestic flocks and the ripening crops. So he is represented not only as smiting the Asiatic bedouin of Sinai and the Eastern Desert, or the Libyans of the northwest and the Nubians of the south, but also as the intrepid hunter of the lion and wild cattle. In his guise as Horus, the harpooner of the hippopotamus foe into which Seth has transformed himself, he seeks his enemy among the marshlands. On death he is assimilated to the Creator of whom he is an incarnation, and his tomb becomes holy ground.

A concomitant of such beliefs was the practice of sacrificing subsidiary wives and servants with their equipment to accompany the king into the next world and so achieve immortality by ministering to him in the hereafter. Around the tombs of the kings, queens, and certain nobles of the First Dynasty are ranged the pit burials of their women and retainers, dwarf attendants, even pet dogs. The custom reached its peak in the reign of Djer. Thereafter it declined and ceased at Saqqara by the end of the dynasty. It lingered on at Abydos into the Second Dynasty, when a solitary pair of servants was buried with Khasekhemwy.

The civil service

Land in Egypt was made suitable for cultivation as much by seasonal organized human effort on a large scale as by natural conditions. This circumstance favored the emergence of technocrats who directed labor, determined the right moment for raising dams and piercing dikes, cutting canals, and redefining boundaries. They organized the collection and storage of harvests and decided how much of it was to be allocated to imposts and to the next season's seed.

FIRST BOATS
Made in the Thinite period, this terra cotta boat model reminds us of the importance of navigation on the Nile, the only way to travel quickly.

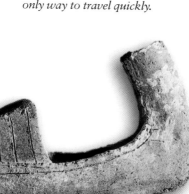

Apart from the companions of the king, who assisted him in his administrative duties and in the affairs of his household, there were the two chancellors in charge of the Red and White Treasuries, as the storehouses of Lower and Upper Egypt were designated from their national colors. The collection and distribution of supplies of all kinds—from wine and oil to corn and honey—were under their direction and that of the two Controllers of the Granaries. The distribution of supplies to the temples, and to a privileged elite of courtiers and officials, was administered from the Office of the Overseer of the King's Bounty.

The development of Egypt as a powerful political entity under a divine king would not have been possible, even with a dedicated bureaucracy of competent offi-

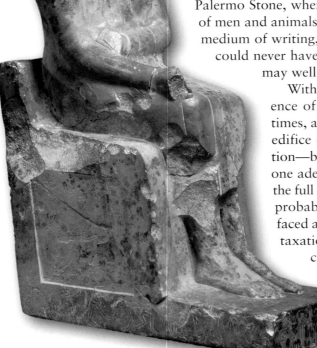

ROYAL STATUE
The pharaoh Khasekhem,
who reigned at the end
of the 2nd Dynasty, is
immortalized in this fine
limestone sculpture. He
wears the White Crown,
symbol of Upper Egypt.

cials, in the absence of another element—a staff of learned scribes, skilled in the magic arts of reading, writing, and mathematics. It is the ubiquitous scribe with his writing-palette and papyrus roll who obtrudes himself upon the notice at most periods of the Egyptian past. Papyrus paper had already been invented by the beginning of the First Dynasty; two rolls of blank papyrus were found in a store-chamber of the tomb of Hemaka at Saqqara. A rapid and cursive system of writing adapted to the use of pen and ink upon papyrus was soon evolved from the hesitant glyphs carved on the Narmer Palette. Writing, as elsewhere, was developed in Egypt not for the purpose of enshrining great thoughts in a memorable literary form, but for the utilitarian purpose of recording the minutiae of state business in a portable and durable form, and not entrusting it to fallible human memory. Precise instructions could be issued at a distance and reports received from afar.

The early use of data preserved by such a system is evident in entries on the Palermo Stone, where the heights of the inundation and the periodical censuses of men and animals are noted over a period of some five centuries. Without the medium of writing, the highly centralized administration of the Egyptian state could never have been devised; in fact, the creation of a unified government may well have had to await the invention and spread of writing.

With the art of writing there was a parallel development in the science of calculation. A decimal system had existed in predynastic times, and it is possible that during the Archaic Period nearly all the edifice of later Egyptian mathematics was raised on this foundation—but since most scribal learning was transmitted verbally from one adept to his pupil as a mystery, we have no means of assessing the full extent of their theoretical knowledge. The incentives were also probably utilitarian, the need for solving the many problems that faced a centralizing state dependent for its wealth upon a scheme of taxation that was ultimately determined from measurements and calculations of possible and actual yields. The bureaucrat would also be required to solve problems connected with such matters as the distribution of rations or seed-corn, the number of bricks required to build a given structure, and the number of men necessary to perform different kinds of laboring work. The Rhind Mathematical Papyrus in the British Museum (written about 1600 B.C.) and other similar texts reveal that by the end of the third millennium B.C. the Egyptians had developed a system of numeration with which they could make arithmetical calculations involving complicated fractions with comparative ease and accuracy. They were also familiar with elementary solid geometry and the properties of circles, cylinders, triangles, and pyramids. Since they could find the area of a circle with tolerable accuracy, they could also calculate the volume of a cylinder. They could also determine the volume of a pyramid or truncated pyramid.

The inundations of the Nile often swept away old landmarks, and an accurate survey periodically had to be made to reestablish former boundaries according to the written records. While linear measure, like that of Europe before the introduction of the metric system, was based upon the dimensions of the human body—the finger, palm, forearm, and so forth—measurements of capacity also existed for assessing the corn, oil, and wine harvests.

The science of computing time did not lag behind that of measuring space. The prosperity of Egypt depended upon forecasting the annual rise of the Nile and its probable volume, and what in a pre-scientific society was just as important—the auspicious moment for a feat or religious ceremony to ensure the success of an undertaking. Astronomy was studied with particular attention at the temple of the sun-god at Heliopolis, where the ritual was closely concerned with time-measurement and the movement of heavenly bodies. Architects and engineers of Heliopolitan origin seem to have been responsible for the accurate orientation of pyramids and their geometrical perfection during the early Old Kingdom.

It was observed at an early date that the dog-star Sirius, regarded as the goddess Sopdet (Greek, Sothis), vanished from sight for a period of seventy days in midsummer and then rose on the eastern horizon for the first time before dawn, and this appearance foretold the rising of the Egyptian Nile in inundation a few days later. This annual heliacal, or first, rising of Sothis was regarded as a prime event, the beginning of a new year and the means of fixing the first of the month of the old Egyptian calendar.

Like many other primitive peoples and the nations of antiquity, the Egyptians had an original lunar calendar determined by the phases of the moon during the cycle of growing, fruiting, and resting that made up the agricultural year. They early realized that four lunar months went to the season of inundation *(akhet),* another four to the season of planting and growth *(peret),* and a further four to the season of harvest and low water *(shomu).* It was some unknown genius during the Archaic Period who devised a schematic lunar year of 365 days and fixed its inception upon the rising of Sirius. The new calendar, called by modern scholars the civil calendar, had a year consisting of twelve months of thirty days each, with five extra days at the end regarded as the birthdays of the gods of the Osiris cycle. Each month of thirty days was divided into three ten-day weeks, an arrangement which involved a day of twenty-four hours. The resulting calendar has been described as "the only intelligent calendar which has ever existed in human history."

WINE JARS
The Egyptians had vineyards as early as the Thinite Period. They knew how to cultivate them and make good wine, conserving and transporting it in terra cotta jars.

It was some time before Egyptians realized that their civil calendar was lagging behind the astronomical year. They never corrected this discrepancy by intercalating, or inserting, an additional day every four years but allowed the civil year to get out of phase until in 4 x 365 years, it came into conjunction again. This occurred at the end of the Eighteenth Dynasty (ca. 1317 B.C.). Instead of a leap year, the Egyptians introduced (ca. 2500 B.C.) a second lunar calendar tied not to Sothis, but to the civil year. For most of its existence, therefore, the pharaonic state had three calendars—the civil year and its lunar counterpart for administrative and fiscal purposes, and the original lunar year to fix the dates of religious festivals and temple services.

The struggles that preceded the union and which are reflected in the design of the votive palettes from Abydos and Hierakonpolis show the importance of the nomes as the allies of the king. But thereafter their influence wanes, except as representatives of the various districts of the land at the coronation and at its repetition during the jubilees of the pharaoh. In their place, the figure of the king towers over all, just as his tomb outrivals those of any others, apart perhaps from one or two belonging to chief queens or queen mothers. The presence of the large mastabas of such women bearing names compounded with Neith, the great goddess of Sais in Lower Egypt, is redolent of the importance assumed by royal women at all subsequent periods in Egypt.

The age was one of ferment in the theological field, too, evident in the dispute between the cults of Horus and Seth, with its effect upon the politics of the kingship. Elsewhere the Palermo Stone speaks of the "birth" of various gods during the early reigns, by which we are to understand that the iconography of the pantheon was being settled by devising the image of individual deities, installing them in shrines built for their cult, and endowing them with a priesthood and revenues.

Little of the art of the age has survived intact, but the two statues of King Khasekhem (ca. 2680 B.C.) show a progressive mastery in carving soft limestone and hard schist. The great glory of the two dynasties is their wealth of fine stone vessels cut from selected boulders in breccia, rock crystal, diorite, slate, alabaster, and other hard stones. The introduction of the potter's wheel and the consequent production of fine pottery in the Second Dynasty reduced the quantity and quality of later stone vessels.

THE LEGEND OF THE YEAR'S FIVE ADDITIONAL DAYS

While inventing a remarkably precise calendar that formed a lunar year consisting of 365 days (12 months of 30 days, plus 5), the Egyptians also invented a legend to explain the surplus.

Geb (the god of the earth) and his sister Nut (the goddess of the heavens) fought so often that their father Shu (god of the air) decided that they would have to be separated. Yet the two met in secret, and soon Nut became pregnant. Informed of their illicit affair, an angry Re (the sun god) forbade Nut to give birth at any time during the month or year. Plagued with worry and despair, Nut asked Thoth, the god with an ibis head, for help.

A magician and reputed man of knowledge, Thoth decided to circumvent the divine ban. To accomplish this, he went to see the Moon and proposed to play with her on the chess board of 30 squares; the challenge was to win hours and minutes. The Moon accepted, and the game began. Thoth quickly took the lead. When he had won enough hours to total five days, he stopped the game and took his leave. Thoth then suggested that Nut give birth during these five days offered by the Moon.

This she did. On the first day, Nut gave birth to Osiris; on the second to Horus the Elder, who had a falcon head; on the third to Seth, who tore his mother's belly; on the fourth to Isis; and on the fifth to Nephthys. In using the additional days won by Thoth, Nut had not disobeyed, and so Re could not complain. He was touched by these three gods and two goddesses, young and beautiful and as large as giants. Their bodies were made of gold, their bones of silver, and their hair of lapis lazuli. Since this day, the Egyptian calendar keeps 12 months of 30 days, plus five—that is, a total of 365, even if in myth these extra days were thought to be dangerous.

CHAPTER 7

The pyramid age of the Old Kingdom I

Imhotep and Egyptian culture

With the Third Dynasty, Egypt entered fully and gloriously into those five centuries of high culture to which modern historians have given the name of the Old Kingdom. Khasekhemwy was followed on the throne by Sanakht and Djoser; although apparently Khasekhemwy's sons by Queen Nimaethap, they were regarded by posterity as beginning a new dynasty. Reliefs on the rocks near the turquoise and copper-ore mines in Sinai show these kings and their successor Sekhemkhet in the now classic pose of keeping evil from their borders by smiting the local bedouin. All the figures reveal the dour, heavy portraits of the Third Dynasty kings and their followers.

It is, however, more in the art of peace than in war that the Third Dynasty kings are celebrated, and here the chief actor is not a king but a king's man, the chancellor Imhotep, preeminent in his time and renowned in later ages as an astronomer, architect, writer, sage, and physician, being eventually deified. As a heroic instigator of Egyptian culture, his reputation never lost its luster, until in Ptolemaic times, as Manetho records, he was famed for the invention of building in dressed stone in the reign of Djoser.

The truth of this traditional association was vindicated when excavations at the Step Pyramid at Saqqara brought to light a statue base of Djoser on which the name and titles of Imhotep are given equal pride of place with those of the king. Actually, stone flooring, walling, lintels, and jambs had appeared sporadically during the Archaic Period, but a great building made entirely of cut stone appeared first in the world during the reign of Djoser, to remain for ever the wonder of its age.

The tombs of the kings and nobles of the Archaic Period show a steady evolution in size and design. The burial chambers were soon located below ground,

THE CHAPELS OF DJOSER
The architecture of these "dummy" chapels, decorated with three small fluted columns, is reminiscent of ancient celebration houses built from reeds and covered with a vaulted roof.

DJOSER IN SAQQARA
(Saqqara, mortuary complex of King Djoser) Bordering the Great Court to the east, between the entrance and the Step Pyramid, still stand the ruins of the "temple with three fluted columns," a small rectangular building decorated with tori, or convex moldings, around the four outside corners.

while the magazines for grave goods were built into the mass of the superstructure, the rectangular mound, or mastaba, of mud brick which surmounted the private tombs. The faces of such mastabas were built in a panelled design similar to the façades of great houses, and the presumption is that in their complete state each would have represented a great mansion in which the dead eternally rested. What sort of superstructure overlaid the ruined Abydos royal tombs is uncertain, but it may also have been a rectangular mound surrounded by trees.

The funerary enclosures which complemented them were the truly monumental elements. These brick walls enclosed a large open area that seems to have contained a variety of buildings constructed in wood and reeds. The latest of these structures added inside it a brick-skinned mound. It was the genius of Imhotep to take the basic plane of the funerary monuments of the kings of the Second Dynasty and by introducing new elements develop it into a funerary complex of great originality. He chose a site at Saqqara, opposite the capital at Memphis, where its position on an escarpment on the Western Desert verges would ensure that it would dominate the skyline. Furthermore, he eventually developed the mound of the super-structure into a stepped construction rising in six diminishing tiers to a height of almost 240 feet, like a giant double staircase reaching into the sky, each face orientated to a cardinal point. The various buildings associated with this central feature were enclosed by a wall of palace-façade pattern over a mile in its perimeter and covering a rectangular area more than sixty times the extent of Khasekhemwy's tomb at Abydos.

Of the fourteen great portals that interrupt the pattern of the paneled walls, only one is a true entrance, its doors represented as though folded back, giving access to a vast *dromos* through an impressive colonnade of engaged piers. The mortuary temple adjoining the pyramid on its northern side is an elaboration of a sim-ilar structure in the brick mastaba tomb of Merka, dating to the end of the First Dynasty. There are also other familiar features, such as the magazine housing provisions and furnishings on the north side and (in galleries and chambers) beneath the pyramid. But there are also a number of elements that appear for the first time, such as a jubilee court, with the attendant throne-podium and vestries. On the south side of the pyra-mid was an extensive *dromos,* with its hoof-shaped markers for defining the course that the king would encircle in a running ceremony at his coronation when he took possession of the land. He repeated this rite at his jubilees.

A remarkable feature was a large mastaba-type tomb on the southern boundary (nearest to Abydos), with its adjacent chapel and subterranean apart-ments that duplicated the funerary chambers beneath the pyramid itself. In addition, there was a wealth of precious objects and furnishings, such as the pan-els of blue glazed tiles that decorated some of the subterranean rooms in imi-tation of rush-mat hangings. Statues of gods and of the king, either alone or with members of his family, in standing and seated poses, were installed, includ-ing a life-size statue of Djoser upon his throne. There were also delicate low-relief panels of the king performing his running ceremony. In various chambers were stored over 40,000 stone vessels, evidently royal heirlooms of the Archaic Period. In addition to all this, of course, was the more costly treasure which was doubtless pillaged from it long ago.

In his great design, it is evident that Imhotep incorporated and expanded the ele-ments previously separately provided at Abydos within the same complex, and

DJOSER IN HELIOPOLIS
The pharaoh is represented on this mural fragment from the building devoted to him in Heliopolis. Nothing remains of this large center for the cult of the sun god, Re. It was also the birthplace of the Egyptian monarchy.

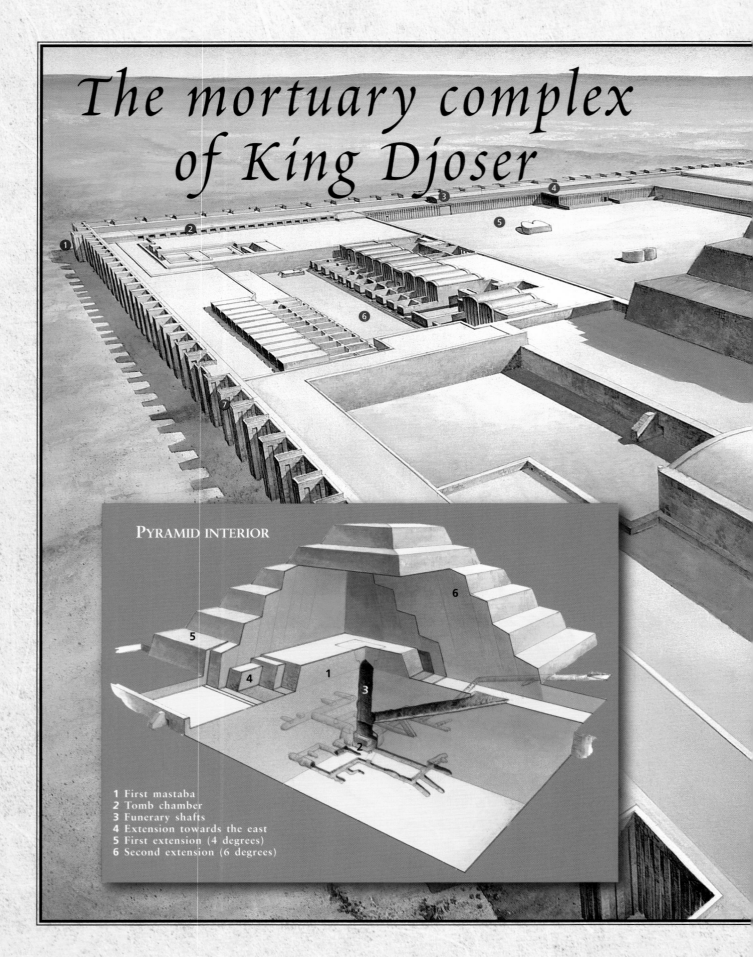

The mortuary complex of King Djoser

PYRAMID INTERIOR

1 First mastaba
2 Tomb chamber
3 Funerary shafts
4 Extension towards the east
5 First extension (4 degrees)
6 Second extension (6 degrees)

THE MORTUARY COMPLEX OF KING DJOSER *(Saqqara)*
Djoser organized his tomb over 15 hectares of desert. It was surrounded by a redan fortification. A single door in the enclosure opened onto a covered corridor that led to a court, in the middle of which stood two altars. The South Tomb most likely held the urns containing the royal innards. The pyramid, a traditional mastaba with a shaft leading to a tomb, expanded to the east into another shaft to bury the royal family. It was first raised 4 degrees, then 6, which indicates that Imhotep, the architect, experimented with his designs. The first pyramid was born.
To the north stood the mortuary temple and the serdab, the secret chamber that contained the ka royal statue. To the east stood the House of the North and the House of the South. To the west was Heb-Sed Court, bordered with "dummy" chapels, which allowed the deceased to celebrate the jubilee festivities. Stone cobras sculpted on the wall protected the king's tomb.

❶ Entrance
❷ Entry colonnade
❸ South tomb
❹ Wall of cobras
❺ Great Court
❻ Heb-Sed Court
❼ Enclosure wall
❽ House of the South
❾ Mortuary temple and entrance to the pyramid
❿ Serdab
⓫ Serdab Court
⓬ House of the North

89

included also such traditional features as subsidiary tombs for members of the royal family. The monument, in fact, was a vast city of the dead, enclosed within a *temenos*, the walls of which imitated the white walls which Menes had built around his residence four centuries earlier. But the various components were buildings by magic only. They were mere dummies, façades behind which lay rubble fillings. Imitation doors, whith their cross-battens, hinges, and bolts, stand open where approach is permitted. Stake fences carved in high relief on blocking walls bar access where entry is forbidden.

The truly novel aspect of the Step Pyramid complex, however, marking a turning point in the development of architecture, was that there sprung complete from the mind of Imhotep a system of building entirely in quarried stone, in local limestone for the mass of the various structures and fine limestone from Tura across the river for the casings and claddings. The burial chambers were constructed of pink granite from distant Aswan, and black granite from the same quarries was used for such features as corbels carved as the heads of foreign foemen.

The Step Pyramid of Djoser was a translation into stone of a technique of building in wood and vegetable products, such as bundles of reeds, stalks of papyrus rush and palm fronds stripped of all but their uppermost leaves, coated with mud. It is doubtful, however, whether the domestic architecture which Imhotep immortalized in stone reproduced contemporary buildings, except perhaps in the more secluded and primitive areas of the marshlands. Houses had been made of mud brick from Amratian times. The design of the structures that Imhotep raised for Djoser at Saqqara seems to harken back to a very remote past, deliberately recalling the occasion of the First Time, when creation arose in the primeval marsh, to which Djoser would return on death. This was a style of architecture that would never be seen again in Egypt—a giant stage-set for the enactment of a miracle-play of the king's resurrection as a great god in the hereafter. Only in one feature did subsequent architecture preserve the same principles of design: The holy-of-holies of the Egyptian temple is a rendering in stone of the primitive rush-work cabin that arose on the primeval mound at the First Time to shelter the Creator at his work.

RE'S VOYAGES IN THE BOATS OF DAWN AND DUSK

Clothed all in red, his falcon head topped with the solar disc, Re burrowed under the gate of heaven. He emerged behind the desert uplands, behind the distant eastern coasts. It was dawn. At once, fish leapt in the waters and birds beat their wings in his honor. A chorus of joyful baboons sang songs of praise in greeting. Awakened by the gentleness of his rays, the animals danced for joy. Men lifted up their hands to him and praised the great sun god.

Re immediately boarded the Bark of Day and sailed across the sky until nightfall. The craft he had chosen to navigate was a magnificent creation of solid gold. Built by the gods, who escorted it day and night, it measured 770 cubits (1,300 feet) long. The stars were its crew. Re encountered many dangers along the way, but he easily dispelled the gale, drove off the rain, shattered the hail, and repulsed the fearsome snake Apopis, his eternal enemy.

In 12 hours, Re reached the edge of the world, far beyond the western desert. It was dusk.

Now the sun god changed vessels and boarded the Bark of Night. From there he shone his brilliant rays on the god Osiris, lord of the beyond and the dead.

As soon as they saw the sun god, the deceased called out joyful greetings, their eyes opened and their hearts exulted. When their prayers reached Re, he at once dispelled their pains and sorrows. Since the winds from the world of the living could not penetrate the world of the dead, the deceased took hold of the rope and hauled it trough the 12 hours of the night.

As soon as he left the world of the dead, Re washed off the dark colors of night in Lake Iaru. Once again dressed all in red, the sun god made his way back under the gate of heaven.

The rise of Heliopolis

There is, however, another and scarcely less important aspect of the entry upon the scene of Imhotep, the architect. He was also the high priest of the sun god in Heliopolis, where Djoser also built a temple decorated with elegant stone reliefs. We are now confronted with the clear emergence of the powerful and widespread influence of the solar cult that was to dominate Egyptian civilization thereafter.

The priesthood of Heliopolis served the office of an intelligentsia. It was from their study of the heavens in which their god was lord that they derived their knowledge of the movement of celestial bodies, the calculation of time-spans from the rising and setting of stars, the geometry of angles, the measurement of space, and similar studies. Such science was jealously preserved as the mysteries of their religion and handed down from one adept to another, like the secrets of writing, reading, mathematics, and any other craft. Such knowledge too conferred power and ensured that in the developing technology of the Egyptian state, the wise men of On would be paramount.

The learning of such pundits had its effect upon the politics of the kingship from an early date. Nebre, a king of the Second Dynasty, incorporated the name of the sun god in his own. The doctrines of Ptah were greatly influenced by the teaching of Heliopolis, 20 miles to the north of Memphis. Above all, the fusion of the sun religion with the cult of the pharaoh is shown in the design of a comb of Djet, incised with a design of Horus in the barque of the sun god sailing across the heavens in the form of the outspread wings of the sky goddess Nut. The king is an incarnation of Horus, and thus arises the idea of the sun god as a heavenly king, Re-Herakhty. The pharaoh rules on earth as his representative.

The sun cult of Heliopolis taught that out of the waters of Chaos arose the primeval mound in the shape of the pyramidal stone, the *ben-ben*, or High Sand, in the sanctuary at Heliopolis. It was on the *ben-ben* that the Creator first manifested himself as Atum, the demiurge in human form. Atum immediately created from himself by masturbation two other deities, Shu and Tefnut, to form a trinity. Shu, the god of Air or the Void, and Tefnut, the goddess of Moisture, created by their coupling another pair, Geb the earth, and Nut, the heavens. Four others were added to these quintessential gods to form the great *ennead*, or group of the nine gods of Heliopolis. Shu, by interposing himself between Geb and Nut, separated the heavens from the recumbent earth—which was regarded as male in Egypt, against the universal concept elsewhere of mother earth. By lowering the goddess every evening

SNOFERU'S PYRAMID
In Dahshur, Snoferu's rhomboid pyramid did not contain any sarcophaguses. Its long corridor descended into a vaulted chamber.

91

on to the earth, Shu brought about the pro-creation of two pairs of other deities—the gods Osiris and Seth and the goddesses Isis and Nephthys.

These legends reveal a very early syn-cretization, for fusion, between different sets of beliefs, in which the divinities of the Osiris cycle of Abydos and Busiris were assimilated into the Heliopolitan pantheon, this process doubtless reflecting the political unions of city-states that preceded the consolidation of the country under one ruler. By historic times the sun god was gen-erally represented in his active role as a heav-enly king Re, or Re-Herakhty, and usually appears in the form of a king with the head of the falcon Horus bearing on his vertex the solar disk.

Djoser in one inscription is hailed as the sun god himself, but by the Fourth Dynasty it was established that the pharaoh was the son of Re, who would on death journey to the horizon, where he would be assimilated to the god who had begot-ten him. Re-Herakhty sailed over the waters of heaven in a day-bark, bringing light and life to a sleeping world that imitated that moribund state that existed before there was light at the First Time. At sunset he stepped into the night-bark and contin-ued his circuit over the waters that are under the earth in the form of Flesh, an inert ram-headed manifestation of the Creator, undergoing various transformations, like the phases of a long dream, that ensured that he would awake in the redness of dawn as a child-king within the uterine sun-disk.

CHEOPS'S BOAT
At the foot of the royal pyramid, a huge pit contained all the pieces necessary for building a boat—for after his death, the king had to navigate with the gods. This boat was entirely reassembled.

The influence of Heliopolitan theology can be seen in the conversion of the super-structure of the royal tomb from a palace to the High Sand of the sun cult. The design did not develop without several changes of plan, and the Step Pyramid even-tually appeared as a staircase whereby the dead king could mount up into the sky to join the crew of the solar barque as it sailed across the heavens from the moment that the rising sun lit up its topmost stage. Subsequent kings of the Third Dynasty adopted the same pattern of superstructure for their tomb complexes, though none of them succeeded in completing his monument.

Snuferu, first king of the Fourth Dynasty, was responsible for erecting the first true pyramids, at Dahshur. The earlier of these, the Bent Pyramid, changes its angle halfway up; the later, the Red Pyramid, is the earliest structure with an uninterrupted slope. The building of two such monuments by one king was the result of structural failure at the Bent Pyramid; Sneferu was interred in the Red Pyramid, where some of his body was found.

With his son and successor, Cheops, the pyramid age fairly gets into its stride. Cheops built at Giza the Great Pyramid, and this, together with its two compan-ions on the same site, was considered one of the wonders of the ancient world. It is still able to stun the spectator into silence despite all its ruin, its casing-stones having been stripped off to build medieval Cairo. It contained well over 2,000,000 blocks of limestone, some of them weighing 15 tons apiece. The core blocks were quarried on the spot, but the finer casing blocks were cut at Tura and ferried to the site during the times of high flood. In addition, granite boulders were hewn as jambs, and relieving beams and basalt blocks were used to floor the mortuary temple, where the cloister was supported by granite piers.

Internally, the Great Pyramid is the most elaborate of its period. This seems to have been the result of a series of changes of plan which the late I. E. S. Edwards convincingly argued was the result of a decision to employ a stone sarcophagus for the first time in a royal tomb since the early Third Dynasty.

The original burial chamber was deep underground, reached by a passage far too narrow to allow the passage of such an item. A new chamber was thus constructed in the superstructure, through whose roof the sarcophagus could be introduced (this room is now known erroneously as the "Queen's Chamber") but this was abandoned in favor of a further, much grander, new chamber, in which the king was ultimately buried (the "King's Chamber").

From these rooms lead apparently unique "air shafts," although traces of beginnings were found in Chephren's pyramid. They are generally assumed to have had some astronomical significance; when investigated using a robot in 1990, one of the small channels in the Queen's Chamber, 8 inches square, was found to be blocked with a piece of stone to which two copper items were attached. This led to much ridiculous media speculation about a "secret door"; investigation of the blocking has yet to take place.

Another discovery made during the same decade was that of the foundations of the lost subsidiary pyramid of Cheops by the Director of the Giza Plateau, Zahi Hawass. All pyramids of the Old Kingdom have small pyramids on their south/southeast sides, which should not be confused with those built for queens, some of which have subsidiaries of their own. The meaning of these subsidiary monuments remains wholly obscure, none having revealed any material that might provide a proper explanation.

KING KHAFRE
This diorite royal statue was discovered inside a grave in the vestibule of the temple of the Valley of Khafre, not far from the sphinx.

THE MORTUARY CITY AROUND THE PYRAMID

The sands of Giza are dominated by the pyramids of Cheops and his successors. As striking as the monuments themselves was the architectural complex surrounding the Great Pyramid. In it were a funerary temple linked by a long causeway to a second temple on the borders of cultivated fields, recesses hewn from the rock to house five wooden ships, smaller pyramids (often wrongly call queens' pyramids), and the countless flat-roofed tombs known as mastabas. The complex was laid out in streets of tombs built for the nobility, officials, and dignitaries, who thus escorted their master in the beyond as they had escorted him on earth.

From the time of the Old Kingdom, when the king ascended into heaven, he joined Re's companions on his heavenly vessel, bringing with him into the beyond all those who had been under his care on earth. Everyone sought this pharaonic protection as the voyage into eternity began. Nobles, courtiers, and officials gave enduring assurance of their devotion to the king, from whom they expected many benefits in the beyond.

The social heirarchy, so rigidly respected in Pharaonic Egypt, was thus perpetuated in the next world—hence the funeral cities that sprang up, their streets and neighborhoods segregated by class, with the noblest housed closest to the pyramid.

The choicest places were undoubtedly allotted by royal consent. Of those who lived by the sovereign's favors, some received his support for the building and upkeep of their mastabas; the pharaoh might offer a whole tomb to one, a false door or stone sarcophagus to another. Some prayed that they would receive "the offering the king makes by the thousand: bread, beer, cattle, geese, and all good things"—an inscription found in many mastabas.

Each pyramid had its ancillary buildings within its complex. Nearby, in the royal tradition, the mastaba tombs of relatives and high court officials clustered around their kings in death as they had attended them in life. Two such cemeteries that Cheops built to the east and west of the Great Pyramid were particularly grand in their design and use of rich materials. The dilapidated condition in which many of these monuments have come down to us, however, gives an impression of cold austerity, though in their original state it is now clear that the mortuary temples and causeways were decorated with the most delicate low reliefs, brilliantly colored, of which only small, scattered fragments remain. The Valley Temple of Chephren, the best preserved of the subsidiary buildings at Giza, is indeed impressive in its stark simplicity, with severe granite piers upholding equally massive architraves, and with the cyclopean limestone walls clad inside and out with large granite ashlars, or squared stones, unrelieved by any ornamentation apart from a hieroglyphic inscription deeply incised around each entrance doorway. In its original condition, however, it must have been tremendously impressive with the sunlight streaming through louvers cut at ceiling level and falling upon the polished alabaster floor, scattering a diffused glow upon the twenty-three statues of the king—carved from alabaster, graywacke, and green diorite from the Nubian desert—that stood before the piers in the interior hall.

In the uncompromising severity and nicely calculated effects of this, the most complete realization of the mortuary concept in Egyptian architecture, we are aware of the same intelligence at work that raised the pyramids at Giza in all their accuracy and orientated them with great precision. In the impressive portrait statue of Cheops' cousin, the vizier Hemon, who was evidently responsible for the building of the Great Pyramid, there is more than a hint of that supreme assurance and intellectual ruthlessness which these early engineers must have possessed to plan, organize and complete such mighty works.

The Giza monuments, of course, were also repositories of statuary, reliefs, furniture, vessels, and other funerary equipment upon which the best artists of the day were encouraged to lavish their talents. Most of it has been destroyed without trace, but we are fortunate that some samples have survived of the brilliant art of this classic period of Egypt's past. In particular, the painstaking work of the Boston-Harvard Expedition has succeeded in accurately reconstructing the magnificent gold-covered furniture of Queen Hetepheres, the mother of Cheops, from her greatly decayed secondary burial. The superb design, proportions, and workmanship of her boxes, chairs, bed, and canopy—with their fine work in carved ebony and cedarwoods; their overlays of cast, chased and tooled gold; and their inlays of blue and black faience and red carnelian—display a taste that is both opulent yet under perfect restraint.

The immense necropolis of the Giza plateau, a veritable city of the dead élite of their time, was protected by a guardian colossus, the Great Sphinx. This huge statue of a recumbent lion with the head of a king—in this example, Chephren—is hewn out of a knoll of rock left after the extraction of stone from a local quarry. It is the

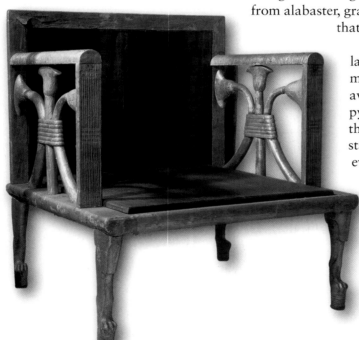

ROYAL ARMCHAIR
Queen Hetepheres (4th Dynasty) sat in this armchair. Its legs are shaped like lion paws, and it most likely had a cushion.

first known version, and the largest, of a type of representation that haunted the imagination of the ancients, and attracted legends around it in Egypt, before the days of Oedipus. According to Egyptian belief, the lion and its derivative, the sphinx, were the protectors of thresholds and would seize any intruder who violated sacred precincts. By the New Kingdom at the latest, however, the Great Sphinx was regarded as a manifestation of Re-Herakhty, the sponsor of the ruling king, and its connection with Chephren had been almost entirely lost.

The heavy drain upon human and material resources that the building of the Giza pyramids evidently imposed was not demanded of their subjects by later pharaohs. Even before the end of the Fourth Dynasty, a decline in the royal pretensions is discernible. The courtiers of Chephren and Mycerinus are buried in modest rock-hewn tombs, and the pyramid of the latter king is a third of the size of either of its giant companions. Shepseskaf, the last king of the dynasty, rejected the pyramid design for the superstructure of his tomb and was buried beneath a monument in the form of a massive sarcophagus resting upon a podium. Mud brick was also substituted for stone in some of his funerary works.

GIZA

A long corridor joined the Khafre mortuary temple, guarded by the sphinx, to its pyramid. The smallest of the three Giza pyramids in the distance belongs to King Mycerinus.

Masterpieces of Egyptian art

TOMB OF PTAHHOTEP
(Old Kingdom, Saqqara)
The vizier Ptahhotep directed that these painted bas-reliefs depict offering bearers carrying fruit, fresh vegetables, and tasty animals like gazelles and ducks. In this way, he would never be in need if his descendants forgot to prepare the necessary food.

PRINCESS NEFRET
(Old Kingdom) Nefret was the wife of the high priest of Heliopolis, the royal prince and probably the son of Pharaoh Sneferu. Protected for centuries by the darkness of her tomb, her statue retained its color and appearance of being alive. One can understand why the ancient Egyptians called the sculptor "he who makes live."

A DIGNITARY

(Old Kingdom)
The great presence,
nobility, and robust-
ness of this man—
with his stick, he
could keep back a
dog, threaten an
idler, or kill a snake
—indicate his social
status. His stout figure
confirms his wealth—
"one who grows fat
is one who eats until
one is full"—and is the
proof of his respectability.

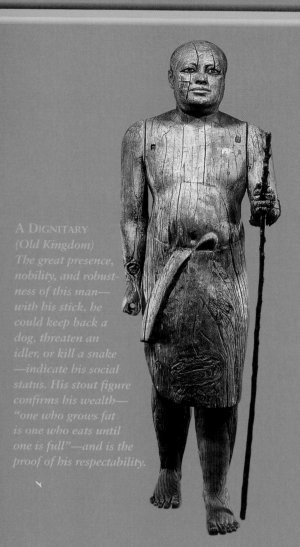

THE FALCON OF HIERAKONPOLIS

(Old Kingdom, 6th
or 12th Dynasty)
Discovered beneath the
pavement of the temple
of Kom el-Ahmar, this
statue represents the
god Horus of Nekhen,
capital of Upper Egypt.
A single vertical line
of obsidian crosses
its golden head to
form the eyes.

TOMB OF METCHETCHI

(Old Kingdom, Saqqara) Representations
of agricultural scenes were very common in
the tombs of Saqqara. Raising cattle for meat
and milk assured that Metchetchi, Director
of Cloth and owner of this tomb, would
have everything he needed in the afterlife.

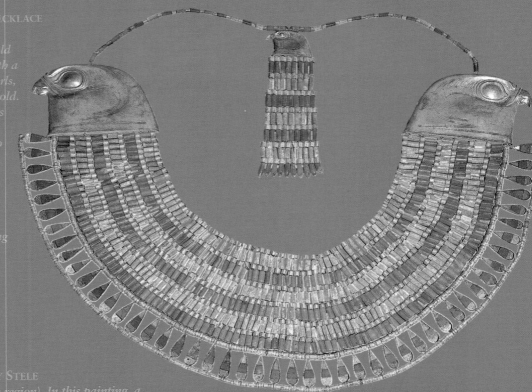

QUEEN NEFERUPTAH'S NECKLACE

(Middle Kingdom) Falcon heads made of engraved gold are tastefully combined with a skillful combination of pearls, turquoise, carnelian, and gold. It is edged by a row of tears made of the same material. This necklace dates back to the golden age of Egyptian goldsmiths, who perfectly mastered the techniques of working metal (casting, molding, stamping, and soldering) and of decorating (engraving, chasing, and encrustation).

AMENEMHET'S FUNERARY STELE

(Middle Kingdom, Theban region) In this painting, a charming family reunion takes place in the afterlife. The parents are overjoyed to talk with their son. During the tender gatherings, the daughter-in-law (to the side, with her hand on her heart) watches the others from behind the table of offerings. The table is so full that two loaves of bread have been put on the floor.

STATUE OF IYMERU
(Middle Kingdom) Iymeru was a royal vizier. Supreme head of the executive, under the direct authority of the king, he was the "will of the master, the ears and eyes of the ruler." Serious and austere, his stone face suggests the importance of his position. His long robe is one of the distinctive signs of this high rank.

PILLAR OF SESOSTRIS I
(Middle Kingdom) Second king of the 12th Dynasty, Sesostris I established unmatched expansion policies. He went beyond the 4th Cataract and strengthened his domination in Asia. He was also avid about building monuments to the glory of the gods. Here, on this pillar from the temple at Karnak, he honors Ptah, the demiurge and great god of Memphis.

STATUE OF NAKHTI
(Middle·Kingdom) Discovered in the entryway of his tomb's chapel, this standing statue of the chancellor Nakhti, Treasury Officer for the king, is made from a single acacia trunk. This kind of tree was very common in Egypt. Despite the fact that the material was fragile, Nakhti is represented life size (about 5 feet).

SARCOPHAGUS OF GENERAL SEPI *(Middle Kingdom)* *Equipped with a door so that the deceased could come and go, having décor that combines geometric motifs and Sarcophagus Texts, and with its frieze depicting the objects necessary for the afterlife, General Sepi's sarcophagus is a genuine house. Sepi could also look out through the eyes, which were placed at the right height.*

QUEEN AHHOTEP'S NECKLACE *(Middle Kingdom)* *The three gold flies on this chain of braided gold threads were a military decoration offered by the pharaoh to his most valiant soldiers. The necklace belonged to Queen Ahhotep, perhaps because she played a role in the battle against the Hyksos at her husband's or sons' side. They were the founders of the 18th Dynasty.*

QUEEN NEFERTITI

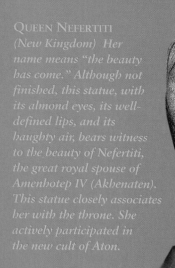

(New Kingdom) Her name means "the beauty has come." Although not finished, this statue, with its almond eyes, its well-defined lips, and its haughty air, bears witness to the beauty of Nefertiti, the great royal spouse of Amenhotep IV (Akhenaten). This statue closely associates her with the throne. She actively participated in the new cult of Aton.

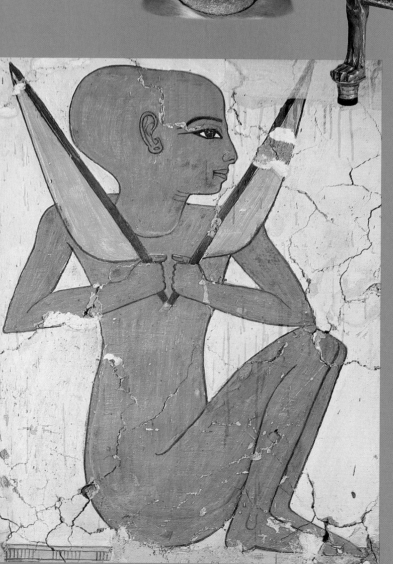

TUTANKHAMUN'S THRONE

(New Kingdom) Two gold-plated wooden thrones encrusted with fine stones, molten glass, ebony, and ivory decorated Tutankhamun's tomb. This one, with its wildcat legs and winged-serpent arms, was used for the palace's ceremonies. The second one, which has crossed legs in the form of duck heads, was meant for religious ceremonies.

NEFERTARI'S TOMB

(New Kingdom, Valley of the Queens) This very young deity is forever protecting Nefertari, the great royal spouse of Ramses II. Holding a long knife in each hand and clutching them to her breast, she is ready to kill any enemy who dares enter the tomb.

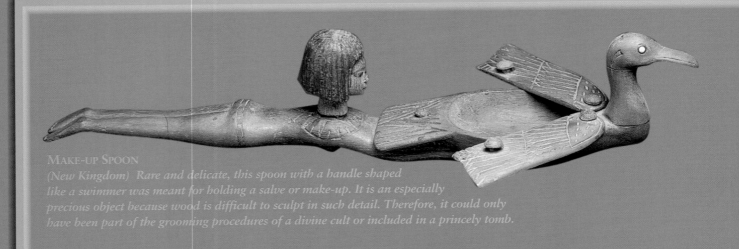

MAKE-UP SPOON
(New Kingdom) Rare and delicate, this spoon with a handle shaped like a swimmer was meant for holding a salve or make-up. It is an especially precious object because wood is difficult to sculpt in such detail. Therefore, it could only have been part of the grooming procedures of a divine cult or included in a princely tomb.

SENNEFER'S TOMB
(New Kingdom, Valley of the Kings) Stemming from the ground, a vine climbs up the wall and covers the ceiling. This is how this nobleman planned on having shade for eternity. From the vine hang black grapes, which will provide fresh grape juice and especially good wine.

THOUTII'S GOLDEN CUP
(New Kingdom) The goldsmith hammered the gold using a round stone. He then completed the fish and water lily motifs, applying the repoussé technique before engraving the details. Only a king could own such a wonder. It was Thutmose II who offered it to his general Thoutii, as thanks for his good and loyal services.

RAMSES II BREASTPLATE
(New Kingdom) This jewel, made from electrum, molten glass, and semi-precious stones, is reminiscent of a temple's architecture. The vulture and the cobra, gods of the north and south of Egypt, spread their protective wings around the royal cartouche.

IMENEMINET'S TOMB
(New Kingdom) The tomb that this bas-relief decorated no longer stands in the sands of Saqqara today. It represents a woman with an almond eye curiously looking to the side. The long curls of her wig still show traces of black paint, and her bouquet still retains some green paint.

THE GODDESS MAAT

(Third Intermediate Period) Represented with an ostrich feather in her hair, the goddess Maat was the daughter of Re, the sun god. Goddess of truth and justice, she was the symbol of the balance of the universe (which was created by the deities) and a certain moral and social order. She incarnated a very conformist vision of the world, a vision to which the Egyptians were meant to adhere.

DOG-HEAD LID

(Third Intermediate Period, Treasure of Tanis, painted alabaster) When the dead were mummified, their intestines were placed in stone vases (or urns). The lids were decorated with the heads of the four sons of Horus and his mother Isis: man (Amset), baboon (Hapy), falcon (Qebhenuef), and dog (Duamutef).

BRACELET OF SHESHONK II
(Third Intermediate Period, Treasure of Tanis) Very decorative, the outlined eye of the celestial god is underlined by a strange mark that marks falcon cheeks. A symbol of good sight, physical plenitude, and fertility, it is present on thousands of amulets and pieces of jewelry, like this bracelet found in the tomb of Pharaoh Sheshonk II, in Tunis.

THE OSIRIS TRIAD
(Third Intermediate Period) This tiny gold jewel (less than 4 inches high) has loops in the back so that it can be worn as a pendant. Squatting on a lapislazuli pillar, the god Osiris is surrounded by Isis, his wife (right), and Horus, his son (left). Their hands are open as a sign of protection.

BREASTPLATE OF PSUSENNES I
(Third Intermediate Period, Treasure of Tanis) Nothing has survived of the beautiful city of Tanis, near Menzaleh, but the ruins of a brick rampart, crumbling temples, and broken colossi. Intact royal tombs were discovered here in 1939–40. King Psusennes I was wearing this superb breastplate with a winged scarab.

CHAPTER 8

The pyramid age of the Old Kingdom II

The triumph of Heliopolis

THE KING AND THE BIRD
The 5th-Dynasty pharaoh Neferefre was protected by a falcon, the king of the birds of Egypt. Many gods liked to take its form, including Horus, Re, and Montu.

The influence of the sun cult, increasing throughout the Fourth Dynasty, as may be seen in the names compounded with Re of some of its kings, makes a full impact in the Fifth with the appearance of the myth of the theogamous (born of god) birth of the pharaoh. According to the folk story recounted in the Westcar Papyrus, the first three kings of this dynasty were the offspring of the wife of a priest of Re, by the sun god himself, and were destined to rule in turn after the eldest had become High Priest in Heliopolis. The sun kings of this dynasty returned to the tradition of building pyramid tombs, though on a more modest scale and to a lower constructional standard, which is why their monuments exist today as mere mounds of rubble after the loss of their casing stones.

Although the dynastic founder, Userkaf, built his pyramid at Saqqara, close to the Step Pyramid, at least four of his successors erected their monuments at Abusir. Since 1976, excavations by a Czech expedition have revealed much new information about the royal necropolis, in particular through the clearance of the mortuary temple of Neferefre. Back in 1893 and 1903, important fragments of temple papyri had been found in the Abusir temple of Neferirkare; in the 1980s, yet more came to light in that of Neferefre. The latter, although of mud brick and attached to a pyramid that had been hurriedly finished off as a mastaba, was exceptionally well-preserved and also contained a cache of exceptional statuary, a pair of ritual boats, and various other elements of the temple furnishings.

Besides their pyramids, at the least six Fifth Dynasty kings also built special temples to the sun god, of which two have been found in the Abusir area. The construction of such buildings ceased from the reign of Isesi onwards, perhaps for the reason that they diverted resources away from the building of the royal pyramids.

Despite their ruinous condition, it is clear from their shattered fragments that the monuments of this dynasty must be numbered among the architectural gems of ancient Egypt. The reliefs of Userkaf and Sahure are drawn by gifted artists with complete assurance and carved in low relief with great sensitivity.

The beauty of the materials also continues the best traditions of earlier works. With pavements and dadoes of black basalt; monolithic chambers hewn out of banded alabaster; red granite columns imitating palm trees or bundles of papyrus rush; architraves also of red granite; painted reliefs of Tura limestone; and ceilings which were vaulted or flat, colored blue, and sown with yellow five-pointed stars, they must have presented an appearance at once rich and harmonious. Names and titles were elegantly spaced and carved and inlaid with colored paste. Of all this glory, little now remains among the sand-engulfed ruins.

The great innovations of the age are the sun temples, of which the badly dilapidated example built by Niuserre at Abu Gurab near Abusir remains the most complete. They are presumed to be based upon the design of the temple of Re at Heliopolis. The main feature of these temples was a court open to the sky with a colonnade around two of the walls, sheltering reliefs and giving access to a large courtyards with a great altar positioned in front of an abstract symbol of the cult—the gilded *benben* elevated upon a podium like a squat obelisk. The most striking feature of the complex, however, was a long, narrow chamber, now known as the "Room of the Seasons" from the subject of its reliefs, which portray all the activities during the Egyptian agricultural year as a kind of visual hymn of praise to the sun god for all his bounty. Only disjointed fragments of these scenes have survived, but they can be supplemented by versions in contemporary mastaba tombs of the king's courtiers.

A somewhat bizarre element in Niuserre's temple was a brick-built version of the boat of the sun god. The imagery of the cult envisaged the journey of the gods across the waters of heaven by boat, the natural form of transport in Egypt on the Nile waterway. From prehistoric times, models and pictures of boats for the use of the dead had been included in the grave goods.

The royal tombs included two or more great boats, representing not only the day and night barque of the sun god but also actual examples used in life, as for instance

UNAS'S CAUSEWAY
In Saqqara, a 2,100 foot-long causeway leads from Unas's pyramid—he was the last king of the 5th Dynasty—to his Temple of the Valley. It was protected by two walls that were 9 feet high. They were covered in inscriptions and finely engraved drawings and held up a blue ceiling with golden stars.

the dismantled state barge of Cheops, some 170 feet long, discovered in a sealed pit adjacent to the Great Pyramid in 1954. Those who could not afford such expensive items made do with models, including those of the two simple reed floats that according to the sacred texts the deceased would need when he struck out upon the waters for the Field of Reeds where the gods dwelt.

The two boat-pits near the pyramid of Unas (ca. 2385–2355 B.C.), the last king of the Fifth Dynasty, may not be enclosures for actual wooden boats, but giant models in stone. The pyramid of Unas at Saqqara, in fact, shows all the features of the royal tomb in a greatly developed form despite its ruinous state. The Subsidiary Pyramid, employed for still-obscure ritual purposes, is on its southern side. The Valley Temple was built with granite columns in the form of palm trees, similar to those used in the Mortuary Temple, which are pictured being shipped to the site in a relief on the Causeway.

This latter adjunct, greatly dilapidated though it may be, is the best preserved of such structures. Over 2,700 feet long, the Valley Temple changes direction twice. Its walls were embellished with reliefs on the interior which appear to be inspired by scenes from the Room of the Seasons, though there are also subjects representing the procuring and manufacture of all the goods used in the building, furnishings, and the functionings of the temple and the services associated with it.

The Mortuary Temple follows what is now a fairly standard pattern of being located on the east side of the pyramid, with the colonnaded court surrounding an altar open to the sky and separated from the inner chambers by a corridor, all embellished with reliefs.

The entrance to the burial chamber was on the north side of the pyramid facing the circumpolar stars, which according to some beliefs, the soul of the king would eventually join. A subterranean corridor, blocked by three granite portcullises, led to an offering chamber adjoining the burial chamber, and here in 1881, Maspero found its most impressive feature—columns of elegantly drawn and spaced hieroglyphs cut into the white limestone walls and gables and colored blue.

These inscriptions are the earliest and the best preserved of a corpus, or collection, of magic spells and prayers which were henceforth to be carved in the burial chambers of subsequent kings and queens and some high officials. These writings, to which the name "Pyramid Texts" has been given, show the preponderant influence of Heliopolitan theology, although some of them hark back to primitive beliefs of a very remote past.

Generally, the texts are selected and positioned on the tomb walls to ensure that the *Ba*, or spirit of the dead king, shall mount to heaven, shall join the entourage of the sun god, and eventually become absorbed by the Lord of All, or the demiurge. But there is also another deity whose influence is beginning to obtrude in some of the texts—and that is Osiris, the god of Abydos, whose cult will have to be discussed later.

While the soul of the king was aloft in the heavenly circuit, his body remained on earth, and the persistence of the Lower Egyptian belief that some aspect of the deceased could live on in his mansion of eternity is evident in the design of the sarcophagus of wood or stone as a house. Unas was buried in a severely plain

A FALSE-STELE DOOR
(5th Dynasty) This stele made of acacia wood allowed the dead to keep in contact with the living. The deceased could come and go from his tomb and profit from the offerings left in his chapel.

sarcophagus of black basalt, but this was housed in a part of the burial chamber walled with alabaster and painted to resemble the mat-hung chamber of a palace.

The pyramids of the Sixth Dynasty followed much the same pattern until the last of the series, the complex of Pepy II. In later years, this seems to have been especially hallowed as the last classic utterance of the Old Kingdom. Its reliefs were copied both in style and substance by pharaohs of the Middle and New Kingdoms, eager to return to the traditions of what seemed in retrospect to have been a veritable Golden Age.

Country life

While the kings were provided for so handsomely, their relatives and officials were buried in mastaba tombs or rock-hewn hypogea in the vicinity. The superstructure of such private tombs usually preserved the rectangular bench-like form, at first in mud brick but later in stone, with two dummy doorways on the eastern façade. The southernmost doorway soon became a niche where prayers and offerings could be made by pious relatives or priests endowed for the purpose. As the idea of the afterlife became more spiritualized there was a tendency for the tomb stela to be carved in relief with a likeness of the deceased seated at a table on which the staples of bread and beer were represented. The spirit *(ka)* of the owner received its sustenance by magic invocation, and once this idea took root, by the Second Dynasty other items were added to the bread and beer in quantity such as flesh,

fowl, wine, milk, vegetables, even sacramental oils and linen, and eventually "everything good and pure on which immortals live."

The offering niche with stela, or inscripted walls, was gradually expanded to a small cruciform chapel, and by the Fourth Dynasty into a simple chamber with the stela filling the upper part of a false door on the rear wall, with reliefs of the deceased on the jambs as though coming forth from the tomb to partake of the offerings. The walls of this chamber were carved with scenes of the children and servants of the owner bearing offerings. This basic idea is the motive for the decoration of the innermost chamber of the chapel, whether in the mastaba tomb or hypogeum of the private person or in the mortuary temple of the pharaoh. But in the Fifth Dynasty, such tomb decoration was greatly extended under the influence of

THE PYRAMID TEXTS
Built during the 6th Dynasty, the pyramid of King Teti in Saqqara is famous for the inscriptions engraved on the inside walls. King Unas (end of the 5th Dynasty) was the first to employ this mode of mortuary inscriptions.

A BURIAL

After his death, the family and friends of an important man invoked his virtues and wept loud and long to the accompaniment of professional wailers. Then it was time to leave the dead man's home. The procession took shape. Servants bore flowers, food and drink, chests, chairs, beds, statues, jewels. The mummy of the deceased, lying in a sarcophagus protected by a curtained catafalque, was placed aboard a funerary bark drawn by oxen.

Boats awaited them on the banks of the Nile. The biggest ship was reserved for the deceased, the priests, and the mourners; part of the procession squeezed aboard the other vessels. Another sledboat awaited them on the far shore. Everyone took his place and, with dragging feet, amid wailing, weeping, and clouds of dust, trudged across the fields to the tomb. Then the procession reached the desert. There, men unharnessed the oxen and carried the catafalque up increasingly steep slopes to the cemetery. There, many workers toiled at restoring or building tombs, sawing, hammering, and carving. Private citizens bore a letter or offerings to the departed, while priests performed the funeral rituals of the mighty.

At the entrance to the tomb, the sarcophagus was set upright before the door. This was the moment for farewell to the dead man— for the Opening of the Mouth, a rite that would permit him to recover the use of speech, to eat, and to move his arms and legs. They then lowered the sarcophagus, the funereal furnishings, and the offerings into the grave, whose entrance a mason then sealed. The living, meanwhile, settled themselves close to the tomb to share the funeral repast before returning home.

Such were the funeral ceremonies of Egypt's great—rites that were denied to the vast majority of the population.

Heliopolitan doctrines. The size and number of rooms in the superstructure increased until, by the Sixth Dynasty, the mastabas of the great officials contained suites of rooms, some large enough to have their ceilings held up by piers. The figure of the owner, too, in the stela-cum-false-door became a life-size statue almost in the round.

The walls of these chapels were lined with fine limestone from Tura, and the reliefs that were carved on them are among the glories of the Pyramid Age. They vary in style from the precise drawing and delicate carving of the Fifth Dynasty to the bolder, more lively, if often less elegant, work of the Sixth Dynasty. The subject matter is largely inspired by scenes in the Room of the Seasons, with its pictures of the cycle of work throughout the agricultural year. But the various activities represented, such as the sowing and harvesting of grain, the baking of bread, the brewing of beer, the raising and butchering of cattle, the trapping and fattening of birds and poultry, are dynamic elaborations of the idea of materializing a funerary meal by a magic invocation. Similarly, shipwrights are shown building the boats for the pilgrimage to Buto or for the last journey across the Nile to the West. Other craftsmen make the furniture, jewels, clothes, and similar wordly goods that may accompany the owner to the tomb. All the components for a full life in the hereafter, like that passed on earth, are provided in a magic sublimation.

MAKING BREAD
Bakers from the Old Kingdom (5th Dynasty) made the bread, providing the basic food for Egyptians. They sifted the flour, prepared the dough, heated the clay molds over the flame, and did the baking.

The main participant in all these activities is of course the owner, supporting the slighter figure of his wife. But his role is strictly passive; he merely "inspects" with a benevolent eye all the work done on his country estates. Only in the royal sports of harpooning the hippopotamus, spearing fish in the pools, or fowling with the throw-stick in the reed thickets does he find an active role worthy of his dignity.

Apart from such borrowings, the events depicted show nothing of the owner's relations with royalty, even though his wife may be the daughter of the king. The life of the pharaoh and his entourage remains a closed book. By contrast, the activities of the peasantry and the lower orders are recorded, as nowhere else, with a sardonic humor. Their toil-worn physiques, their ill-shaven jowls, their bald heads, their trouble with the refractory ass or the no less stubborn tax collector, their cheerful banter, their work songs, are faithfully reported. Lively figurines of servants at their various duties in all their homeliness often accompany the handsome painted wood or limestone statues of their masters and mistresses in the *serdabs,* or funerary chapels, of the great mastabas.

In addition, such themes as the entertainment of the owner with music and dancing may be illustrated; also the cult of the dead with the funerary cortège and bands of mourners may be represented. Throughout all these scenes, there runs the connective thread of the private life of the owner, from nursing at his mother's breast through the games of his childhood to the pride of his vigorous youth, the corpulence of his prosperity, and the final farewell at the tomb door.

The intention of all these scenes was not only to re-create the past by magic. The tomb chapels were the resort of relatives and descendants of the deceased, who were accustomed to visit the necropolis on feast days—as is often the practice in Egypt today—and there partake of a meal in memory of their ancestor.

This ceremony was a two-way affair, as much for the benefit of the living as for the dead. In antiquity, when premature death could suddenly arrive, the continuance of the family was a prime concern, and its fertility was thought to reside with the ancestral spirit. By this communion with the ancestor in a sepulchral meal, the family's future could be assured.

External affairs

While thus our picture of life in Egypt on the great country estates seems sharply in focus, our knowledge of affairs elsewhere is nebulous indeed. Some control was evidently exercised over Nubia and the Lower Sudan, largely for trading purposes and for the recruitment of fighting men like the Medjay folk (later synonymous with police) and other renowned bowmen, but it is doubtful whether the Egyptians were able to subdue for long the warlike, though more primitive, tribes of the region, who had the advantage of inhabiting difficult terrain through which progress even by boat was hazardous.

By the Fourth Dynasty, a town had been established at Buhen, near the head of the Second Cataract, and included a copper-smelting works among its industries. This seems to have been under control of Egyptian officials until the reign of Isesi (ca. 2413–2385 B.C.), when it was abandoned. By that time, Nubia was under the suzerainty of the agents of pharaoh— the Keepers of the Gateway of the South, the local barons at Elephantine, whose for-

NAVIGATING THE NILE
The boats from the Old Kingdom had a row of oars on each side of the hull. In addition, they were equipped with two enormous oars that could be folded. They served as both a rudder and a mast, to which was attached a trapezoidal sail.

ays into Africa were chiefly concerned with trade and maintaining peace among the rival tribes of the region, as much by diplomacy as by police action.

Trading ventures by sea to the mysterious spice land of Punt, thought to lie on the Somali coast or opposite it, were undertaken for the sake of the incense gums and resins demanded by temple ritual. These expeditions included the transport in sections of seagoing ships across the Eastern Desert, their reassembly on the coast of the Red Sea, and a reversal of this onerous procedure on the return journey. As we have noted, the great ship of Cheops was found carefully dismantled in its boat-pit at Giza and reveals how such operations were made in the absence of a canal from the Nile to the Red Sea.

Mining operations in Sinai for turquoise and copper—and for copper only in the Eastern Desert—were probably in the hands of the indigenous Asiatic bedouin under Egyptian direction. When the less settled bedouin raided Egyptian settlements in times of drought and privation, punitive expeditions had to be dispatched against them. It is doubtful, however, whether the pharaoh took any personal part in these campaigns, though on the monuments he accepts the sole credit for the victorious outcome. Scenes of pharaohs smiting the bedouin, or nomads, are found in Sinai.

The Libyans on the opposite borders of the Delta were also persistent infiltrators into Egypt and had to be repulsed from time to time—although it is almost certain that scenes in the funerary temples of Sahure, Unas, and Pepy II, showing the king plundering them are purely symbolic and refer to events dating back to the dawn of history. All give the same names for the conquered foe, the artificiality of the depiction being shown by its appearance, complete with the same names, under Taharqa—two thousands years later!

There is a little more evidence for Egyptian penetration in Palestine. Two representations have survived in different tombs of the Sixth Dynasty, showing the storming of Asiatic fortresses, with scaling ladders and sappers (soldiers in trenches) undermining the walls, though such scenes could refer to events no farther afield than Sinai. The autobiography which Weni inscribed in his tomb-chapel at Abydos describes more ambitious campaigns, including the conscription of men from Egypt and Nubia in a combined operation which he directed as far north in Palestine as Mount Carmel, during the reign of Pepy I.

The most impressive testimony for Egyptian activity in Asia, however, comes from the great timber-exporting region around Byblos, where objects bearing the names of pharaohs from Chasekhemwy to Pepy II have been brought to light suggesting a long and continuous association between Lebanon and Egypt. This was doubtless the result of close trading relations rather than colonization, though it may be that there was an influential Edgyptian settlement in Byblos, where a temple existed to Hathor, the equivalent of the local goddess Anath.

PRISONERS OF WAR
Throughout the many military campaigns, Pepy I (4th Dynasty) won victories and took in prisoners. The latter accompanied him in his mortuary temple (Saqqara), in the form of statuettes.

The rise of feudalism

From the time of the first kings of the unified Egypt, it would seem that the pharaoh ruled over the whole of Egypt as his demesne, or estate, and this system reached its greatest development in the Fourth Dynasty, when Snoferu appears to have initiated the policy of administering the country directly through members of his immediate family. The office of vizier, from his reign onwards, became the most important office under the crown in this centralizing process. At the same time, the kingship appears to have become more remote and hedged around with divinity, a difference well illustrated by the towering bulk of the royal pyramid over the neighboring mastabas of the king's relatives. These were also his officials whom he had brought up and educated, maintained during their lifetimes, and granted decent burial on death. The king may be traditionally pictured as the Protector of Egypt, treading down the national foes, but there is little evidence that any pharaohs of the Old Kingdom led any expeditions into the field. Such enterprises were the concern either of accomplished administrators, such as Weni, who was a mere magistrate before he was appointed governor of Upper Egypt, or experienced agents such as the half-Nubian border barons of Elephantine. The picture received from such vestiges that have survived from the Old Kingdom is one of an Egypt enjoying security, prosperity, and internal peace under the rule of the pharaoh. The change of dynasties appears to have occurred not as the result of strife but through the extinction of the male line.

The arrival of the Fifth Dynasty, however, marks a distinct diminution in the power and prestige of the pharaoh. The great officials were no longer princes of the blood royal, or other near relatives, but claim a greater familiarity with the god-king by boasting of their privilege in being allowed to kiss the royal foot, rather than the ground on which it trod, and similar favors. The inscriptions in the private tombs, which become progressively larger as the age advances, now expand from a laconic list of titles and honorifics to more revelatory statements—and even, as in the case of Weni, a modest autobiography.

With the rise in the importance of the nobility, there was a diminution in the stature of the pharaoh. Favored courtiers were rewarded with gifts of land as endowments for the upkeep of their tombs and funerary services. Such gifts were often exempted from taxation in perpetuity, and the silent cities of the dead received large shares of the national resources at the expense of the Royal Treasury, when there were not lapses or misappropriations of funds. Much of this expenditure was upon activities, which only encouraged economic stagnation.

While the kings became the poorer by these donations, their subjects reaped the benefits. The district governors, once they felt themselves secure in posts that became hereditary, handed on their offices to their children, according to the Egyptian ideal of appointing the son to the place of his father, in the belief that they owed their appointments to right of birth and not to royal favor. They no longer sought burial

THE CROUCHING SCRIBE
This funerary statue of a scribe, whose name has disappeared—he was definitely a dignitary, since he could read and write—was rendered in painted limestone with encrusted eyes. He is not crouching, but is seated cross-legged and seems almost to be alive. He is considered one of the wonders of ancient Egyptian sculpture.

near the king's pyramid but cut their own rock tombs at the provincial capital.

From the middle of the Fifth Dynasty, the beginnings of a feudal state may be traced with an increase in the power and status of these provincial lords, particularly in Upper Egypt. The possibility of rivalry between them cannot be ignored, nor an attempt on the part of the Crown, evidently under Isesi, to come to terms with them by appointing one of their number to a new post—governor of Upper Egypt. This office exercised a check upon them by conferring upon the holder the duty of collecting their taxes, but it was not long before it, too, became hereditary.

THE QUEEN
AND HER SON
*Sculpted in calcite, Queen
Ankhnesmeryre holds her
son Pepy II on her lap. This
child-pharaoh, who already
wears the royal headdress,
does not know that he will
reign for more than 90
years—a record.*

The chasm that separated the pharaoh from such magnates was spanned when Pepy I late in his reign married two sisters, the daughters of a mere governor of the Thinite nome, who became in turn the mothers of his successors, Nemtyemsaf I (Merenre) and Pepy II. Their brother was appointed to the vizierate, and other members of the family held high office in Thinis. Thus, by the middle of the Sixth Dynasty, the foundations of a feudal state had already been laid. Following Pepy II's death, a series of obscure kings held the Memphite throne, outshone by the provincial nobles of Middle and Upper Egypt.

Egypt during the Old Kingdom enjoyed a virile and self-assured culture which is the most characteristic expression of the national ethos. The calm faces that gaze out from so many statues and reliefs are untroubled by doubts, and the voices that speak from the scanty writings of the period, the books of precepts and etiquette and the complacent autobiographies, are unfaltering in their belief that the good life consisted in being discreet, modest, honest, and patient; prudent in friendship; and not covetous, or envious, or violent, but respectful to superiors and inferiors alike—in short, keeping one's proper station and exercising moderation in all things.

Such an ideal of the golden mean was essentially aristocratic. The king and his court—mostly his relatives and high officials who proclaimed their kinship with him, and inherited therefore in some degree his divine right to rule—were the educated elite for whom the economic and artistic enterprises of the state were created. But while forming a privileged class, they were no idle nobility. They comprised the architects, engineers, writers, theologians, administrators—all the men of action and intelligence of their day.

CHAPTER 9

The time of troubles

Collapse of the Old Kingdom

At this distance of time, the disintegration of the Old Kingdom at the end of the Sixth Dynasty has all the appearance of being sudden and complete. Egyptologists had attributed this downfall to the decline in the sole authority of the pharaoh after the Fourth Dynasty, when the rise of provincial governors resulted in the emergence of a hereditary caste of feudal potentates seeking a growing independence from control.

More recent research, however, has attributed the abrupt nature of the collapse to contemporary changes in the climate of Africa and the Near East. With the cessation of the Neolithic Wet Phase about 2350 B.C., the specter of famine begins to haunt the region. An isolated block from the Unas Causeway, and an earlier example from that of Sahure at Abusir, showing piteously emaciated people weakened by famine and dying of hunger, might be an early portent of the evils to come. Egypt was protected from the worst of such irregular calamities by its unique irrigation system and the central control it could exercise over its granaries and supplies of corn. It is fairly evident, however, that a change in the pattern of monsoon rains falling on the Abyssinian plateau could lead to a series of low Niles which the basin system of cultivation in Egypt could do nothing to counteract, and the results would have been disastrous for the entire population.

Hot winds from the south, similar to the stifling *khamsin*, which today blows for two or three days at a time in the spring, apparently accompanied this climatic aberration. The high winds assisted the denudation by creating dust bowls and shifting sand dunes on to the cultivation. The whole political and economic system of Egypt, whereby a god incarnate was believed to control the Nile flood by his magic powers for the benefit of the nation, would have been discredited in a very short time. As we have remarked, the king-lists refer to many pharaohs during the three decades of the Seventh and Eighth Dynasties, each ruling for a year or two before presumably paying the penalty for being unable to make the Nile flow copiously—and disappearing without trace.

In these conditions, "when the Nile was empty and men crossed over it on foot," Egypt splintered into a number of feudal states under the purely nominal suzerainty of the pharaoh, each governed by a petty ruler who tried to promote the welfare of his own principality without much concern for that of his neighbors. There are cryptic references in the meager records that have survived to marauding bands of starving people searching for food in more favored localities, and in at least one

FAMINE VICTIMS
The thinness of the figures on this bas-relief from the Unas Causeway reminds us of the famine that sometimes struck Egypt when the floods were either too light or too heavy.

115

THE REVOLTS OF THE HUNGRY

As early as Pepy II's long reign (6th Dynasty), royal power was on the wane. In Memphis in particular, the pharaohs began to lose control. There, the governors of the province no longer obeyed Pharaoh's orders, acting more and more like kings. Did they hope to become the pharaoh? Perhaps. It appears, however, that the governors were not so much wanting to change the social system as to use it to their advantage.

This would explain why no revolts against established organizations or any form of injustice took place. Instead, there were pillages and riots born of years of poor harvests and subsequent food shortages—and even famine. The peasants were hungry, and the homes of the rich were attacked and pillaged, as were their tombs.

One record has survived from this period of unrest—a text called the *Lamentations*. In it, the writer Ipuwer longs for past times, when Pharaoh reigned as an absolute master.

"The king was overthrown by the mobs!" Ipuwer wrote. "He who was buried as a falcon was torn from his sarcophagus! The tomb of the pyramid was raided! A handful of men who understood nothing of the government stripped the country of its monarchy. The royal palace was ravaged in one hour, and those who had wardrobes are now in rags."

instance there is an account of cannibalism. This dismal phase in the fortunes of Egypt in fact seems to have been the first recorded instance of one of those periods of drought which have ravaged the land from time to time, as in 502 A.D. and especially in 1085 A.D., when the Nile inundation failed for seven years and brought dire famine and pestilence to the population.

In the twentieth century B.C., the local governors took what measures were open to them to succor their own districts by conserving water supplies and reducing the number of hungry mouths by driving out famine-stricken invaders—whether natives, Libyans, or Asiatics—from their provinces. The internecine strife further restricted the areas of cultivation. The perils of these times are reflected in the boasts of the local rulers on their crude tomb stelae that only by their organizing abilities and their strong right arms had they been able to preserve their people, their crops, and their herds. The cataclysm is plain for all to see. The monuments of the period are very sparse. The materials are of poor quality, with pottery, for instance, replacing stone, faience, and metal in the manufacture of vessels. A ruler in Asyut was buried with a painted wooden model of a company of Egyptian spearmen and another of Nubian bowmen to render him service in some troubled afterlife. Macabre reminders of the civil strife of these days are the bodies of some sixty shock troops who were accorded an honored mass burial at Thebes. Their wounds showed that they had fallen in the desperate storming of some key fortress.

With Egypt divided against itself, there was the inevitable immigration of foreigners into the pastures of the Delta. Famine in their own lands always drove Libyans and the bedouin of Sinai and the Negeb to graze their flocks on the borders of the Delta in the manner of Abraham and Jacob.

The evils caused by famine, poverty, social upheaval, and anarchy brought others in their train, such as plague and sterility. A deep and lasting impression was left on the ancient Egyptians by the trauma of these times, so that in later literary works, such as *The Prophecy of Neferti* and *The Admonitions of Ipumer*, when the writer wished to depict mankind tormented by intolerable miseries, it was most probably the sufferings of this period that he recalled.

The recovery

The history of the First Intermediate Period is concerned with the painful struggle by successive strong men to restore the divine power of the pharaoh, which had been so effective for centuries in the past. The most notable of these efforts was made by a powerful family living at Herakleopolis near the Faiyum who regarded themselves as the legitimate successors of Pepy II. They appear to have united all Egypt under their sway for a brief interlude. Upper Egypt, however, from a little south of Abydos to the border at Elephantine, seems to have preserved some kind of nominal independence under princes ruling at Thebes.

The Herakleopolitans from the Ninth and Tenth Dynasties (ca. 2160–2040 B.C.) —and, according to Manetho, founder of their line, Akhtoes—achieved supreme power "by great cruelty which wrought woes for Egypt." His name survived on a number of small monuments, but there is a significant reference to a book of instruction in statecraft which he wrote for his descendants, though it has not so far come to light.

After a century in which the Herakleopolitans appear to have consolidated their power by expelling the Asiatic immigrants in the Delta, fortifying the eastern borders, reestablishing the importance of Memphis, improving irrigation works, and reopening trade with Byblos, the rising pretensions of the aggressive Thebans constituted a threat which could not be ignored. Sporadic fighting broke out between the rival powers with varying fortunes until the Theban prince Mentuhotep II (Nebhepetre) decisively defeated the Herakleopolitans and reunited Egypt under the rule of one pharaoh.

THE PIKEMEN
This painted wood model from the 1st Intermediate Period depicts a platoon of 40 Egyptian soldiers carrying pikes and shields made of wood and leather.

The interludes between the great epochs of civilization in Egypt had their birth pangs as well as their death agonies. Out of the social revolution of the time, which cast aside the old accepted forms of expression, and out of the acute suffering which moved men to cry out with a new voice, there was born a secular literature quite different from what had preceded it—a literature, moreover, which continued to inspire Egyptian writers for centuries afterwards and helped to sustain an accepted style. An appeal was made through the emotions by artistic processes, and the pessimistic literature that now flowered is cast in a poetic and elegant form.

The ability of writing to influence men's minds is shrewdly recognized by a Herakleopolitan king who exhorts his son to be a craftsman in speech so that he might prevail, "for power is in the tongue; and speech is mightier than fighting." Such feelings fathered a genre of pessimistic writing which was to prevail even when it no longer reflected external circumstances in the high noon of the Middle Kingdom.

117

In this category is *An Argument between a Man Contemplating Suicide and His Soul* and *The Complaints of the Peasant*. These writings appear to have emanated from the court of the Herakleopolitans; it is one of these kings, probably Wahkare, who has left us another of these Egyptian literary classics, *The Instruction for King Merykare*. In this work, ideas appear which are different from the recipes for worldly success compiled by the Old Kingdom sages. There is, for instance, a confession of wrongdoing and repentance for past misdeeds. A warning is also given of retribution on the Day of Judgment, when even the king will have to account for his deeds on earth. "He that cometh before [the judges] without having done wrong, he shall continue like a god." This is a distinct change from the assertions in the Pyramid Texts that the dead king will not be tried before any tribunal. While much of the "instruction" takes the form of practical advice from a ruler who has few illusions about the frailty and treachery of the human species, there is a distinct preoccupation with a code of conduct determined by abstract moral factors:

THE ARCHERS
Found in a prince's tomb, this Nubian platoon is armed with bows and arrows and advances in rows of four.

"Do right as long as you are on earth. Calm the afflicted, oppress no widow, expel no man from his father's possessions…Do not kill; but punish with beatings or imprisonment. Then shall this land be well established. Leave vengeance to God…More acceptable to Him is the virtue of one who is upright of heart than the ox of the wrong-doer."

This last extract refers to another transformation that was taking place in the social and religious heritage of the past. The promise of immortality in the Old Kingdom was greatly restricted, and it is doubtful whether in origin it extended beyond the divine king. What kind of afterlife was enjoyed by his subjects is less clear. The queens and members of the royal family were naturally interred in tombs near the mastaba or pyramid of the king they had served in life and to whom they expected to stand in the same relationship after death. Such tombs and the immortality they assured were in the gift of the king. But when local governors began to make tombs in their own districts, they inevitably took over something of the divine privileges of the pharaoh himself. The process was greatly accelerated during the First Intermediate Period, when so many minor lords regarded themselves as little inferior to kings.

At the same time, the general poverty made it necessary to find substitutes for all the lavish furnishings of the royal burials. Thus, instead of painted reliefs in fine limestone showing the procession of estates bringing their produce to the deceased, or the brewers, bakers, and butchers preparing the funerary meal, a few servant-statues—often crudely hacked out of wood—were provided to perform

WORKING WITH WOOD

During the turbulent times of the 1st Intermediate Period, artisans no longer had enough commissions, or material—alabaster, fine limestone, sandstone, and granite—to continue to produce enormous false doors, delicate bas-reliefs, statues, and hard stone vases. To make matters worse, the pharaoh was no longer financing expeditions to desert mines and faraway countries. But there was still a need for funerary materials: The eternal life of the deceased depended on it. The artisans therefore had to break new ground by working with the wood in the country (acacia and sycamore), which was soft and abundant.

In the process, the creativity of artists was stimulated. Eyes were made of encrusted materials. Coffins were painted with two eyes for the deceased to see with, a door for coming and going, and religious formulas in handsome hieroglyphic script.

In the tombs that were later made in the desert mountains, bas-reliefs were replaced by paintings that illustrated the concerns of the period—for example, warrior dances and hand to hand combat. Statuettes rendered in poor wood and covered in paint were also used. These were genuine "models," little forms made from multiple pieces that represented scenes from daily life—a house, a boat, a butcher, a cowshed, offering-bearers, musicians, fishermen, or a parade of soldiers.

Not a single detail was missing from these statuettes. The fishermen's net was filled with fish, pieces of meat hung from cords, and the baskets of peasants were overflowing with vegetables and breads. Naïve, moving, and sometimes humorous, these humble yet intricate works are the fruit of the hard work the Egyptians performed day after day beneath a burning sun.

their offices by magic. Rectangular wooden coffins, decorated externally in a manner reminiscent of houses, were painted internally with pictures of equipment which had formerly been the exclusive trappings of royalty—crowns, headdresses, staves, scepters, kilts, girdles, aprons, and tails. Even the Uraeus-cobra, the essential symbol of royalty, which the pharaoh wore on his brow so that it might spit fire in the eyes of his enemies, was faithfully represented.

This wholesale usurpation did not stop at forms and emblems. The liturgy of the Pyramid Texts was altered to make it suitable for use by private persons to protect them from the hazards and terrors of the underworld and to imbue them with special influence and potency. New spells referring to contemporary conditions were added, and archaic utterances that could no longer be understood were omitted. In the impoverished burials of the period, in which the offering-chamber is often very modest or nonexistent, the practice arose of writing these texts in cursive hieroglyphs upon the interior of the coffins below the painted frieze of accoutrements, and the name "Coffin Texts" is given by Egyptologists to this new group of religious writings. The custom appears to have arisen in Herakleopolis. It was continued throughout the ensuing Middle Kingdom for some royal as well as private burials, although several of the more opulent tombs had their chapel walls inscribed with the old Pyramid Texts (in this, probably aping royal burials in which, however, funerary inscriptions have not survived).

It seems clear, therefore, that whatever impediments there were to achieving the supreme office of pharaoh in life, few of the new governors and officials had any doubt about their becoming as kings at death.

A population of peasants

~

PRODUCING BEER
(End of the Old Kingdom)
*This woman is blending
a mixture of barley, water,
and yeast which—once
fermented, filtered, and
sweetened with a few
dates—turns into beer, a
favorite of the Egyptians.*

Peasants worked the lands of the pharaoh, the only landowner in Egypt. They did not hope for rain because rain was so rare for the country. Rather, they hoped for a good Nile flood. The river would set the rhythm of their lives, and every year they engaged in the same routine of essential work.

When the valley disappeared under the water, only the villages and dikes were not submerged. During these periods, the peasants fished, repaired their tools, wove baskets, and performed other tasks. They prepared the fields and repaired the flood damage by rebuilding embankments, dams, and riverbanks and canals. They redug gutters, saw to the reservoirs, and marked the extent of the lands with poles. Every one of these tasks had to be finished before the land dried.

Then came the time for tilling, for which they used a simple plow made from a pole; the lower end was tied to a wooden plowshare with a cord. They plowed furrows in the land, which was still drenched in water. Behind them, men hoed lumps of earth. Finally, the peasants sowed the wheat or barley and then let goats or sheep into the fields to stamp the seeds into the ground.

The arduous irrigation work came after the water had totally receded. For days on end, the canals had to be supervised and the fields constantly watered to ensure a good harvest.

Come harvesting time, the peasants cut the sheaves with a sickle, which had a wood handle and flint blade. Donkeys or oxen walked around the threshing floor, tirelessly treading on the ears to extract the grain. The peasants then tossed the grain to separate it from the husks, which were carried off by the wind.

That work done, the harvest had to be gathered. It was at this time that the scribes evaluated the crop, taking whatever was necessary to pay taxes.

Constantly tending to the wheat, barley, flax, vegetables, vineyards, and fruit trees, Egyptian peasants spent most of their time in the fields and gardens. The shepherds, on the other hand, moved to the edge of the marsh. Isolated, shaggy-haired, and clothed in a reed skirt or nothing at all, they would take care of the pharaohs's livestock. On their return from the marsh, they would give an account to their employers. The herd would walk in front of them while a scribe noted the number of animals in writing.

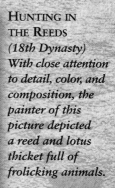

PASTORAL SCENE
(Old Kingdom)
While goats graze at a sycamore, a shepherd quenches his thirst. One of the goats is giving birth, and a dog sniffs the kid. To convey the size of the herd, the artist has rendered the animals on two planes.

HUNTING IN THE REEDS
(18th Dynasty)
With close attention to detail, color, and composition, the painter of this picture depicted a reed and lotus thicket full of frolicking animals.

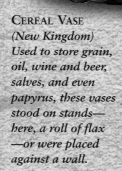

CEREAL VASE
(New Kingdom)
Used to store grain, oil, wine and beer, salves, and even papyrus, these vases stood on stands— here, a roll of flax —or were placed against a wall.

SKILLED FISHERMEN

Fishing was an important activity in Egypt. It was said that fish "were more plentiful than sand on the banks." During the Middle Kingdom, fishing scenes were often depicted in tombs, both painted and sculpted (as small wooden figures). Egyptians loved fish— especially since they were free and untaxed. They would eat them fresh, dried, or salted; only religious officials (kings or priests) refrained from eating them. There were as many recipes for fish as there were fishing techniques. Standing on small papyrus boats, the men dragged a net—hoop or other— between their vessels. Lone fishermen dangled four-pronged fishing hooks by hand, knocking a fish out with a hammer as soon as it bit. Athletic fishermen chose to use a harpoon, while clumsy ones went with a landing net. The fishing pole became popular during the New Kingdom.

GATHERING PAPYRUS
(Old Kingdom)
After cutting papyrus, often 20 feet in height, field hands took their harvest in heavy bundles to the workshops.

THE HARVEST
In this painting from a Theban tomb dating back to the New Kingdom, men cut long stalks for the papyrus harvest. In a part of the painting not visible in this photograph, two young workers behind the men glean the fallen tufts and slip them into their baskets.

CHAPTER 10

The Middle Kingdom

The feudal rivalry

Throughout the Herakleopolitan period, the princes of Thebes had been able to exercise an uneasy suzerainty over the five southernmost districts of Upper Egypt, enclosing their names in cartouches like any pharaoh. Their border with the northern powers was at the city of Abydos, now coming into even greater importance as the principal holy seat of the god Osiris. In sporadic fighting this town changed hands several times, and it was not until their prince, Mentuhotep II (Nebhepetre), came to power that the Thebans began to prevail over the loyalist powers. After several years of hard fighting, however, Mentuhotep found himself the first effective pharaoh of a united Egypt since the reign of Pepy II.

His gradual advance from a provincial kinglet to the "Lord of the Two Lands" is reflected in the funerary monument he built at Deir el-Bahri, with its early reliefs carved in a primly rustic yet curiously attractive style. His activities are recorded in many parts of the country, but he remained a devotee of southern culture, making his residence at Thebes and building largely in Upper Egypt. There is more than a flavor of Nubian culture in his entourage, with his dark-skinned womenfolk tattooed on their bodies, and in some of the artifacts that were buried with them. Mentuhotep II celebrated a jubilee in his thirty-ninth regnal year and died after a long reign of fifty-one years, during which he had a good opportunity of pacifying the land and guiding it back to some of its former prosperity. His eldest surviving son, Mentuhotep III (S'ankhkare), inherited a united and tranquil state populated by a new generation to whom civil war was only a legend, and he devoted his short reign of twelve years to the arts of peace.

A trading expedition was sent to Punt, a voyage which involved the conscription of an expeditionary force of 3,000 men, the digging of wells and the cutting of stone in the Wadi Hammamat, the rounding up of hostile bedouin en route, and the building of a ship on the Red Sea coast for the transport of the myrrh resins from Punt. The blocks of cut stone were for the sanctuaries in temples which Mentuhotep III built at Elephantine, Abydos, and hamlets near Thebes. Some of the reliefs with which they were adorned have survived and show that the refined carving and drawing characteristic of the last years of Mentuhotep II continued to be followed—but with even greater skill and subtlety—and were not surpassed even by the sculptors of the Twelfth Dynasty.

As with the long reign of Pepy II, the fifty-one-year rule of Mentuhotep II seemingly created confusion in the dynastic succession. After the death of Mentuhotep III we catch a brief glimpse of a fourth Mentuhotep and find that during his short reign another expedition—this time of 10,000 men under the command of the vizier and governor of the South, Amenemhet—in the Wadi Hammamat quarrying hard stone for the king's sarcophagus and its lid; then the mists of history come down again. When the scene clears, it is presumably the vizier who is now on the throne, ruling as Ammenemes I, the first pharaoh of the powerful Twelfth Dynasty.

The new king found the wearing of the crowns of Upper and Lower Egypt an uneasy privilege. Mentuhotep II had evidently curbed the claims of his fellow nomarchs in climbing to supreme power, but Ammenemes may have had to come to terms with them in order to obtain the throne. Under the early rulers of the new dynasty, the feudal structures of the First Intermediate Period remained

A USURPER'S WORRIES

Amenemhet, the vizier of Mentuhotep IV (the last representative of the 11th Dynasty), seized the throne after a short interim reign. Did he hasten Mentuotep's death? Perhaps. In any case, he was aware of the dangers that threaten all usurpers and wanted to solidify his power. He even added the name Ouhem-Mesut (he who revives births, or he who founds a dynasty) to his own.

Still worried, the usurper sought solace in literature. This is how the premonitory story of the wise man Neferti of Heliopolis arrived at the royal court, a tale conceived and written on his orders. The writer goes into great detail about the country's tragedies (especially in the north) before announcing the arrival of a good pharaoh who reestablished order; he was nicknamed Ameni: "Heliopolis will no longer be the birthplace of any god," he explained. "A king will come. He will be from the south and will be named Ameni. He will receive the White Crown and will take the Red Crown. He will bring together the Two Crowns."

Finally, to solidify his new dynasty, Amenemhet abdicated to his oldest son, Sesostris, in the twentieth year of his reign. He was the first king to take such an action, and many other kings would follow suit.

in place, the nomarchs of Hermopolis arrogantly dating events to their own years, like kings. Some provincial governors maintained their own armed forces and fleets of ships, quarrying stone for their own monuments, some of considerable size.

The difficulties that confronted Ammenemes I are sufficiently underlined by the co-opting of his eldest son, Sesostris, to act as his co-regent in his twentieth regnal year, a practice in which he was followed by the subsequent kings of the dynasty. Ammenemes died suddenly in his jubilee year, and according to Manetho he was murdered by his own chamberlains. There is further evidence for his violent end in a political testament, *The Teaching of King Ammenemes,* and in a fictionalized autobiography, *The Story of Sinuhe,* which have survived as literary classics. The policies that he inaugurated, however, were carried out by his successors. While a southerner, he abandoned the attempt to govern all Egypt from Thebes and moved his capital to the fulcrum of Upper and Lower Egypt, some thirty miles south of Memphis, to Itj-tawi ("Seizing the Two Lands") near the modern el Lisht. Here he revived the Old Kingdom form of a pyramid for his tomb.

Ammenemes made a determined attempt to subjugate Upper Nubia and the Sudan by building a string of fortified townships in the region all the way to Semna and planting trading posts in the lands beyond, as at Kerma above the Third Cataract. The climax of this development was reached with Sesostris III, who rebuilt most of the forts and was so intimately associated with the region that in later years, he was worshipped there as the local god. While the southern border was pushed farther upstream by a deliberate policy of expansion, the northeastern frontier of Egypt, which had so frequently been penetrated by Asiatics, was consolidated by means of a fortified barrier known as "The Walls of the Prince," doubtless a series of strongholds set up at strategic points to command all the usual routes in and out of Egypt. During the last year of the co-regency, Sesostris I seems to have fought a campaign in Libya to repress raids on the western borders of the Delta, evidently with complete success, since the later resettlement and development of the Faiyum would only have been possible in the absence of Libyan incursions into the western oases. Political activity to protect the frontiers is matched by greatly increased intercourse with Palestine and Syria, where objects bearing the names of different kings of the Twelfth and Thirteenth Dynasties have been found at Gaza, Byblos, Ras Shamra (Ugarit), Megiddo, and elsewhere. *The Story of Sinuhe* acquaints us with the fact that regular journeys by king's envoys were made to Syria by the beginning of the dynasty, and a deposit of Asiatic treasure in a temple near Thebes shows that the trade was not all in one direction.

BLOODY FINERY
On this breastplate, which belonged to a 12th-Dynasty princess, Nekhbet—the vulture-goddess from Upper Egypt—protects the kings who joyfully massacre their enemies.

Generally speaking, relations with Asia during this period seem to have been peaceful and largely concerned with trade. It was doubtless from Byblos or some such entrepôt that Aegean products reached Egypt; conversely, Egyptian objects of Middle Kingdom date have been excavated in Crete. The mining centers in Sinai also show evidence of the tremendous vigor with which the kings of this period increased the supplies of copper ores and turquoise from this source. The extent of this foreign trade is an index of the prosperity in Egypt itself. The capital at Lisht was near the Faiyum, and kings of the Twelfth Dynasty devoted much attention to land settlement and improved irrigation in this region, turning it into one of the most fertile districts of Egypt.

Sesostris I proved to be a most energetic builder, founding a great new temple at Heliopolis, where, to commemorate his jubilee obelisks were erected, one of which still stands. He built or rebuilt on sites all over Egypt, not neglecting the family seat at Thebes whose obscure god, Amun, now begins to come to the fore, as the names of several kings of the dynasty proudly proclaim. The Theban buildings of the Middle Kingdom were used as quarries. The vitality shown by the architects of Sesostris I was shared in differing measure by their successors and reached its apogee during the reign of Ammenemes III (ca. 1842–1794 B.C.), for whom building and sculpture on a truly colossal scale was created.

By that time, however, the pharaoh had once more gained a lonely and unchallenged preeminence thanks to the policies pursued by his predecessors, particularly his father, Sesostris III, under whom a restructuring of national administration had diminished the power of the nomarchs in favor of more centralized departments of state. In place of the former grandees, we find crown officials bearing their titles but governing mere townships as local mayors. It is during Sesostris III's reign that the great series of provincial tombs at Beni Hasan and Deir el-Bersha come to a sudden end, as those at Asyut and Meir had ceased a generation earlier.

The half-century-long reign of Ammenemes III, the last great king of the Twelfth Dynasty, stored up troubles for the succession soon after, and the following dynasty ruled for a confused century during which we have scant details of too many kings to suggest that it was either prosperous or tranquil. Fluctuating climatic conditions seem to have returned to Egypt and caused irregularities in the flow of the Nile. High floods, slow to fall and allow seed to be sown at the proper time, were as disastrous in their effects as feeble inundations. The manifest inability of the pharaoh to control the Nile may have been the chief reason for another slump in the prestige of the kingship, which is apparent throughout the Thirteenth Dynasty, with a host of pharaohs each ruling in obscurity for a short time and leaving few memorials behind him. During interludes when more stable conditions prevailed, some kings were able to erect monuments, including large statues and even a small pyramid tomb, but the general picture is one of slow decline. Unlike the similar crisis at the end of the Old Kingdom, however, the climatic changes were not so severe or protracted, and the bureaucracy established by the last two kings of the Twelfth Dynasty was able to carry on the government of the country under the direction of powerful viziers and chancellors who enjoyed a long continuity of office over several reigns.

The capital remained at Lisht despite the Theban names of many of these rulers. At times, some kind of control seems to have been exercised by more vigorous kings or co-regents. Building operations went on at the old centers and trade continued with Byblos, but a steady decline in artistic and technical standards and a gradual poverty in ideas and materials tell their own story. A significant portent is the appearance of several Asiatic names in the king-lists of this period, and under a certain Dudumose, an event occurred which receives special mention by Josephus, who quotes Manetho at length:

"Tutimaeus. In his reign, for what cause I know not, a blast of God smote us; and unexpectedly, from the regions of the East, invaders of obscure race marched in confidence of victory against our land. By main force they easily seized it without striking a blow; and having overpowered the rulers of the land, they then burned our cities ruthlessly, razed to the ground the temples of the gods, and treated all the natives with a cruel hostility..."

Thus ended ingloriously, according to the official accounts, the second great period in the history of Egyptian culture destroyed by the Hyksos invaders.

Funerary beliefs and practices

While the nomarchs of the First Intermediate Period had taken over most of the style and ritual of royal burial, they were still interred in rock-cut tombs. The

SESOSTRIS
More than 30 years of reign mark the face of Sesostris III, the powerful pharaoh immortalized in this diorite statue.

princes of Thebes followed general custom, having tombs cut in the desert surface of the west bank opposite Karnak. They took the form of great colonnaded courtyards, the tombs of the nobility occupying the flanks, with the chapel and burial chambers of the king to the rear.

Mentuhotep II adapted such a conception to fill the whole valley of Deir el-Bahri: Nobles' tombs occupied the cliffs at the north and south margins, while the king erected a temple-tomb at the western end, under the cliffs. This comprised a porticoed structure rising in three tiers, the uppermost comprising a section that may be interpreted as a square mastaba (the base for a mound) topped by trees. Its unknown architect showed a remarkable eye for the picturesque exploitation of a site with his use of terraces and colonnades. A curious feature of the monument was a dummy tomb with an entrance in the dromos of the temple, leading by way of a long corridor to a burial chamber under the mastaba containing a statue of the king in jubilee costume wrapped in linen like a mummy. The statue, with its flesh painted black, the crown red, and the jubilee-cloak white, is well calculated to give a savage force to what has been regarded as a substitute for the corpse of the divine king. In the precincts and vicinity of this temple were cut the rock-tombs of several relatives and officials, including the pit-tombs and adjacent shrines of six of the royal women, some of whose funerary equipment has survived.

LAMENTATIONS
If this mourner from the Middle Kingdom were not made of terra cotta, she would cry, beat her breast, sprinkle herself with dust, and undo her long hair to properly grieve the deceased.

Also near at hand was the famous chapel of his half-sister, Queen Neferu, with its painted limestone reliefs, the walls of the burial chamber decorated with offerings, friezes of objects, and versions of the Coffin Texts, like the interior of a huge contemporary coffin. The chapel was a tourist attraction for sightseers in the New Kingdom, who showed their appreciation by scribbling on the walls after the manner of their kind.

With the transfer of the capital from Thebes to Itj-tawi in the Twelfth Dynasty, there came a return to the Memphite form of a royal tomb—particularly under Sesostris I, who followed the example of his father by erecting a pyramid at Lisht which shows the direct inspiration of the funerary monument of Pepy II. While the monolithic sarcophaguses, chests, and tomb chambers made of granite or quartzite are often of superb workmanship, the pyramids themselves are of an inferior standard of construction. These pyramids have ill resisted the hand of the stone-robber, and with the loss of their casings have collapsed into eroded black mounds. The pharaohs of the dynasty also renewed the old practice of building the mastabas of their high officials and mortuary priests around their own pyramids, but on a reduced scale, for the truth was that burial near the king had now become something of an anachronism with the rise to importance of the cult of the god Osiris.

Osiris had become prominent in the Delta town of Busiris. He was also adopted into the solar cult of Heliopolis, his companion deities Seth, Isis, and Nephthys becoming the third generation of gods. By the end of the Fifth Dynasty, he was prominently identified with the dead king in the Pyramid Texts, but Abydos was his probable place of origin and had become a town of political importance as well as religious significance under the pharaohs of the Sixth Dynasty. With the increase in the power of the Thebans in the later years of the First Intermediate Period and their capture of Abydos, the claims of Osiris were greatly extended. From being a chthonic god of agriculture and of the Nile, Osiris in the Middle Kingdom became

THE EPIC OF OSIRIS, GOD OF THE DEAD

When age overtook him Geb, god of the earth, bequeathed his throne to his eldest son, Osiris. This young king of the world decided to sever the Egyptians from their savage state. He taught them to till the soil and respect laws and the gods.

Alas, his brother Seth envied his royal status. Devoured by jealousy, he set a trap for him with the help of the ibis-headed god Thoth, killed him, and threw his corpse into the Nile. The current bore the body away. As soon as it reached this colder water it changed color, turning black and green. Ever afterwards, the Egyptians called the sea the "Great Black" or the "Great Green."

The sad news reached the gods. They wept, beat their breasts and tore out their hair in token of their sorrow. Only Seth and Thoth failed to mourn. Osiris's two sisters, Isis and Nephthys, sobbed inconsolably as they wandered the land in search of the body. At last they found it, bobbing in the water, and took it back to the gods. But long immersion in the water had decomposed Osiris's body and detached his limbs. Nut, goddess of the heavens, bent over him, realigning his bones, putting his head back in place, and replacing his heart. Geb, god of the earth, then washed away the mud coating the body. And finally Re, the sun god, supported his head while the assembled deities ordered him to wake.

At once Osiris—the god who loathed sleep and inactivity—awoke to a new life. But death had made final his earthly reign. Henceforth he would rule the world of the dead. His sister and spouse Isis, in the form of a vulture with outspread wings, flew down to settle on him and became miraculously pregnant. Soon the goddess gave birth to their son, Horus. With the help of her sister Nephthys, Isis raised him in the calm of the marshes.

the god of the dead *par excellence*. While the cult of Osiris was concerned entirely with the life after death and did not challenge that of other deities, a certain amount of encroachment was inevitable as Osiris took over the judicial powers—which the sun god Re, for instance, had exercised over the Heliopolitan tribunal—and became the supreme judge of the dead, before whom all wandering souls after death had to account for their deeds on earth. The prestige of the pharaoh as a divinity, already sadly eroded from the last years of the Old Kingdom, suffered further decay with the ascendancy of Osiris as the deification of the idea of kingship. From now on, all men who were worthy had the promise of immortality in the realms ruled over by the kingly divinity Osiris—not merely those who had known the pharaoh in life. There was of course no revolutionary cleavage of thought, since the pharaoh, on his death, was assimilated to Osiris.

The cultural achievement

The decline which this religious development and the new political circumstances wrought in the kingship during the First Intermediate Period was arrested and reversed during the Twelfth Dynasty, when a series of remarkable literary works were written in praise of various kings. It has become the custom in recent years to regard these writings as deliberate attempts at propaganda on behalf of the pharaohs who are the protagonists in these works. The first of them is a sort of post-hoc prophecy, known to Egyptologists as *The Prophecy of Neferti*, and describes how in the spacious days of King Snoferu of the Fourth Dynasty, a great prophet, Neferti, is called to the court to divert the king with "choice speeches." He describes what is to happen in the land in the distant future:

"I show thee the land wailing and weeping...a man's spirit will be concerned with his own welfare... Every mouth is full of, 'Pity me!' All good things have departed. The land is destroyed."

A 50-Year Reign
This sandstone statue of Mentuhotep I, founder of the Middle Kingdom, comes from his tomb in Deir el-Bahri. Outfitted in jubilee costume, he wears the Red Crown of Lower Egypt.

The prophecy ends, however, on a more cheerful note:

"A king shall come from Upper Egypt called Ameni, the son of a woman of the south...He shall receive the White Crown and wear the Red Crown...Be glad, ye people of his time! The son of a high-born man will make his name for all eternity. They who would make mischief and devise enmity have suppressed their mutterings through fear of him...There shall be built the 'Walls of the Prince' and the Asiatics shall not again be suffered to go down to Egypt. They shall beg again for water their cattle after their custom...And Right [Ma'et] shall come into its own again and Wrong shall be cast out."

The Ameni of the prophecy is undoubtedly Ammenemes I, and his Upper Egyptian parentage, which was noble, is stressed as an apologia for his seizure of supreme power to end the miseries of anarchy at the close of the Eleventh Dynasty.

The second work, *The Teaching of King Ammenemes*, already mentioned, is concerned with events at the end of the reign of the same king, who was apparently murdered or ritually killed by his chamberlains. In *The Teaching*, the dead king is made to appear in a dream to his son Sesostris I in order to give him some sage advice:

"Be on thy guard against subordinates...Trust not a brother, know not a friend and make not for thyself intimates..."

But *The Teaching* then goes on to justify this skepticism on the strength of the experiences of the king himself, who had received nothing but ingratitude from those he had promoted. The major part of the work is, in fact, not a "teaching" but an apologia for the king's life and a eulogy of his achievements. It could also be in the nature of an official explanation and excuse for any extreme measures that the young co-regent may have had to take on the sudden and violent death of his father.

The third of these works of propaganda, *The Story of Sinuhe*, is cast in a typically Egyptian literary form—the novel—and is a simple success story told with an elegance, dramatic conciseness, and humor that we can still appreciate. The scene opens in the camp of the co-regent Sesostris I, who is returning from a successful campaign in Libya when the news of his father's death is brought to him. Sinuhe, an official in the service of the queen, overhears the dire report and flees from the camp in panic, so beginning his odyssey. The justification he gives for this flight is that "it was like the dispensation of God... after the manner of a dream," and it is as a god-struck man that he continues his adventures. Fate takes him to the Lebanon, where he prospers. But as a good Egyptian, he is sick for home and eventually returns to the court, where he is received by a gracious king.

The Story of Sinuhe is remarkable for the semblance of actuality that is given to all the incidents in the tale, suggesting a real tomb-autobiography rather than a work of the imagination. Although the setting is fairyland—to the court Egyptian of the Twelfth Dynasty, Asia was *terra incognita* where all things were possible—all the dramatis personae behave in a completely rational manner. Sesostris is shown first as the dutiful son and valiant warrior conquering through love as much as might, and finally as the god-like ruler, forgiving and generous.

These and some minor works—hymns in praise of the kings and so forth—form the classical literature of Egypt. They were painfully learnt by schoolboys even half a millennium later. That the kings of the Twelfth Dynasty should accept the services

of skillful writers to sustain their power and glamour may seem startling—and probably it was no explicit directive that brought such literature into being—but the plastic arts reveal the same subconscious desire to show the king as a superman.

The royal statues of this reign are remarkable for their forceful portrayal of the king as either the ruthless or regal overlord of the nation, or later as the world-weary "good shepherd" of his people. Most of this sculpture in hard stones, such as obsidian, granites, quartzites, and basalts, is of magnificent workmanship, both technically and artistically, with a haunting inner power.

While royal statuary is differentiated by individual portraiture, private sculpture merely follows the fashion of a particular reign. Much of it was shop-work and on a small scale, and it varies from the competent to the frankly inept. The chasm between the superb creations of the court sculptors and this mediocre hack-work only emphasizes the gulf which had opened again by the end of the Twelfth Dynasty between the king, aloof at the head of affairs, and the mass of the people.

It was only in the early Thirteenth Dynasty, when royal commissions were once more in decline, that superior statuary for private owners reappears. At the same time, the great number of votive stelae and statuettes suggests that the little man had increased his prosperity at the expense of the great feudal lords.

GROOMING
The tombs of the women in Mentuhotep I's harem are near the entrance of the pharaoh's tomb. In the sarcophagus belonging to Queen Kawit (above), the reliefs show us her daily grooming routine.

CHAPTER 11

The time of Hyksos

The immigrations

Manetho's account of the appearance of the Hyksos on the Egyptian scene as the eruption of a conquering horde spreading fire and destruction was colored by memories of more recent Assyrian and Persian invasions in his own time and has had to be discounted. As early as the First Intermediate Period, western Semites from Palestine, driven from their own pastures by famine to seek sanctuary elsewhere, had infiltrated the Delta. The Egyptians referred to the tribal chiefs of these people as Hikau khasut, or "Princes of Desert Uplands," a term which Manetho by false etymology translated as Hyksos, or "Shepherd Kings," a name which has clung tenaciously ever since to the entire people rather than its rulers. At Beni Hasan, a group of Hikau khasut are shown in their coats of many colors, being received by the nomarch Khnumhotep in his capacity as governor of the Eastern Desert in the reign of Sesostris II (ca. 1890 B.C.).

Such bedouin were no more than wandering Semites trading their products with Egypt or going down there for sanctuary, to buy corn, or to water their flocks according to an age-old tradition referred to in *The Prophecy of Neferti*. By the Thirteenth Dynasty, the number of Asiatics, even in Upper Egypt, was considerable. They acted as cooks, brewers, seamstresses, vine-dressers, and the like. One official, for instance, had no fewer than forty-five Asiatics in his household. Such people were classed as "slaves"—a comparatively new element in Egyptian society, but one that was destined to prevail for a long time as wholesale migrations and foreign wars brought many aliens into Egypt.

Their children often took Egyptian names and so fade from our sight. Asiatic dancers and a doorkeeper in a temple of Sesostris II are known, showing that these foreigners attained positions of importance and trust. It is not difficult to see that by the middle of the Thirteenth Dynasty, the lively and industrious Semites could be in the same positions of responsibility in the Egyptian state as Greek freedmen were to enjoy in the government of Imperial Rome.

Famine or ethnic movements leading to large-scale infiltrations into the Delta of Semites could have resulted in the founding of a Lower Egyptian state with an Asiatic chieftain and officials taking over imperceptibly all the functions and machinery of pharaonic government. At a later stage there must have appeared upon the scene a war-leader similar to a number of condottieri, or leaders of mecenary soldies, who at this time with their aristocracy of chariot warriors—such as Salatis, who seized Memphis and turned the ancient site of Avaris into a formidable stronghold—were seizing power and founding military states all over western Asia. A rather different immigration was also evident at the other end of the country. Nomadic warlike tribes from the eastern highlands of Nubia, particularly the Medjay, entered Egypt as mercenary soldiers and took service with the Theban princelings. They have left traces of their sojourn in the scanty ruins of their settlements, and especially in the characteristic shallow round or oval graves of pan-like formation at various sites in the desert verges of Upper Egypt.

These pan-graves contain the contracted bodies of warrior immigrants dressed in leather garments and simple barbaric jewelery, accompanied by weapons of Egyptian design and make. They were clearly of a more primitive culture than their Egyptian hosts. In time, their burials lose their characteristic features and by the end of this period are indistinguishable from native Egyptian graves.

The pharaohs of the Middle Kingdom had subjugated territories in Nubia and the Lower Sudan as far as the Second Cataract and had established some kind

of outpost as far as Kerma near the Third Cataract. Kerma was probably at this time the capital of Kush, a civilization of native origin but greatly influenced by Egyptian importations. Here a curious hybrid culture flourished, employing Egyptian techniques in faience and metal, yet also using such alien materials as mica and shell, and native-inspired designs. But the more primitive nature of this culture is seen in the burials of its local rulers under great circular tumuli, or artificial mounds,

enclosing subsidiary graves of hundreds of servants and women who had been drugged and suffocated to accompany their masters into the hereafter. Egyptian statues and other treasures looted or traded from sites farther north were also buried as part of the funerary equipment.

The conquest of Nubia and its organization had been the work of the pharaohs, particularly of Sesostris III, and as soon as their interest in their southern properties began to wane in the face of more potent threats in the north, the decay of Egyptian power in Nubia was inevitable. The great forts were gradually abandoned and were occupied by native pastoralists, squatting among the ruins. The acceptance by the Theban rulers in Upper Egypt of the suzerainty of the Hyksos overlords completed the work of disengagement. The Prince of Kush became an independent kinglet, entering into trading relations with the Hyksos and being recognized as in some kind of alliance with them.

THE ARRIVAL OF
THE BEDOUIN
In his tomb at Beni Hasan, Prince Khnumhotep had painters depict the arrival of a parade of 34 Asians. The document in the leader's hand indicates that this event took place in the sixth year of Sesostris II's reign.

Hyksos and Thebans, ca. 1650–1550 B.C.

By the seventeenth century B.C., Lower Egypt was ruled from Avaris by a line of Hyksos kings with their vassals who had wrested Memphis from the last feeble monarchs of the Thirteenth Dynasty. They adopted Egyptian titularies, costume, and traditions, writing their outlandish personal names, such as Yakobher and Khyan, in hieroglyphs and selecting Egyptian throne-names. They dutifully worshipped Re of Heliopolis, as well as Seth or Sutekh, the Egyptian equivalent of their Baal. That they were regarded as legitimate sovereigns in Lower Egypt at least is clear from their inclusion in the Turin king-list written as late as Ramessid times.

SARCOPHAGUS
This body-shaped sarcophagus dates back to the 18th Dynasty. The head has a long wig tucked behind the ears and a false beard under the chin.

The six "Great Hyksos" kings of the Sixteenth Dynasty, who ruled Lower Egypt from Avaris, inherited all the prestige and responsibilities of the Egyptian pharaoh and exerted influence beyond the Delta over territories in Sinai and Palestine. Upper Egypt, from Elephantine to Cusae north of Asyut, enjoyed an uneasy independence under its princes ruling at Thebes by paying tribute to the Hyksos overlord.

While to Manetho the Hyksos seizure of supreme power seemed an unmitigated disaster, we can recognize it as one of the great seminal influences in Egyptian civilization, bringing new ideas into the Nile Valley and ensuring that Egypt played a full part in the development of Bronze Age culture in the eastern Mediterranean. A problematic example of the Mediterranean connections of the Hyksos is provided by the series of Cretan Minoan frescoes found in the ruins of Avaris, the earliest of their kind found anywhere. A number of innovations appear in the archaeological record. Even at the end of the Old Kingdom, a curious perforated hemispherical seal—known to archaeologists as a button-seal or design amulet—made its appearance. During the Middle Kingdom, it was transformed into the characteristic Egyptian scarab, perhaps more of an amulet than a seal, and this artifact was adopted with enthusiasm by the Hyksos, who produced them in enormous numbers.

With the increase in Asiatic influence during the Middle Kingdom, bronze comes into general use. It was easier to work than copper and more effective for weapons and hardware. It had already been used for casting statues in the reign of Ammenemes III—a technique not possible with copper, which was hammered over a wooden core in the only two large examples surviving from the Old Kingdom. Silver, too, of a purity which shows that it was not of native origin but smelted from argentiferous, or silvery, ores, was now imported from Asia in increasing amounts.

In the later phase of the war of liberation that developed between the Hyksos and the Thebans at the end of this period, a whole range of novel weapons was introduced from Asia, such as the horse-drawn chariot, scale armor, and new designs of daggers, swords, and scimitars. It is doubtful whether such weapons as the horse-drawn chariot were fully effective in Egypt, where the inundation and topography gave a greater importance to water-borne operations. But the Thebans certainly adopted all these weapons in their wars against the Hyksos in both Egypt and Palestine. The Asiatic origin of the chariot was preserved in the different woods used in its construction, the Canaanite names for its various parts, and by the tradition of retaining Asiatics to drive and maintain some of them at least. A war helmet, probably made of leather sewn with gilded metal disks, was added to the pharaoh's regalia and is known to Egyptologists as the *khepresh*—the Blue, or War, Crown.

More important than these weapons of destruction were certain abiding inventions of peace, such as improved methods of spinning and weaving, using an upright loom, and new musical instruments—a lyre, the long-necked lute, the oboe, and the

EMBALMING

To live again in the afterlife, the deceased had to preserve his body. His heart and soul could then take their place again and wake up. Embalming varied depending on the period and social rank of the deceased. Lower-ranking Egyptians had to make do with mummification of bodies buried in the sands of the desert, which was free, natural, and effective; but first-class embalming (there were three classes) required considerable care.

The embalmer-priests first prepared the rare and expensive products that were necessary to mummification—beeswax, cedar oil, gum, henna, juniper berries, onions, palm wine, resin, sawdust, pitch, tar, and natron—plus linen strips, jewels, and amulets. They removed the brain and intestines (which they placed in four vases), cleaned the body, filled it with herbs, and placed it in a natron bath. Seventy days later, they washed the dried body and wrapped it in gum-soaked strips. The mummy then received necklaces, bracelets, rings, and protective finger coverings. Starting in the New Kingdom, mummies also received the *Book of the Dead*, an indispensable guide for avoiding the pitfalls of the afterlife.

Amulets were placed on appropriate places: eyes on the lids, a Wedjat eye on the stomach, and a scarab on the place of the heart, which bore a formula that allowed the deceased to not be betrayed by his conscience during the judgment of the dead. After masking his face, the priests wrapped the mummy in a second layer of strips soaked in scented liquid gum. Ritual recitations were uttered: "You live again; you live again forever; you are young again now, forever!" Then came the Opening of the Mouth ceremony, after which the deceased was able to talk. Finally, the mummy was placed in a sarcophagus and was ready to be buried.

tambourine. Hump-backed bulls were imported from an Asiatic source. Other importations included the olive and pomegranate trees.

In Thebes during this period, the poverty and lack of good timber encouraged further changes in funerary customs, and the self-contained burial came into fashion. There had indeed been a shift of emphasis during the last quarter of the Twelfth Dynasty, when a new expression creeps into the funerary prayers to indicate that the deceased was regarded less as a materialization than as a spirit. At the same time, under the impact of the Osiris cult, the coffin as a sort of rectangular wooden house is replaced by the anthropomorphic case decorated to represent the deceased as the mummified and bandaged Osiris, or as the human-headed *ba* bird, a spirit.

With the appearance of this type of coffin, the tomb-statue, already greatly reduced, either disappears or is transformed into the funerary statuette—or shawabti (later ushabti)—figure. The shawabti figure was a specialized form of the servant statue which had disappeared with the triumph of the Osiris faith. Its purpose was to act as a substitute for the deceased whenever onerous toil had to be performed in the fields of the Osirian underworld. As we have already mentioned, from the earliest times a corvée had existed whereby laborers could be drafted en masse for public works at critical moments during the inundation. Similar duties were naturally expected in the agricultural realms of Osiris, and it was to exempt the deceased from such forced labor that the shawabti was provided. By the end of this period, even the king, who on death was assimilated to Osiris, was thought to be subject to this same conscription, and royal shawabtis are many and elaborate.

The lack of good timber as well as changes in doctrine hastened the disappearance of the rectangular outer coffin, and the sole anthropoid containers were now dug out of local trees and are invariably ill-shaped and crude. They were painted with a characteristic feathered decoration representing the wings of the sky-mother, Nut, who, according to a pastiche of several brief spells from the Pyramid Texts, regularly found on the coffin lids of the next dynasty, is exhorted to embrace the deceased with her winged arms so that he might not die a second time but be placed among the Imperishable Stars which were in her.

CHAPTER 12

The New Kingdom

The military state

About the year 1600 B.C., a certain Tetisheri, the daughter of commoners, was married to Taa I (Senakhtenre), the Prince of Thebes who recognized the suzerainty of the Hyksos king in Avaris. By the time she died as a little, white-haired, partially bald old woman, her grandson, Ahmose, was the pharaoh of a united Egypt and the greatest prince of his age.

This dramatic rise from obscurity to supremacy was not achieved without a bitter struggle. A novelette of later years relates how her son Taa II (Seqenenre) fought a diplomatic battle of words with the Hyksos overlord Apophis, who had challenged his pretensions in Upper Egypt. Although the end of the story is missing we are to assume that the verbal victory lay with the Theban.

This is the same Taa II who was less successful on a more active field, for his shattered skull shows that he met a violent end, either in battle or at the hands of assassins. It was probably at this critical juncture that his widow, Queen Ahhotep, took over the reins of government, for a later stele erected in her honor praises her for cherishing Egypt, for tending her soldiers and rallying her fugitives: "She has pacified Upper Egypt and cast out its rebels."

It was left to Kamose, the successor of Taa II, to begin a war of liberation in earnest, and we are fortunate in having his account of the opening of the campaign in two texts. In his third regnal year, the new king sailed downstream with his forces and stormed the stronghold of a Hyksos collaborator, Teti, near Hermopolis, pushing his boundary to within a short distance of the entrance to the Faiyum. Kamose, however, did not live to see the end of the affair, and it was Ahmose, the next in line to the Theban principality, who carried on the struggle, eventually reducing the Hyksos capital Avaris after a long siege.

In order to deter further Asiatic incursions into Egypt, another campaign was necessary, and this was mounted as far as the town of Sharuhen in southwestern Palestine which was destroyed, thus advertising to the Asiatic princes the arrival of a vigorous new actor upon the international scene.

After his capture of Sharuhen, Ahmose was able to turn his attention to consolidating his position in Egypt by replacing the last of the Hyksos collaborators with his own men and by restating claims upon the southern territories, Nubia and Kush.

Both Egypt and Kush were reorganized upon the bureaucratic system of government which had been developed during the last reigns of the Twelfth Dynasty, but with a new logistical efficiency appropriate to a military state. The feudal nomarchs had long since disappeared from political life and no rivals to the supreme rule of the pharaoh were to be tolerated by Ahmose and his successors. His soldiers, both Egyptians and their Medjay auxiliaries, were rewarded for their services by

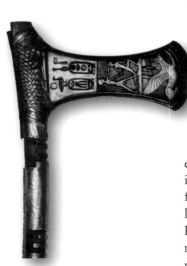

AX OF PRESTIGE
Used as a tool by artisans but also as a weapon of war, the ax was a symbol of power. This ceremonial ax belonged to King Ahmose, founder of the New Kingdom.

134

modest grants of land, with prisoners as slaves and with valuable gold decorations and parade weapons, but the large estates in Lower Egypt were kept in the possession of the king and his family.

Ahmose (ca.1550–1524 B.C.), the son of the last rulers of the Seventeenth Dynasty, was honored by subsequent generations as the founder of a new line and a glorious chapter in Egyptian history. The policies which he initiated were followed by his successors, and during the Eighteenth Dynasty this was a recipe for unparalleled prosperity and imperial expansion in Palestine, Syria, and Kush. It was from the last-named region that new supplies of gold were procured that made Egypt rich and influential among the nations of antiquity. The Hyksos interlude had destroyed forever the Egyptians' belief in their uniqueness and superiority. Their pharaoh, traditionally the incarnation of the god that had created their world and ruled its extent as far as the circuit of the sun, inherited from the Hyksos the leadership of vassal states in Palestine and Syria, but he also shared his sovereignty with "brother" monarchs in Cyprus, Babylonia, and Assyria and the Hittite and Mitannian lands in Anatolia. The triumph of Ahmose on the battlefield introduced a new idea of the pharaoh as the national hero, a personification of Egypt itself, sitting, as Kamose expressed it, between an Asiatic in the north and a black Nubian in the south.

The pharaoh was now regarded as the incarnation of some warrior-god, Baal or Seth or Mentu, at the head of a caste of professional military leaders, chariot-warriors accomplished in athletic feats, the management of horses, and all the skills of a new mobile warfare.

Imperial designs

The Asiatic component in the civilization of the New Kingdom is considerable, extending even to an alteration in the racial type of the Egyptian ruling class. The men and women of the New Kingdom have lost the heavy physiques of their Old Kingdom counterparts and the dour solemnity of their Middle Kingdom forerunners. The countenances of the men are bland, often faintly smiling. The women are slight, their features delicate, with great gala wigs and tip-tilted noses and long almond eyes. An erotic element enters the art of the Eighteenth Dynasty, perhaps as a result of the introduction of the cults of nude goddesses from Asia. The luxury of the age finds expression in the colorful jewels made in new materials, such as faience and glass, worn by both sexes.

The initial Egyptian forays into western Asia brought her armies into sustained contact with the great cultures of the Near East. Against the unified power of Egypt, under the command of a warlord, were opposed loose federations of Syrian and Canaanite principalities lacking cohesion. In Palestine, Lebanon, and Syria, the political unit was the city-state, ruling over the territories in its vicinity and receiving within its walls the local populace in times of trouble.

These various states hardly welcomed the interference of a great power in their constant rivalry with one another, their main aims being to preserve their autonomy, and to extend their frontiers at the expense of their neighbors. They were, however,

LADY TJEPU
This beautiful Theban woman, dressed in the fashion of the Amenhotep III's court, lets a cone of scented fat slowly melt over her wig.

only too ready to turn intervention to their own advantage, following the power whose star was in the ascendant and seeking its assistance in promoting their own local ambitions. But sometimes it was doubtful to whom fortune would incline the supremacy, and in such cases one big power was played off against the other, vows of loyalty given to both, and sides changed and rechanged with little compunction. This is the world of Palestine and Syria that has been revealed to us from the Amarna diplomatic correspondence, which also apprises us of the intrusions of a mysterious people known as the Sa-Gaz or Apiru, whom some scholars regard as the immediate ancestors of the Hebrews. Apiru appear to have been displaced persons of both sexes moving around like robber-bands, probably keeping to difficult country away from the high-roads and intervening in the local politics by accepting services as mercenaries when they were not fighting on their own account.

WAR SCENE

In this bas-relief, Pharaoh is prancing on his chariot, proud of his many prisoners. He wears a khepresh *on his head, which is the Blue Crown decorated with the frightening Uraeus serpent.*

Egyptian campaigns in western Asia quickly made their impression on the local rulers who hastened to show their submission by sending tribute. But by the time Thutmose III attained sole rule (ca. 1457 B.C.), the Egyptian position in Asia was threatened by a confederation of petty kingdoms under the leadership of the Mitanni, a Hurrian people ruled by an Aryan-speaking aristocracy who worshipped Indo-European gods and inhabited the land of Nahrina, the watershed of the Euphrates. On the east they were bounded by the young nation of Assyria and on the west by the Hittites, a mixed people occupying most of Anatolia, with an Indo-European ruling class speaking a language akin to Greek and Latin. At the beginning of this period, the Mitanni were the dominant power in north Syria, having conquered the eastern Hittite territories.

Thutmose III found it necessary to fight seventeen campaigns over a period of some twenty years before his claims in Palestine and Syria could be recognized and the pretensions of the Mitanni checked. In the course of these wars, Egypt was forced to organize her Asiatic sphere of influence into a virtual dependency, forming garrison-towns at strategic points and removing the sons of local rulers to Egypt as hostages for their fathers' good behavior. These sons were brought up with the Egyptian royal children "to serve their lord and stand at the portal of the king." Eventually they went back to rule their states after having been anointed by the pharaoh himself.

As part of his foreign policy, Thutmose III had concluded a treaty with the Hittites, the rivals of the Mitanni, and a similar strategy was pursued by his successors. A pact of mutual assistance was also negotiated with Babylonia to keep the Canaanite vassals in check. Such treaties were cemented by marriages between the daughters of the various royal houses and the pharaoh. Even the daughters of the less exalted princes also entered the royal harems and played their part in the diplomacy of the age. This traffic was all in one direction. When the King of Babylon attempted to make a reciprocal arrangement, he was haughtily reminded that it was not the custom for Egyptian princesses to be married to foreigners.

After the conclusion of peace between Egypt and the Mitanni, such treaties brought a century of comparative calm and stability to Palestine and south Syria during the middle reigns of the Eighteenth Dynasty.

This balance of power was however upset by the accession of the energetic and able King Suppiluliumas to the Hittite throne (ca. 1350 B.C.). He was to remold the political structure of the region for the next century. The struggle between the Hittites and the Mitanni was renewed. After a long contest, the Mitanni capital was sacked and its king subsequently assassinated. Syria came under the dominance of the Hittites, who fostered intrigue and dissension farther south by means of their vassals, all anxious to take advantage of a situation that once more had become fluid. At this moment, the pharaoh, the ally of the Mitanni, issued no effective challenge to the Hittite threat, an indifference which has been accredited to the preoccupation of the religious reformer Akhenaten with events at home. Egypt, however, had treaties with both powers, and it may have been of little account to the pharaoh which of the two rivals had authority over north Syria. His chief concern was in preserving Egyptian influence in a coastal trading region stretching from Byblos in the south to Ugarit in the north. In this, however, the Egyptians were thwarted by the wily Amorite vassals of the Hittites, and although a serious attempt to win back territory and influence was undertaken by the immediate successors of Akhenaten, they did not achieve any lasting success. The powerful kingdom of the Mitanni riven by civil strife became a mere satellite of the Hittites and was eventually incorporated into the expanding state of Assyria on the death of Suppiluliumas, and it disappears from history.

While events in Asia followed a fluctuating course, the more important southern dependencies of Nubia and Kush, the biblical Ethiopia, came under effective Egyptian government as never before. The entire territory was now put in charge

A TRIUMPHANT
RAMESES II
In one hand, Pharaoh is holding the ceremonial ax, in the other, the hair of those conquered: a Nubian, a Libyan, and an Asian. All the border regions of Egypt are therefore represented, and all enemies are defeated.

of a high official or viceroy, "the king's son (= prince) of Kush," appointed by the pharaoh and responsible to him alone.

Under a peaceful and efficient rule, the region prospered. The Egyptianization of Nubia and Kush was so effective that at the end of the New Kingdom, ca. 1075 B.C., the viceroy intervened decisively in the affairs of Egypt proper in the name of law and order. The products of Nubia and Kush added greatly to the wealth of Egypt, particularly gold, ivory, ebony, cattle, gums, resins, and semi-precious stones.

Most of these same commodities were also obtained by trading ventures to Punt, always an indication of the health and vigor of the Egyptian state, and during this period such voyages became commonplace. The first of these expeditions during the Eighteenth Dynasty, in the reign of Hatshepsut, is the most noteworthy for the detailed representation of it carved in relief on the queen's funerary temple at Deir el-Bahri. This is the first known example of an anthropological study of an alien culture, with its record of the flora and fauna of the region, the human types, their physique, dress, and habitations. The final sequence in the scenes shows the triumphant return from Punt with gold, ivory, apes, and precious myrrh-trees, their root balls carefully protected in baskets, and the dedication of measured heaps of myrrh to Amun of Thebes.

THE QUEEN OF PUNT
Queen Hatshepsut saw to it that the story of her maritime expedition was sculpted in her temple at Deir el-Bahri. Her body deformed from sickness, the queen of Punt watches over the commercial trade of gold, ebony, ivory, and rare animals like giraffes.

The advent (ca. 1298 B.C.) of the Nineteenth Dynasty, a family of evident Semitic descent from the eastern Delta, brought a new dynamic into the affairs of Western Asia, and in the first year of his reign, Sethos I set forth to follow the sacrosanct patterns of the campaigns of Thutmose III and win back the Syrian dominions. While Sethos was successful in re-establishing Egyptian authority in Canaan and in capturing the key fortress of Qadesh on the Orontes, his battle with the Hittites was inconclusive, and it was left to his impetuous son Rameses II to try conclusions with the prime enemy. In the latter's fifth regnal year (ca. 1274 B.C.), the Egyptian forces fell into a trap set by the astute Hittite king north of Qadesh and were extricated from disaster only by the chance arrival of one of their army corps and by the personal valor of Rameses in persistently charging the enemy to rally his demoralized forces. Thereafter, no serious challenge was made to Hittite ascendancy in northern Syria. The two powers in fact entered into increasingly friendly relations culminating in a defensive alliance between them, which is an important landmark in the history of diplomacy. In the treaty, of which a Hittite copy exists as well as Egyptian versions of the original inscribed silver tablet, both powers act as equals; their spheres of influence are carefully defined, with south Syria going to Egypt and the north to the Hittites; each pledges the other not to support its enemies; and there are provisions for the extradition of criminals or emigrés.

138

A GRANDIOSE WEDDING

In year 33 of his reign, Rameses II, at age 50, received an envoy from the Hittite king, who suggested they strengthen the peace agreement signed 13 years earlier with a marriage. He offered his daughter and a very good dowry. At the beginning of the summer, the princess set out for the south, accompanied by an impressive cortège composed of a few noblemen; well-armed soldiers; carts overflowing with gold, silver, copper, and bronze; fine cloth; hundreds of slaves; and horses, cattle, and rams.

Rameses also prepared. He sent part of his army and a few noblemen officials to meet her. Unfortunately, by the fall, the snow had already covered the provinces of the North. Pharaoh worried and, unwilling to wait any longer, went to the temple of Seth, the frightening god of thunder and the deserts. He brought him offerings and begged him to send neither rain, icy wind, nor snow to the regions the princess was crossing. Seth seemed to have answered the royal prayers: The sky of Asia calmed along the fiancée's path. And soon, along the border between the two kingdoms, the troops, chariots, and dignitaries of Egypt joined the troops, chariots, and dignitaries of the Hittite country. Those who once clashed now embraced, eating and drinking together like brothers. They then took their leave of each other and went either north or south.

This incredible cortège finally arrived in Pi-Ramesse, the Egyptian capital, during the third month of the winter of the 34th year of the reign of Rameses II. Although he already had dozens of wives and concubines, Rameses found the princess to be very beautiful. Days and days of banquets, dancing, music, and enjoyment took place to celebrate their marriage, and there is no doubt that the princess was mesmerized by such splendor.

The treaty was sealed by a marriage between Rameses II and the daughter of the Hittite king—an affair which breathed fresh inspiration into a continuous romance of the Near East. The marriage was celebrated alike in the scarab of regnal year ten of Amenhotep III, when he was married to the daughter of the Kings of Nahrina, and in the story of Solomon and the Queen of Sheba—though in the case of the Hittite princess, we have a more tangible memorial in a scrap of papyrus found by Petrie at Gurob, listing part of her wardrobe.

Loss of empire

It may be that both powers realized the futility of warring against each other in the face of a common menace.

In the fifth regnal year of Rameses II's successor Merenptah (ca. 1207 B.C.), new tribes of Libyans appeared in force on the western frontier, penetrating the defenses as far as the oasis of Farafra and the Canopic branch of the Nile. This was no plundering incursion, but a migration of peoples moving with their families, cattle, household goods, and treasure to settle in the rich pastures of the Delta, in the face of increasing aridity in their own lands. Merenptah's forces drove them back with great losses. This heavy defeat gave Egypt nearly half a century of uneasy peace, but in his time, Rameses III (ca. 1185–1153 B.C.), the first effective king of the Twentieth Dynasty and the last great pharaoh of Egypt, was called upon to repulse two more desperate invasions of immigrants from Libya, again accompanied by their families, cattle, and possessions. Even these disasters did not deter these land-hungry peoples from settling in Egypt. Throughout the Twentieth Dynasty, wandering bands of Libyans filtered across the western borders, striking terror in the valley-dwellers as far south as Thebes and Aswan. Many of them took service with the Egyptian armies and, as veterans, were eventually settled on the land. Their descendants constituted an influential military caste and later became powerful enough to intervene decisively in Egyptian affairs and form several dynasties of pharaohs.

THE YOUNG KHAMOUAST
On the walls of his tomb in the Valley of the Queens, the young prince is accompanied by his father in the afterlife. The king precedes him to introduce him to the gods who guard the world of the dead.

These various incursions from Libya had a feature that was new and soon to prove of a calamitous significance. The Libyans who had invaded the Delta in the reign of Merenptah had been accompanied by foreign contingents of "northerners coming from all lands," mainly Lycia, Etruria, Sicily, and Sardinia. Similar groups of piratical adventurers appear again in strength in the next great crisis that Rameses III had to meet—the invasions of the Sea Peoples (ca. 1177 B.C.) This is a name which the Egyptians applied to the loose federation of roving corsairs that now overwhelmed the old nations of the Levant and cast them into a newer mold. According to the only account of these events, given on the walls of the mortuary temple of Rameses III at Medinet Habu, a league of these northern peoples had evidently been formed to replace sporadic raiding by a concerted drive against the great powers of Anatolia, Syria, and Palestine. "All at once," says Rameses, "these peoples were on the move...No country could stand up to them. The Hittites, Cilicia, Carchemish, Cyprus, and others were cut off. A camp was established in Amor, and they desolated its people and annihilated its land. Their confederacy was Peleset, Tjeker, Shekelesh, Denyen, and Weshesh..." Egypt lay before them rich in spoils and ripe for settlement. Rameses met the invasion on two fronts. A fierce land battle was

140

fought near the Egyptian frontier in Palestine. The Egyptians with their auxiliaries claimed a great victory. The second assault was fought upon the sea—and evidently, in order to avoid single scattered actions, the enemy were enticed, "like birds into a clap-net," to enter the Nile mouths where boomships had been stationed and a single decisive engagement could be fought. Once more, Egypt was victorious and the dire threat dispelled.

Much has to be read between the lines of the Egyptian account, but the victory seems to have been complete. The Egyptian strategy was correct in tempting these essentially small, individual bands of marauders to commit their forces to a concerted attack against which a unified command would have the advantage. But while the Egyptian frontiers may have been preserved, the map of the Near East was considerably altered in the process. Priam's Troy had traditionally fallen to the Achaeans a year or two before the advent of Rameses III.

The Hittite empire now disappeared from Anatolia together with its maritime vassals Ugarit and Amor. Despite the total victory claimed by Rameses III over the land forces of the Sea Peoples, accompanied by their women and children in bullock carts, the Peleset and the Tjeker settled in the coastal towns of Palestine during the next half-century. The former are often equated with the Philistines, and the latter with the Teucri of the Troad. Whether the Weshesh originated in Illios (Troy), and the Akawash were Mycenaean Greeks, may be beyond all conjecture. But what is more evident is that the 12th century B.C. in the Levant was a time of the breaking of nations, when in the words of the Egyptians, their peoples were on the march, scattered in war.

This was indeed a proto-Armageddon, the end of an epoch. During the last three centuries of the Bronze Age, there had been established all over the New East great and little principalities of indigenous farmers ruled by divine warlords and their *maryannu*, an aristocracy of chariot-using warriors dedicated to the service of their leaders. These élites were usually Aryan-speaking and devoted to military sports.

The character of these stratified societies is as much revealed in the epics of Homer as in the Amarna Letters. They were feudal, contentious, boastful, and aggressive, living in splendid palaces and cultivating the luxurious arts. Their leaders engaged in commerce, but were dependent upon a palace bureaucracy for organizing their trading ventures as much for prestige as profit. They exchanged their oil, corn, copper, and timber for such luxury goods as gold and silver, lapis lazuli, fine furniture, and horses.

In the 13th century B.C., this world began to disintegrate. The reasons are complex; probably climatic change, leading to drought and the movement of starving peoples, was at the root of the deterioration. Plague had been endemic in Anatolia since the 14th century, doubtless reducing the farming community and restricting the supply of grain. The area was also subject to severe earthquakes.

As such, catastrophes had their political effects upon settled communities and the commerce in which they were engaged. As trade began to decline, maritime adventurers unable to trade as before took to piracy—an endemic feature of the Mediterranean seaways until very recent times. Such assaults led to reprisals and ever bolder brigandage. A governing caste that had been nurtured upon the military arts knew only how to fight and plunder. The kings of men became the sackers of cities. From this boiling cauldron of nations on the move, the Mediterranean lands were eventually colonized by warrior groups preserving legends of a former greatness, when their heroic ancestors were in pursuit of glory.

PAYING TRIBUTE
(New Kingdom) A Syrian prince pays the tribute owed by his country in the form of rare products lacking in Egypt—copper, silver, iron, and certain semi-precious stones or good-quality wood.

The decline and fall of the divine kings of Asia and their *maryannu*, or chariot warriors of noble birth, had its repercussions upon the position of the pharaoh. His prestige waned in the later years of the Twentieth Dynasty, when revolt against authority was in fashion. There was trouble on the frontiers in the north and west and a need for constant vigilance. Late in the reign of Rameses XI, civil war broke out between the king and Pinhasi, his viceroy of Kush. Pinhasi was driven out of Thebes by the king's generals Herihor and Piankh, not without inflicting deplorable damage in the process, and retired to Kush, where he kept up such an effective resistance that the province was thereafter permanently lost to Egypt. Asia had been abandoned a little earlier, probably in the reign of Rameses VI, and the Faiyum—and possibly other northern oases—had become indefensible through Libyan raids. By the end of the New Kingdom, Egypt was back behind her old frontiers.

The cultural heritage

The civilization of the New Kingdom seems the most golden of all the epochs of Egyptian history, and the nearest to us, probably because of the wealth of its remains. Its great pharaohs are more than mere names: We have many of their personal possessions, their scepters, weapons, chariots, jewels, and finery, their very paint-boxes and toys.

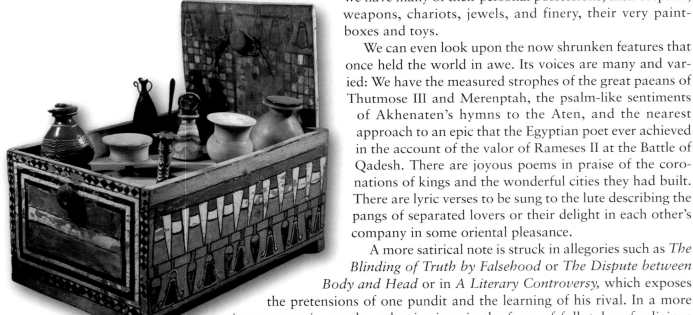

We can even look upon the now shrunken features that once held the world in awe. Its voices are many and varied: We have the measured strophes of the great paeans of Thutmose III and Merenptah, the psalm-like sentiments of Akhenaten's hymns to the Aten, and the nearest approach to an epic that the Egyptian poet ever achieved in the account of the valor of Rameses II at the Battle of Qadesh. There are joyous poems in praise of the coronations of kings and the wonderful cities they had built. There are lyric verses to be sung to the lute describing the pangs of separated lovers or their delight in each other's company in some oriental pleasance.

A more satirical note is struck in allegories such as *The Blinding of Truth by Falsehood* or *The Dispute between Body and Head* or in *A Literary Controversy*, which exposes the pretensions of one pundit and the learning of his rival. In a more irreverent vein are the vulgarizations in the form of folk-tales of religious myths such as *The Outwitting of Re by Isis* and the Rabelaisian *Contendings of Horus and Seth*. The wars of liberation and conquest engendered a crop of popular historical romances such as *Apophis and Sekenenre* and *The Taking of Joppa*, besides the fairy tales set in Syria, such as *The Foredoomed Prince*.

SALVES AND PERFUMES
Kha, one of the head workers of Deir el-Medina under Amenhotep III, placed this superb toilette case in his tomb. It was sure to be quite useful in the afterlife.

In addition to these literary works, there are autobiographies, model letters, books of proverbs and maxims in the tradition of the "teachings" of earlier ages, accounts, taxation-rolls, horoscopes, dream interpretations, juridical papyri, the reports of a royal commission which investigated the harem conspiracy that may have ended the life of Rameses III, and the proceedings of other tribunals. *The Adventures of Wenamun* retells the misfortunes that befell a priest of Amun when he set forth for Lebanon in the sunset years of the New Kingdom to buy cedarwood

for the barque of Amun. For its vivid character-drawing and descriptive force, this narrative is unequaled in the literature of the pre-Classical world.

The artistic legacy is vast, from colossal statues in granite and quartzite to small articles of luxury in ivory and gold. New materials make their appearance. A factory for the manufacture of vessels in brilliant polychrome glass seems to have been attached to the royal palaces, and great skill was shown in casting glass to imitate semi-precious stones for inlay in jewelry and furniture. Fine work in various colored faiences is a prominent feature of architectural decoration, especially during Ramessid times. The art of the goldsmith hardly reaches the high standard of the court jewellers of the Middle Kingdom, but a process of coloring gold in tones from pink to crimson was invented during this period. The rich store of treasure from the tomb of Tutankhamun has given us a dazzling conspectus of court art at the period of its most opulent development and acquainted us with the skill and resource of the craftsmen of the day whose taste was often a little too exuberant.

All this heritage has survived by the accident that the founders of the New Kingdom were princes of Thebes, who made that city the virtual capital of Upper Egypt

DAYS OF MOURNING
These weepers are mourning Maia, the painter who lived in Deir el-Medina in the 18th Dynasty. Could Maia himself have painted these mourners on his tomb wall?

THE LAST RESIDENCE
OF SENNEDJEM
*It was in Deir el-Medina
that Sennedjem, an official
in the 14th Dynasty, was
interred. In his tomb, richly
decorated, was traced "the
life of a faithful servant in
the place of truth."*

and lavished much of their wealth upon its god Amun, who had promoted their success. Above all, they returned to the birthplace of their dynasty after death, to the tombs that had been prepared for them there.

The tradition begun by Amenhotep I or Thutmose I (late sixteenth century B.C.) of abandoning the pyramid in favor of a rock-hewn sepulchre in the crags of western Thebes was followed by their successors, who for the next four centuries cut their tombs in the lonely Valley of the Kings and built their mortuary temples on the plain below. Other wadis were subsequently used for the tombs of some queens and princes. In the adjacent hills, overlooking the mortuary temples of the kings they had served, the court officials were granted burial in the old tradition, and the painted walls of their chapels have bequeathed us a most lively picture of life in the Eighteenth Dynasty—the royal investitures and scenes of military life and the

A REST STOP

The foremen, scribes, artisans, and workers who dug and decorated the royal tombs lived in the village of Deir el-Medina, between the Valley of the Queens and the Valley of the Kings. Divided into two teams, they worked ten days in a row before resting. From the village to the tombs, the shortest route was through the desert mountain. It took one hour by foot!

To overcome the problem, the workers built a small hamlet half way—a "rest stop." It included 78 little houses and a chapel dedicated to Amun-Re. No longer did they have to return every night to Deir el-Medina. These huts were pressed up against one another and were made of limestone blocks and mortar. They had branch roofs that were made heavy with flat stones. They were equipped with doors but no windows, and their two tiny rooms were furnished with a bench and a bed-couch. In the corner stood a large jug for fresh water.

Every day, inhabitants of the village brought provisions loaded on donkeys. At night, some workers would talk, others would engrave statuettes or steles, and others would make offerings to Amun-Re, "Amun of the good encounter." For in the desert, danger was always present at night. Ferocious animals, evil spirits, and the menacing dead roamed about.

professional occupations of the owners. After the Amarna interlude, the subjects lose their pagan delight in the world and its joys and show a more somber preoccupation with funerary scenes and magic rites, in this probably being influenced by the decoration of contemporary royal tombs as well as by a change of mood. To cater for the construction of the royal tombs, a village was established at what is now Deir el-Medina, housing generations of necropolis workers; and it is from the ruins of this hamlet that many of the Theban objects in our museums have come. We owe the preservation of the New Kingdom past almost entirely to the dry climate of Thebes.

The new ideal of the pharaoh as the heroic champion of Egypt is expressed in representations of him on a colossal scale. Huge statues and reliefs of kings, and sometimes of their queens, dominate the ancient sites. The ambitions and tastes of the kings and their courtiers instigated the building of great temples to the gods in the main towns, and to the royal funerary cult at western Thebes.

There were two main reasons for this growth in the size and volume of such works, apart from the great increase in wealth and the delusions of grandeur of the entire contemporary world. The reorganization of the government of Egypt as a military autocracy, with its bureaucracy reshaped to deal with the logistics of a military state, meant that a large professional standing army could be used at home as a labor corps whenever field operations were in abeyance. Reinforced with criminals and prisoners captured in the imperial wars, it provided the means of exploiting the new gold mines in Nubia and Kush on which so much of the prestige of the new Egyptian state depended. The use of the army ensured that a disciplined labor force could function without affecting vital agricultural operations.

Deir el-Medina

DEIR EL-MEDINA
Once called Set Maat (the Place of Truth), this village was protected from the dangers of the desert by a brick wall of about 400 by 150 feet. A wooden portal gave access to it. By being isolated, the artisans and their families were sure to keep the secret of the precious contents of the royal tombs. In the north section (left) were the simplest houses, which had a kitchen, a terrace, and a cellar. More spacious homes were found in the south quarter, and were for the foremen and a few more fortunate men. Outside the wall, there were tombs for the artisans. These had a pylon entrance, a court, a chapel topped by a pyramidion, and, in the back, shafts leading to the tomb.

❶ Enclosing wall
❷ Kitchen
❸ Cellar
❹ Stairs to access terrace
❺ Oven
❻ Storage rooms, work-rooms, or bedrooms
❼ Main street
❽ Entry room
❾ Room with altar, stele, and table of offerings
❿ Pylon
⓫ Pyramidion
⓬ Chapel
⓭ Court
⓮ Terrace
⓯ Village entrance

147

SEKHMET, THE DANGEROUS GODDESS

The goddess Sekhmet—the name means "Powerful One"—was depicted as a woman with the head of a lioness, surmounted by the sun disk. She was the spouse of Ptah, god of Memphis, to whom she bore the delicate Nefertum, the perfumed lotus, who occasionally turned into one of the ferocious deities protecting the eastern frontiers. At such times he became a lion, resembling his mother.

A fearsome warrior, Sekhmet was feared throughout the land. When the situation required it, she placed all her energies at the service of political and social order. Identified with Re's eye, spewing terrifying flames, she slaughtered all who threatened the royal status of the gods (it was she who suppressed the revolt of men against Re, the sun god, when he reigned on earth) or of kings, annihilating their enemies and glorying in the carnage of battle. Punishments meted out for the evil deeds of men were recorded in a ledger kept by the gods and entrusted to Sekhmet. She worked alone, shooting off arrows that never missed their mark or sending in her swift-running genie emissaries. These Slaughterers (also known as Executioners, Destroyers, or Evildoers) obeyed her orders without question. Armed with long knives, bows, and arrows, they spread disease, tore out hearts, bundled the dead into their caldrons, polluted the waters of the Nile, or generated infectious vapors, heat waves, and searing sandstorms.

Although she was especially to be feared during the six extra days of the calendar, Sekhmet punished on every day of the year—whence the 355 altars raised by kings in her honor. Luckily, the priests had the secret of appeasing her with prayers and offerings. They transformed Sekhmet the lioness into Bastet the cat, and the goddess, now moved to compassion, set about healing the sick.

SEKHMET
During the 18th Dynasty, the number of statues of the goddess Sekhmet multiplied. It was in this way that Egyptians hoped to appease the wrath of the goddess.

The second factor was the use of sandstone in place of limestone as the prime building material, allowing wider spaces to be spanned. The opening of new quarries at Gebel es-Silsila, on the very banks of the Nile, enabled fine-quality sandstone to be easily extracted and transported in great quantities and sizes with comparatively little effort and in a relatively short time.

It is in fact the great temples of the New Kingdom that reveal the full extent of the wealth and power of the reformed state. The tradition began with Queen Hatshepsut who, after dutifully serving for seven years as regent for her young nephew Thutmose III, assumed pharaonic titles and ruled as his co-regent for a further fifteen years. She was particularly devoted to the worship of Amun of Thebes, and she built a splendid temple dedicated to him and to her own funerary cult at Deir el-Bahri. Her architect and favorite, Senenmut, was obviously influenced by the adjacent temple of Mentuhotep II and also used limestone for his own construction, but he transformed the design of his predecessor into a more satisfactory architectural unity. The reliefs which embellish the colonnades commemorate the great events of Hatshepsut's reign in conformity with the heroic ideals of the age: They show her expedition to Punt, her divine birth, and the erection at Thebes of colossal granite obelisks brought from Aswan by river transport. In addition, over 200 statues in various stones of different sizes were furnished for the temple precincts.

The architects and sculptors trained on the queen's pioneer constructions were available for the undertakings of Thutmose III in his sole reign, during whose long tenure the buoyancy of the new Egypt, confident and wealthy as a result of its military successes, is expressed in widespread building. The climax of this development was reached in the reign of Amenhotep III, who devoted most of his reign of nearly forty years to the arts of peace. His buildings at Thebes are still impressive, even in their ruin, though they were once lavishly decorated with gold and silver. Thus we read of "numerous royal statues in granite of Elephantine, in quartize and every splendid and costly stone, established as everlasting memorials and shining in the sight of men like the morning sun." He furnished the temple of Mut, the consort of Amun, with some 600 statues of the lion-headed goddess Sekhmet. With him, stat-

uary on an enormous scale makes its appearance, the most notable perhaps being the pair of colossi—the so-called Colossi of Memnon, still dominating the Theban plain before the vanished portal of his funerary temple. The temple of Amenhotep III at Luxor is still standing, and the fame of this and other great monuments won for the king's master of works, Amenhotep-son-of-Hapu, the unprecedented honor of a funerary temple in his lifetime and deification in the Ptolemaic Period.

The reformed sun cult

A feature of the age was the greatly enhanced influence of the cult of the sun god Re-Herakhty of Heliopolis. The worship of the sun god was observed at an altar under the open sky within a peristyle, or colonnaded court, and such adjuncts were now added to every primal temple containing the sanctuary of the original local god and his associated deities. Above all, two symbolic hills forming the towers flanking a main entrance to the colonnaded court were erected to represent the twin mountains of Bakhu and Manu, between which the sun god rose daily to shine upon the temple and bring it to life.

THE TEMPLE OF LUXOR
A simple chapel of the temple at Karnak, the temple of Luxor was used only once a year, when the god Amun would go there in a procession. The Egyptians referred to it as the southern harem of Amun.

Another testimony to the fresh currents circulating in religious thought, perhaps as a result of ideas coming from Asia, were the new theological works that decorate the tombs of the kings at Thebes, *The Book of What Is in the Underworld,* *The Litany of the Sun,* and *The Book of Gates.* These writings reveal a new emphasis upon a monotheistic syncretism of ancient beliefs. Re is not only the sun god, he is "the sole god who has made myriads from himself: all gods came into being from him." He is invoked as "he whose active forms are his eternal transformations when he assumes the aspect of his Great Disk." This disk, or Aten, which illumines the world of the dead as well as the living and daily brings both to life from death or sleep, is the constant element in these transformations which the active day-sun undergoes to become the inert night-sun and vice versa. The power immanent in the disk is Re, the supreme god whose son—the pharaoh, his representative on earth—will return to him on death.

The effect of these doctrines is seen in the sun worship which the pharaoh Akhenaten introduced at his advent. He departed from the pundits of the orthodox sun cult in placing more emphasis upon the Aten, or visible manifestation of godhead, than he did upon Re-Herakhty, the hidden power that motivated it. Where he differed from the sun cult was that instead of incorporating all the old gods in his sole deity, he rigidly excluded them in an uncompromising monotheism. Where this idea came from in a world which tolerated so many diverse forms of godhead is unknown. They were presumably Akhenaten's own, the logical result of regarding the Aten as a self-created heavenly king, whose son, the pharaoh, was also "unique, without a peer." The Aten was made the supreme state-god, achieving the position of a heavenly pharaoh.

The cult of the Aten became more uncompromising as the reign of Akhenaten wore on. Almost from the first, the Aten ceased to be represented in the old iconic form of Re-Herakhty but was symbolized as the abstract glyph for sunlight—a rayed disk, each sunbeam ending in a ministering hand. Other gods, particularly the influential Amun and Osiris, were abolished, their images smashed, their names excised, their temples abandoned, their revenues impounded. The plural form of the word for god was suppressed. At the same time, however, the prayers to the Aten were usually addressed through the intermediary of the king; the icons of the new faith in the tombs he gave to his followers are concerned only with the doings of the royal family. The participation of the tomb owner, even the most exalted, is minimal.

This increase in the power and glory of the kingship, in conformity with the spirit of the time, was the inevitable outcome of Akhenaten's religious ideas. The closing of the temples would have had the effect of transferring all their property and income to the ownership of the pharaoh. The administration of this great accession of property evidently ceased to be in the hands of the many local temple officials for fiscal purposes, and the king had to call upon the army as the only source of manpower capable of enforcing tax collection in the absence of the former officials. Without proper supervision, and the sanction of traditional practice, corruption, arbitrary exactions, and other malpractices soon took a firm hold and had to be savagely suppressed by subsequent kings in restoring the former system of taxation.

The rapid building of new temples to the Aten at Karnak and on other major sites, and particularly the erection of a new residence-city on virgin ground at Amarna, must have drained the land of its labor and economic resources. The lavish offerings

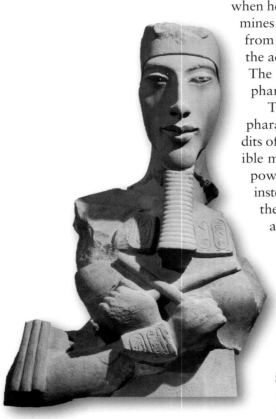

AKHENATEN

On the head of this colossal statue of Akhenaten (the fragment is about 4 feet high), the sculptor accented the shape of the royal face to the point of caricature. Its thinness and strange length are accentuated by the false beard.

OFFERINGS
In this relief, Queen Nefertiti is present as King Akhenaten (not visible in the photograph) makes offerings to the god Aten, the solar disk.

to the Aten that were such a feature of the daily worship in the temples at Amarna, and doubtless elsewhere as well, must have hastened economic collapse that probably more than anything ensured the abandonment of Akhenaten's religious ideas right after his death. Even in his capital city, his ambitions outran his resources. Only two of the tombs he lavished upon his followers were completely cut and decorated; even his own sepulchre is unfinished. When his successor, Tutankhamun, attempted to return to the policies that had succeeded in the past, he reported that the temples of the land, from one end to the other, were abandoned, weeds grew in their sanctuaries, and their courts were as a trodden path. If one petitioned a god or goddess, one's prayers went unanswered, for they were angry at what had been done. His remedial measures were to restore the morale of the nation by appeasing the offended gods. Temples were therefore to be cleaned and repaired, new images made, priesthoods appointed, and endowments restored.

Decline of the pharaonate

Despite this rehabilitation and reforms in the army and fiscal service later introduced by Horemheb, it was left to the Ramessids of the next dynasty to repair much of the damage, Sethos I restoring desecrated buildings at Thebes and embellishing Abydos and other centers. His son, Rameses II, was the most vigorous builder to have worn the Double Crown, nearly half the temples remaining in Egypt dating from his reign. His mortuary temple at Thebes (popularly known as the Ramesseum), the huge Hypostyle Hall at Karnak, the rock-hewn temple at Abu Simbel, and many other erections would have contented lesser men. But in addition he usurped a great deal of the work of earlier kings to adorn the new capital city of Pi-Ramesse, on which he expended so much treasure.

These appropriations have won him the reputation in modern times of being the arch-plunderer of others' monuments. But he left so universal and impressive a legend of superhuman qualities that his successors could only attempt a pale reflection of it. Rameses III, for instance, named his sons after those of his idol, and in his mortuary temple at Medinet Habu copied much of the decoration and texts of the Rameseum. Despite an evident decline in enterprise and invention during the Twentieth Dynasty, the royal sepulchres continue to be vast excavations, such as those of Rameses VI. The fine granite sarcophagus made for Rameses IV, and the one made for his father, Rameses III, testify to the vigor of the pharaonic tradition, which could still command such resources in what seem to be a period of decline.

Under their fighting pharaohs, the Egyptians in the early Eighteenth Dynasty had shown a new-found zest for war and conquest. The professional soldier, as distinct from the unwilling conscripted peasant, had made a sudden appearance. The Asiatic campaigns introduced many exotic novelties into the Nile Valley—strange people, fashions of dress, Canaanite words and phrases, and foreign religious cults. It was from Syria that Thutmose III imported curious plants, animals, and birds, represented in reliefs adorning a chamber of his great festival temple at Karnak.

THE RAMESSEUM
Bordering cultivated lands on the west bank of the Nile in front of Luxor, stand the ruins of the mortuary temple of Rameses II.

In all this, Egyptian horizons were widened and an optimistic spirit prevailed. The Egyptians shared in the delight in personal greatness and the pride in worldly success which is the spirit abroad over the entire civilized Near East in the Late Bronze Age. The procession to grandeur reached its apogee with the reign of Akhenaten. But after the failure of his policies, both at home and abroad, a loss of self-confidence can be sensed in the Egyptian psyche.

The military career tended to be left to foreigners—mercenaries from Nubia, the Sudan, Canaan, Libya, and the lands of the Sea Peoples. The Egyptians turned more to the professions of scribe and priest, especially with the great increase in the

wealth of Amun of Thebes, being content to fill or create some comfortable office which they could hand on to their sons.

The loss of Asia, Kush, and some of the western oases turned the vision of the Egyptians inwards upon themselves, and their pharaoh ceased to be regarded as the heroic champion of the entire nation, successfully challenging the insolent foreigner.

The change in the Egyptian outlook is reflected in the tomb-chapels of the age where gay, painted scenes of everyday life are discarded in favor of the icons of a funerary mythology permeated with magic. The self-contained burial within the coffin of Hyksos times had been elaborated in the wealthy days of the Eighteenth Dynasty to comprise nests of coffins, stone sarcophaguses, Canopic chests, copies of *The Book of the Dead*. But in the necessitous times that followed the reign of Rameses II, only a coffin or a set of coffins was provided, painted with selected religious scenes and short extracts from *The Book of the Dead*.

This vogue, with variations in style and elaboration, persisted thereafter, in all but the wealthiest burials, even into the Christian period. At the same time, there was a tendency to create family burial places by making intrusive interments in the ancestral tomb, or in locations within its precincts. Intrusive burial in fact became very much the common practice at Thebes after the wholesale pillaging of the necropolises during the disorders at the end of the New Kingdom. Very many of the earlier tombs had been desecrated and were then standing open, ready for appropriation. Even the despoiled bodies of past royalty were to be hidden away in this manner during the following decades in two or more mass burials.

THE TEMPLE OF HATHOR
The ceiling of the small temple of Abu Simbel, cut into the mountain, is supported by pillars. The capitals represent the goddess Hathor, who has a woman's face and cow ears.

The treasure of Tutankhamun

~ ~

When Akhenaten died, Egypt was in a period of turmoil. Tutankhaten, age nine, then took the throne. As the cousin or nephew of the deceased and the sole male heir, he legitimized his power by marrying Princess Ankhsanpaaten, one of the daughters of the deceased king. This was common practice.

Soon after, Tutankhaten left Amarna for Thebes, restored the cult of Amun, and—to exemplify his willingness to return to tradition—changed his name. Tutankhaten became Tutankhamun, which meant "living image of Amun." In the south of the country, the pharaoh had begun the building of his mortuary temple not far from Amenhotep III, and his tomb, in the Valley of the Kings.

But the 19-year-old king suddenly died, childless. This shocking turn of events, along with his hasty burial, explain the incredible disorder found in his tomb. It also explains why the funerary furnishings were in part "borrowed" from his predecessors. This "little" king, buried too soon in a sparsely decorated tomb, was surrounded by luxurious objects that had survived the pillagers until the arrival of Carter and his workers in November of 1922.

Howard Carter, head of Lord Carnarvon's expedition, was exploring the Valley of the Kings when he discovered this forgotten pharaoh's tomb. He then proceeded to open the only tomb that survived to our times semi-intact. We do know that it was visited in the 20th Dynasty. Fortunately, after having stopped the pillagers and verified the contents, the royal scribe of the time reestablished some order in the rooms plundered by thieves. He then resealed the door between the funerary chamber and the antechamber. He also affixed seals to the doors and piled up furnishings and statues before covering the entrance with rocks and sand. Thanks to his exertions, the tomb of the young king would be forgotten for centuries.

Tutankhamun's final resting place is a tiny tomb consisting of a corridor on a steep grade that leads to a vestibule. It opens onto the sarcophagus chamber (the only decorated room) and onto two other rooms used for storage. It was here that Carter discovered a real treasure: large catafalques, encased sarcophaguses, jewels, statues, weapons, vases, chariots, and chairs or beds made of precious materials like gold, silver, lapis lazuli, turquoise, and alabaster.

SARCOPHAGUS FOR ENTRAILS *In an alabaster case wrapped in the manner of mummies, four miniature gold sarcophaguses, encrusted with carnelian and molten glass, contain the king's entrails for eternity.*

ROYAL COUPLE

In the chapel that contains the statuettes of the rulers, Tutankhamun is shown pouring a scented liquid into the queen's hand. In her hair, she is wearing the two tall plumes of the great royal spouses.

A HEAVY GOLD EARRING

Tutankhamun is depicted between two Uraeus serpents, which defend kings by spitting fire on enemies. Tutankhamun is also protected by a vulture, perched above him with outstretched wings.

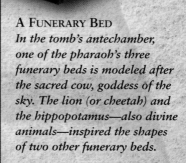

A FUNERARY BED

In the tomb's antechamber, one of the pharaoh's three funerary beds is modeled after the sacred cow, goddess of the sky. The lion (or cheetah) and the hippopotamus—also divine animals—inspired the shapes of two other funerary beds.

THE STATUE OF KA

Ka is the manifestation of the vital energies, the power of the creation of the gods, the necessary strength to maintain existence. The "reservoir" of the king's forces, two statues of his ka frame the door of the young king's mortuary chamber.

THE SARCOPHAGUS CHAMBER

A huge chapel in gilded gold occupies the space of the mortuary chamber opened by Carter in February 1923. There are in fact four chapels that fit together around the vat, in which two mummy-sarcophaguses are tightly placed. On October 28, 1925, when the last sarcophagus was opened, Tutankhamun was revealed. Carter found 143 jewels and amulets while unwrapping the royal mummy. As the room was unearthed, mural decoration was found: the deities of the afterlife, the catafalque on its platform, and further, the deceased being resuscitated by the Opening of the Mouth ritual. Today, the tomb harbors only its vat. Engraved with religious texts and four goddesses with outstretched wings, it protects the royal mummy for eternity.

HEART SCARAB

This jewel—a scarab (the manifestation of the god Khepri, the rising sun) and the wings of the protective falcon—would be very useful to the deceased when being judged in the afterlife.

CHAPTER 13

The end of the pharaohs

Upper and Lower Egypt

The troubles at the end of the Twentieth Dynasty left the Thebaid and much of the southern part of Egypt under the control of the military-priestly regime installed by Piankh and Herihor. The descendants of Piankh combined the offices of high priest of Amun and commander-in-chief of the army, and for a time at least had a residence at el Hiba, the fortress town on their northern border.

The nominal kingship of the whole of Egypt had passed from the last Ramessid (XI) to his son-in-law, Smendes, governor of the Delta city of Tanis, whose authority was recognized by the Thebans. For most of the Twenty-First Dynasty, the soldier-priests of Thebes and the pharaohs in Tanis were closely related, and for a period were even brothers.

The city of Tanis, originally a dependency of Pi-Ramesse, was greatly embellished with new temples, mostly constructed with stone from the older town, whose functions had transferred to the upstart. It was here that the Tanite kings were buried, in stone tombs sunk in the courtyards of the great temple of Amun-re.

One of these tombs, that of Psusennes I himself, was found intact in 1939 and shows us the mixture of riches and poverty that characterizes the Third Intermediate Period: Although the king lay in a silver coffin, a gold mask upon his face, his granite outer coffin and sarcophagus were both second-hand, the latter coming from the tomb of Merenptah in the Valley of the Kings.

Libyan dynasts

THE TREASURE OF TANIS
Discovered in Tanis, in the Delta, this necklace belonged to Psusennes I, king of the 21st Dynasty. Because of internal divisions, he accepted the authority of the priest-kings over the south of Egypt.

About 974 B.C., a family of Libyan descent who had eventually settled at Bubastis became influential enough to secure the throne after the death of King Amenemhopet. Osokhor, the first of these kings, may not have been able to retain the throne for the next generation, but around 948 B.C. Shoshenq I (the biblical Shishak) was able to establish a new dynasty, the Twenty-Second. An energetic ruler, he invaded Palestine in about 930 B.C. and plundered Solomon's temple of its rich treasure (2 Chronicles 12: 2–9), restoring some of Egypt's prestige. He also renewed contacts with Byblos and may have sent an expedition into Nubia to recover lost ground in that region of gold and fighting men. The plunder from his raid into Israel and Judah enabled him to undertake new additions to the temple of Amun at Karnak, especially in the forecourt.

During the next century, the successors of Shoshenq managed to maintain something of his original impetus in the affairs of Egypt. Temples and many of the great centers of the land were richly endowed with furniture and other treasures in gold and silver. However, around 867 B.C., Thebes once again obtained its own king, the former High Priest Harsiese, and, for the next one-and-a-half centuries, each half of Egypt had its own separate pharaoh. The Theban kingdom was soon wracked with internal disputes, with a number of claimants fighting for the throne. Matters were only resolved following the victory of Osorkon III around 800 B.C., when he over-threw the last of the usurpers.

In the north, Tanite power waned in the years following the definitive decoupling of Thebes around 840 B.C. Various fiefdoms were assigned to members of the royal family, which gradually became hereditary prince-doms that owed but nominal allegiance to the king. Thus, by the latter part of the eighth century B.C., Lower Egypt was a patchwork of independent polities, of which the old national capital territory of Tanis was but one of many. Middle Egypt now had its own pharaoh as well, making—together with a king in Leontopolis—a total of four individuals claiming the ancient titles of Egyptian kingship.

Kushite intervention

Since the end of the Twentieth Dynasty, Kush, including its northern province of Nubia, had secured independence from Egypt, its kings ruling from Napata near the Fourth Cataract. When the Kushite king Piye marched from Napata to subdue Egypt in the name of order and orthodoxy, he met with no resistance in Upper Egypt and was in fact welcomed deliriously in Thebes during the great Festival of Opet. His armies defeated one by one the petty kings of Lower Egypt, who submitted to him abjectly, though Tefnakhte of Sais was able to maintain some nominal independence as prince of the western Delta.

The pious Kushite kings favored a provincial version of the Egyptian culture of a purer past, harkening back to the classical arts of the Middle and New Kingdoms. They proved energetic builders, particularly at Thebes, where they restored and repaired many of the monuments of earlier times. They brought some long-needed direction into the affairs of Egypt, though the country was far from being united under their sway, as the prophet Isaiah knew well enough (Isaiah 19:2). Like their Libyan predecessors, they attempted to interfere in the politics of Palestine, proceedings which aroused the enmity of Assyria, the now dominant power in the region. The intrigues of Taharqa, the third successor of Piye, at length brought about a long-

QUEEN KAROMA
This superb bronze statue, discovered in Karnak, dates back to the 22nd Dynasty. It is made of bronze that was damascened—i.e., etched with wavy markings inlaid with gold or silver.

THE ASSYRIANS

Signs of civilization appeared very early between the Tigris and the Euphrates. Rival peoples succeeded one another in the region: Sumerians and Akkadians, founders of Babylon—the city reputed to be the most wondrous in the East—followed by their northern neighbors, the Assyrians. This last group worked in the service of the kings of Babylon before themselves taking power.

From 1150 to 612 B.C., the Assyrians dominated the region. Their armies were composed of infantry and of fighting chariots carrying three men armed with bows and spears. They were trained to besiege strongholds and carry out lightning-swift attacks. To the conquered they were merciless, impaling them, flaying them alive, beheading them, and sometimes deporting them en masse.

Their empire reached its zenith around the 8th and 7th centuries B.C under the rule of Sargon (721-705) and Assurbanipal (669-626). In those years, the Assyrians, thanks to their remarkable administrative system, were masters of the Mediterranean.

In 671, Assyrian King Assarhaddon invaded Egypt and seized the ancient capital of Memphis. He meant to extend his conquests farther, but two years later he died. His successor Assurbanipal won a brilliant victory when he attacked Thebes in 664-663. The Bible describes the sack of the city, the bliblical name of which is No: "Yet was [No] carried away...into captivity: her young children also were dashed in peices at the top of all streets...and all her great men were bound in chains. (Nahum 3: 8–10). Egypt had been conquered.

But the Assyrian kings were finding it harder to control their vast and unwieldy empire, given various palace plots and sporadic uprisings. A year after Assurbanipal's death, a coalition of Babylonians and Medes crushed the Assyrians, and their empire was no more.

---

delayed open confrontation with the Assyrians, whose forces twice marched into Egypt, eventually sacking Thebes (663 B.C.) and driving Taharqa's successor, Tanutamun, into his own Kushite domains, where he and his successors became more and more Africanized and ceased to play any direct role in Egyptian affairs.

The southern theocracy

The Kushites continued a policy—begun by their predecessor, Osorkon III—of neutralizing the powerful *imperium in imperio* of the high priests of Amun of Thebes by appointing one of the royal women as the divine consort of Amun. From the start of the Eighteenth Dynasty, Ahmose-Nefertiry, the chief queen of Ahmose, had also held this position, a wealthy sacerdotal office with great estates and a powerful establishment which rose to paramount importance as the high priests became more and more involved in their military and political roles. The tradition of appointing an heiress daughter of the pharaoh to the position of divine consort was continued by the Kushites, when Piye obliged the Libyan princess Shepenwepet I to adopt his sister Amenirdas I as her successor. Such "god's wives," together with the oracle of Amun to whom they were "married," ruled the Thebaid with the administrative assistance of their high stewards.

The most notable of these latter was Mentuemhet, the fourth prophet of Amun, who governed Thebes in the difficult days of the Assyrian invasions and was one of the chief patrons of the new art that flourished in the Kushite Period and the following dynasty. When the Kushites were displaced by a family of Libyan extraction originating from Sais, the first effective pharaoh of a reunited Upper and Lower Egypt, Psammetikhos I (664–610 B.C.), in turn compelled Shepenwepet II, the reigning divine consort, to adopt his eldest daughter, Nitokris, as her junior partner and eventual successor.

In her later years, about 595 B.C., Nitokris adopted Ankhnesneferibre, the daughter of Psammetikhos II, and she proved to be the last incumbent of this important religious and political office before it lapsed with her death in Persian times.

The king and the gods

Apart from the universal worship of Amun as a state god, not only in Upper Egypt but also in newly developed Delta sites, the tendency was for the populace to turn to their local gods for spiritual support and succor, as they had done in similar situations since the First Intermediate Period. The reason was the sharp decline in the power and prestige of the pharaoh. Since the Egyptian found it difficult to direct his religious feeling to mere abstractions, he tended to worship tangible manifestations of godhead, and preferably something animate.

In the Late Periods there was a vast increase in the worship of divinities incarnate in animals. This feature of Egyptian cultic practice had always been present as a dark warp in the richly colored fabric of its religious life (even the monotheist Akhenaten had not proscribed the worship of the Mnevis bull), but now it erupted in force, to earn the bewilderment of Greek observers and the contempt of such Roman satirists as Juvenal.

The ruling groups of both Upper and Lower Egypt, however, adhered to the worship of Amun-re, the oracles of the god, in fact, so far determining the government of Upper Egypt that it became a theocratic state. The pharaohs in addition extended their patronage to the gods of their residences, such as the cat goddess Bast of Bubastis, the archer goddess Neith of Sais, and Ptah of Memphis. The cult of Osiris, the hope of salvation for all mortals, never lost its impact throughout the period, though the worship of his wife Isis and the child Horus steadily increased in popularity until they had entirely overshadowed him by Roman times.

The Ahmosides, at the beginning of the New Kingdom, had found it difficult to rule Egypt from distant Thebes and transferred their capital to Memphis. Subsequent dynasties found it convenient to move their seats of power even nearer to the Mediterranean shores, where the action was. The dynasties of the Late

RAM MUMMY
A stucco, gilded, and glued cloth covers this ram mummy of Khnum. The god Khnum, protector of the sources of the Nile, near the Elephantine, was the potter who modeled on his wheel the egg from which all life was born.

159

POSING QUESTIONS TO THE GODS

When the Egyptians sought to learn of the intentions of the gods, they had a number of ways to do so. One of the simplest was to wait for a procession day, when priests placed a god's statue on a boat-like structure in the chapel and carried it from the temple. On the way, the statue responded to questions posed by individuals in the crowd. Pushing through the throng, an asker would approach the statue: "My good Lord," he might say, "Is it true that I stole Untel's amulet?" The god considered the question. Suddenly, filled with divine will, the porters bent or moved ahead to say yes, or retreated to say no. The god had spoken.

When there was a question on the order of "My good Lord, where is my goat?" the asker would write the names of those he suspected to have stolen the property on reeds. Inspired by the god, the priest answered by picking a reed without seeing the names.

When the question could not be answered with a yes or no, the god had to speak with his own voice. If someone had a problem to resolve with his neighbor, had an important decision to make, or wanted to know how to cure himself, he walked into a special chapel. Often built on the terrace above the temple, the chapel included two rooms separated by a door.

The man entered the first room, reverently asked his question, and waited. The god filled the second room. Suddenly, a deep voice was heard. It was the voice of a priest, who, according to his divine will, stood behind the door—which was equipped with a tiny window—and spoke in the name of the god.

There were other ways to talk to the deities besides asking questions of their statues. But whatever the way, if the answer was not to the asker's satisfaction, he could consult another god.

Period show a general pattern: They began with vigor and promise, reviving the old dream of exercising suzerainty over Palestine and Phoenicia and so preventing another invasion from Asia across their northeastern borders.

Their campaigns, however, were little better than armed raids in search of plunder and the replacement of hostile princes by willing collaborators. Whenever their forces came up against battle-trained and united enemies with superior weapons, such as the Assyrians, Babylonians, and Persians, they invariably suffered defeat despite often valiant efforts. Constant defeat could not but produce further discouragement at home, as well as the reputation abroad of being a broken reed.

The northern merchant princes, 664-525 B.C.

The Saite kings brought more than a century of order and prosperity to a troubled Egypt. The first Psammetikhos freed himself from the overlordship of Assyria, which was now beset with its own troubles. In their stirring days, the Saites were to see the sack of their own populous "No [Thebes] that was situate among the rivers" (Nahum 3:8) repeated in the destruction of Nineveh and Babylon. Psammetikhos I appointed his own men to key positions in Edfu and Herakleopolis to keep Thebes in check. He also curbed the power of the military caste by employing Ionian, Carian, and Libyan mercenaries.

With this *corps d'élite* and the possession of a strong fleet, probably largely Phoenician, the Saites ruled as merchant princes, restoring prosperity by active commercial ventures and setting a precedent for the export of Egyptian corn and wool, which was to be followed with greater intensity by the Ptolemies. In the interests of trade, Nekho II (610–595 B.C.) began a canal from the Nile to the Red Sea and commissioned Phoenicians to circumnavigate Africa. But the Saites never won the wholehearted cooperation of their subjects by these policies. The favoritism shown to Greek oracles, wives, traders, and soldiers aroused jealousy and revolt in outbursts of xenophobia, and when the Persian Kambyses invaded the country in 525 B.C., it fell into his hands without much trouble. The Persians, who organized their empire with a thoroughness lacking in previous conquerors, ruled Egypt with the aid of efficient satraps and collaborators for nearly two centuries, except for an interlude when native princes with Greek aid were able to snatch half a century of uneasy independence (404–343 B.C). This was, however, the last twitch of dying pharaonic Egypt, and it was only the embalmed corpse that then passed in turn to the Persian kings, the Greek Ptolemies, and the Roman emperors. After Alexander the Great had defeated Darius on the plain of Issus in 333 B.C., the westen satrapies of the vast Persian empire fell into his hands without any great struggle, and Egypt thereafter became a part of the Hellenistic world.

The Kushite kings, with their conservative tastes for Classical standards, are usually adjudged to be the instigators of the antiquarian study of the past which is such a feature of the following dynasties, but the movement began earlier. Looking back in nostalgia to the golden past is, in fact, the malaise of the entire Late Period, which recalled the glorious achievements of former days without any deep commitment to their inner meaning. Not only were the styles of the Old, Middle, and New Kingdoms copied with a more searching technique, but eclectic confections were made by antiquarians almost for other connoisseurs to appreciate. The Pyramid Texts and the Coffin Texts were revived for funerary inscriptions. Reliefs were inspired by those of Hatshepsut at Deir el-Bahri, and fashions of dress and coiffure long out of date were revived. Burial was sought near such hallowed sites as the Step Pyramid at Saqqara, in the vicinity of which its now legendary architect had been buried, or near the Great Pyramid at Giza.

The intensive copying of the past is a prominent feature of the Saite Age—though the tomb-reliefs of Mentuemhet and his temple statues had already set the fashion with sculpture in the style and dress of all periods.

As an idealistic academic art, it has its appeal. Its technique, especially in the cutting of inscriptions in hard stones, is faultless— but as in all art where style has become more important than content, a tendency to emphasize the abstractions underlying form leads to a distinctive mannerism. Egypt had invariably gone back to her past as a point of vigorous departure, but now her return was a permanent retreat from the world of her decline. That monasticism which is so characteristic of Christian Egypt is already inherent in the outlook of the Late Period.

THE COW AND THE KING
Psammetikhos, pharaoh of the 26th Dynasty, was protected by Hathor, the powerful cow-goddess. Between her horns she carried Re, the sun god, and Uraeus, the serpent.

CHAPTER 14

Egyptian social groups

The pharaoh

While Egypt may have been, in the epigram of Hecataeus, "the gift of the Nile," the Egyptian state was the creation of the pharaoh, the divine king whose evolution has been traced in the foregoing pages. Other civilizations had risen and flourished in river valleys elsewhere in the Near East, enjoyed economies based upon agriculture, and had a unifying system of communications afforded by a great river. They, too, had discovered the art of writing and keeping records, without which no civilization can flourish, yet for the most part they remained a congeries of rival city-states, whereas Egypt displayed a national conformity under the leadership of a deity. So powerful, so successful a ruler could not fail to impress other nations with the charisma of his office, and they vied with each other in sending embassies loaded with gifts to beg his blessing at the advent of each new king.

For the pharaoh is a prime example of the god incarnate as king. A tangible deity, whose sole authority could produce results by the exercise of the divine attributes of "creative utterance," superhuman "understanding," and "rightness" *(ma'et),* appealed to the Egyptian mentality and gave the nation confidence to overcome daunting obstacles.

The prehistoric origins of the king as a pastoral chieftain and rainmaker have been outlined earlier. Even in more sophisticated times, his control of water, "which

THE WELLS OF RAMESES II

Rameses II coveted the gold of the Akuyati Desert in the east of Nubia. But traveling the road to the desert was deadly because of the lack of water. As Rameses had understood, drilling for water was useless, as the viceroy of Nubia confirmed.

In the past, various pharaohs had attempted in vain to open water wells in this desolate place. His own earthly father, Set, had given up after digging down very deep. "Send a group of soldiers and workers halfway down this desert road and let one whole month pass," ordered Rameses II to the viceroy. "Let them wait! Then you will send my instructions to these men..."

The viceroy was ready to comply. One month later, after having received the royal orders, workers began to dig in the exact spot that Rameses indicated. After a few days, the hole was well-deep but still dry. The soldiers watched over the workers, yelling at them, pushing the lazy ones, and sometimes beating them. Some of the laborers fell and never got back up.

After weeks of harrowing work, a few drops appeared at the bottom of the well—and finally, water sprang forth. "Oh, my master and ruler," wrote the amazed viceroy. "Everything happened exactly as Your Majesty said it would. Water appeared inside the well at a depth of 12 cubits [more than 18 feet]. It is rising already to 4 cubits [more than 6 feet]. It is springing, gushing. Nothing of this kind has happened before." Thus, in the second year of his reign, Rameses II gained a reputation as the master of the waters. On his orders, they emerged in the desert, flooded the valley, or fell on faraway lands. "His plans are perfect, all that he orders happens," was the official belief. But it was more likely because Rameses II was really the son of Re, the sun god—the true god on earth.

begets all living things, and all things which this earth yields," was often stressed. Akhenaten was apostrophized as "this myriad of Niles." Rameses II is regarded as being able to make rain fall even in the far-off Hittite lands or to withhold it at his pleasure. The advents of Merenptha and Rameses IV are occasions for rejoicing as the Nile then carried a high flood from its source. The connection between the pharaoh and the Nile is particularly evident in the peripteral stone kiosks that Thutmose III, Amenhotep II, and Amenhotep III built on Elephantine Island to celebrate their second jubilees, when Khnum of Elephantine was specially honored as the god who brought forth the Nile from his cavern under the island. At this particular time he was already beginning to be associated with Osiris, later to move to Bigga and become Lord of the Inundation.

Several instances exist where pharaohs acted as water diviners when wells had to be dug in desert places. Sethos I is credited in the Wadi Abad with having saved his gold miners from death from thirst by finding water at Kanayis, where his well still has water in its depths. It is significant that on the nearby rocks are prehistoric drawings of animals, probably indicating an ancient water-hole and acting as an indication to the diviners that water was in the vicinity despite the general aridity. Similarly, Rameses II boasted of having found water for his miners in the Wadi Alaki at a depth of twelve cubits.

As the controller of the Nile and its water, the pharaoh was also a fertility king, an incarnation of the god who had created the Egyptian universe at the First Time, and to whom he would return on death. This demiurge varied from time to time and from place to place, though the sacrosanct traditions of the myth ensured that its fundamentals would not change. Thus the king was an incarnation of Horus, the Remote One, a prehistoric sky-god who was also manifest as a falcon.

This identification of the pharaoh with the falcon is frequently encountered. The king is said to "rule while he was yet in the egg," and his death is spoken of in such terms as "the falcon has flown to the horizon." On solemn occasions, he may wear garments decorated with a feathered pattern.

THE UNION OF
TWO COUNTRIES
On the base of this throne, the gods Horus and Seth tie a knot around the hieroglyphic sma, *which means to unite the lotus and papyrus— symbols of the kingdoms of the south and the north. In this way, the king's authority extended over the entire country.*

163

When the sun cult conceived of its active god as a heavenly king, reflecting the political system on earth, they united their lord of the day-sky with the sky-god Horus in the concept Re-Herakhty. The king became the son of Re. The idea was probably engendered in the Fourth Dynasty that the birth of the king resulted from the union of the gods; the earliest surviving representation of the divine marriage occurs in the reliefs in the temple of Hatshepsut at Deir el-Bahri.

Here we see that the god takes the form of the pharaoh and fills the chief queen with the divine afflatus by holding the sign of life to her nostrils. As a result of this union, the heir apparent will be born. Thoth, the messenger of the gods, is dispatched to announce the good news to the queen.

The Creator, in his active aspect of Khnum, is instructed to fashion the child and its spirit on his potter's wheel, a poetic device for symbolizing the growth of the fetus within the womb. Guardian spirits and birth-gods come to attend the birth. Last, the infant is recognized by its divine father and nursed by the seven Hathors. Other representations of this myth are carved in similar low relief on walls of the temple of Luxor and in the birth-house of Nektanebo I at Dendera. In all cases, it is the sun god, in his aspect of the Upper Egyptian Amun, who acts the role of the progenitor.

Similarly, the coronation of the king, though conducted on earth by chamberlains who had the royal insignia in their charge, was thought to take place in heaven and to be performed by the gods, as is represented on so many temple walls. Thutmose III claimed that it was Amun of Thebes who recognized him as his son while the young prince was serving as a mere acolyte in the temple at Karnak—whereupon he flew like a divine falcon to heaven and was crowned by the sun god, though this is probably a fanciful way of saying that it was his earthly father, Thutmose II, who crowned him in the sanctuary of the temple ("the heaven") as his co-regent.

The harmony between this divine kingship and the natural world is evident not only in the intimate connection between the pharaoh and the Nile, on which the prosperity of Egypt depended, but also on the timing of the various royal ceremonies to conform to the cycle of the agricultural year. Thus the coronation traditionally took place at a time which was heralded by the rising of Sirius at the beginning of the inundation. This moment was the auspicious point for the sympathetic rising of a new king and a new Egypt out of the old land drowned in the chaotic waters of the Nile flood, in which the old king as Osiris was now believed to float.

Therefore, each king was regarded at his advent as re-creating the old universe anew, in the primal pattern that had come down intact from the time when the gods had ruled the earth. Their son and incarnation was on the Horus throne of the living, and when he died and was assimilated to Osiris, the king of the dead, his son —the new Horus—would reign in his stead.

Thus Egypt was eternally under the beneficent rule of God. The idea of this god incarnate, his birth and coronation, bequeathed a legend and a tradition to the nations of the Near East which persisted for centuries.

The chasm that separated the pharaoh from the rest of society was not only symbolized by his pyramid with its gilded capstone; he also underwent ceremonies at his coronation that ensured that his human nature would be entirely absorbed by his divine aspect. As the protector of the land, he combined within his person two rival forces—Horus, the god of Lower Egypt, and Seth, the god of Upper Egypt. This duality is expressed in the different crowns he wore and the titles he assumed. The

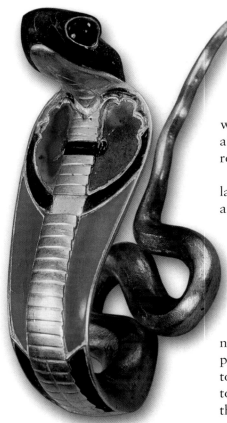

THE COBRA-GODDESS
From the crown of the Middle Kingdom, Ouadjet, the goddess of the north of Egypt, protects the kings. Always on the pharaoh's forehead, she spits burning venom on the enemies of the kingdom.

throne he sat upon had the quality of rendering him divine and royal and was itself personified by the goddess Isis. At his advent, craftsmen from all parts of the kingdom were set the task of preparing a complete outfit for him, with the exception of the White and Red Crowns, which were holy objects—goddesses in their own right, kept in shrines in the charge of special chamberlains.

The protocol that governed his life was as punctilious as that which attended the daily service of a god in a temple. The throne-rooms of the royal palaces at Memphis and Medinet Habu have the effect of isolating the king, as the statue of a god was contained within its shrine. The strict regulation of his life is confirmed in the words of Diodorus: "For there was a set time not only for his holding audience or rendering judgments, but even for his taking a walk, bathing, and sleeping with his wife; in short, for every act of his life."

This concept of the king as the supreme god Horus incarnate reached its fullest development in the Archaic Period and the early Old Kingdom. Probably the Step Pyramid and the pyramids of Giza stand as its greatest memorials, when the entire nation undertook the tremendous travail involved in raising and equipping these huge monuments, not for the sole benefit of their human ruler but to ensure the persistence of their greatest divinity. By the Fourth Dynasty, the thinkers of Heliopolis were beginning to make their influence felt, and became dominant in the next dynasty. The king was now regarded as a descendant of the sun god Re-Herakhty, who had ruled Egypt in the beginning, but weary of mankind had retired to the remote heavens, leaving

the pharaoh as his earthly representative to govern in his stead.

The prestige of the pharaoh received a severe blow during the First Intermediate Period, when droughts and low Niles destroyed belief in the supreme divinity of the pharaoh which had instigated the Egyptian state machine. The exclusiveness of the pharaoh was replaced by a multiplicity of local kinglets, who boasted less of their magic powers than of their ability to preserve their people by their temporal might. This concern for the material well-being of their subjects was carried over into the tenets of government during the Middle Kingdom, when the idea took hold that the king tended his subjects as a good shepherd watched his flock. "God has made me the herdsman of this land, for he knew that I would maintain it in order

ROYAL OFFERINGS
Represented in his tomb in the Valley of the Kings, the last pharaoh of the 18th Dynasty, Horemheb, makes eternal offerings to the gods.

THE PRINCE

*On this limestone
stele, the young
Rameses II is partially
shaved, wears a
braid on his right
temple, and has his
finger in his mouth.
It was traditional to
represent children
in this manner.*

for him," said Sesostris I to his assembled courtiers. "He is full of graciousness, rich in benignity, and through love has he conquered," said Sinuhe of this same king. Though the pharaohs of the Twelfth Dynasty restored the prestige of the kingship, it was more as a powerful champion than as a god that the "living Horus" was esteemed. Much of the reverence for the king as the best hope of immortality for those who were "known" to him had passed to that deification of kingship, Osiris.

The pharaohs of the New Kingdom—true to the ideals of the contemporary warrior society with its aristocracy of armored chariot fighters—had to hack their way to power by feats of arms, and the character of their rule is distinctly martial. The pharaoh himself took the field at the head of his troops—the champion of Egypt, an incarnation of a warrior god Mentu or Baal, as well as sun god. His trophies are the foes he has vanquished and stripped of their inlaid armor, the prisoners he has taken, and the rich booty he has captured. Such heroes had to have memorials that not only sustained their mortuary cults but also left some record of their great deeds to posterity, and the ruined funerary temples on the west bank at Thebes bear witness to these ambitions.

The age reached its climax in the reign of Amenhotep III, when the imperial bounds were widest, the state coffers the richest, and the monuments the most colossal and numerous. Thereafter, only a decline was possible in step with the decay of the heroic age all over the Near East, culminating in the forays of the Sea Peoples and the movements of new settlers in Syria, Anatolia, the Lebanon, and Palestine in the 12th century B.C.

In the Late Periods, the kingship became but a prize for which foreigners—Libyans, Kushites, Persians, and Greeks—fought each other. The fact is that men turned more to the worship of gods in the form of kings—to Amun, Re-Herakhty, and Osiris. Prayers were addressed to gods less and less through the intermediary of the king and more through the agency of the city god, while for the great mass of the people, as the cult of the god incarnate in the king declined, the worship of animals increased to grotesque proportions. The greatness of ancient Egypt was inextricably bound up with her kings, who had created it: They rose and fell together.

The royal family

When Sesostris I encourages the fugitive Sinuhe to return to Egypt, he holds out the inducement that Queen Nofru, whom Sinuhe served, still inhabited the palace and was alive and well. She played her part in the government of the realm and her children were in the council chamber. The position of the chief queen of the pharaoh is thus incidentally defined.

If the king was the incarnation of the supreme god, the queen was also regarded as embodying the goddess Hathor, "the Mansion of Horus"—i.e., the mother of the sky-god Horus. She was early assimilated to Isis, another goddess of kingship, and also to a very ancient goddess of the sky in the form of a cow, her body speckled with stars.

The attributes of Hathor, her headdress with cow-horns, sun-disk and tall plumes, were worn by queens upon their crowns. Her symbols, the sistrum rattle, and the necklace with its menyet counterpoise, were carried by her priestesses, of whom the queen was the leader. Both had the power of bestowing a propitiatory blessing upon all to whom they were held.

The chief queen was a lady of great sanctity, and in a number of cases left a greater impression on posterity than her husband. Besides her biological role, her office carried politico-religious functions, which in some cases led to the title being bestowed upon certain kings' daughters after their mother's or stepmother's death. Whether this always implied a sexual relationship between the pharaoh and his daughter remains the subject of debate.

Alongside the chief queen, however, a king maintained a "harem" of other women. Ideally, the heir to the throne was the eldest son by the chief queen, but where such a child was lacking or had died prematurely, the offspring of one of the "junior" wives would be elevated to the status of crown prince. The queen who had conceived the pharaoh of the divine seed was exceptionally privileged among the royal women as the king's mother, even if she had not previously been the late ruler's chief wife.

It appears that the designation of the heir to the throne was the subject of a public declaration by the king. Where there was an eldest son by the chief queen, this must have been a formality, but where a child of a lesser lady was involved, there may have been some jockeying for position to define who was actually the senior prince.

Even more significant would have been the declaration when no son of the reigning king's body survived. It is unclear how the succession was formally determined in such cases, but indications are that senior political or military figures were the most likely nominees.

A number of pharaohs married their sister- or half-sisters, which once led to a theory that the royal inheritance passed down the female line, princes having to marry the "heiress" to qualify for the throne of pharaoh. It is now quite clear that this was not the case, for too many chief queens were of demonstrably plebeian birth to permit such a conclusion. A more likely explanation for incestuous marriages is the fact that within all systems where a king is divine, a supernatural potential exists in all his progeny. From this would derive a desirability that this be kept within the royal house and not spread too far outside.

However, a number of nobles certainly married royal daughters, and many other cases are doubtless hidden from us. It seems to have been much more acceptable to proclaim one's politico-social relationship with royalty than one's close physical relationship.

Naturally, however, where a queen was also a royal daughter, her status was further elevated, something which can be particularly traced in the early Eighteenth Dynasty. The prominence of Ahhotep, one of the first of a line of such queens during the Seventeenth and Eighteenth Dynasties, has already been mentioned in the honors paid to her as the Savior of Upper Egypt at a time of crisis. Her daughter Ahmose-Nefertiry, married to her son, Ahmose, was even more influential, being the first queen to hold the important post of divine consort of Amun before it was limited to virgin incumbents. She was later deified and became one of the great Theban deities for as long as the New Kingdom lasted. Later queens of the dynasty, however, include numerous ladies of non-royal birth—the principal wives of Thutmose III, Amenhotep II, Amenhotep III, and Akhenaten were in no case kings' daughters. In spite of this lack of lineage, Tiye, spouse of Amenhotep III, and Nefertiti, wife of Akhenaten, attained

MOTHER OF THE KING
The tomb of Ahmose-Nefertiry, the mother of Amenhotep I, is buried in Dra Abu el-Naga, the oldest royal necropolis in Thebes. She is immortalized in this wooden statuette.

a prominence almost unparalleled by their earlier sisters—in the case of Nefertiti, verging on kingly status. Under the Nineteenth Dynasty, yet another commoner, Nefertari, became a pivotal figure as chief queen of Rameses II. Royal blood was thus not a determining factor in the careers of those holding the highest official female status in the pharaonic state.

The very highest office of all—that of king—was not nominally open to females. However, at least four women obtained pharaonic titles prior to the Ptolemaic Period; on the other hand, in the two best-known cases, those of Hatshepsut and Tawosret, the ladies had first come to power as regents for child-kings.

We are ill-informed about the careers of royal sons, particularly crown princes before the Nineteenth Dynasty. They were usually brought up by high-ranking wet-nurses and formed strong attachments to their milk-brothers, who often became companions of their youth and maturity, holding important positions in their house-holds. Royal sons were instructed in the military arts by army veterans appointed for the purpose; military scribes were engaged to teach reading and writing. Princesses also learned to write and paint in watercolor, judging from the ivory writing-palettes of two daughters of Akhenaten that have survived, showing signs of use. Female nurses and male tutors or major-domos were also appointed to attend upon them.

It would appear that all the royal sons received the education of a potential pharaoh, since no one could know whom fate had in store for the succession. There are many instances of heirs apparent who did not survive infancy.

There are occasions on which a king associated his eldest son on the throne with him as co-regent, and the system is well attested for the Twelfth Dynasty in which every king ruled for his later years with a junior partner. Double datings exist to prove the circumstance, and from these it is possible to affirm that Sesostris I ruled with his father, Ammenemes I, for the first ten years of his reign.

The officers of state

In theory, all government was by the king. In practice, of course, he ruled through officials. In the earliest dynasties these appear to have been his near relatives, for, since authority came from the gods, those who partook even in some small degree of the divine essence were best qualified for subordinate rule. In time, offices tended to become hereditary as the Egyptian ideal of appointing the heir to his father's place was generally followed.

Veritable dynasties of officials existed by the side of the kings they served, and the genealogies of some may be traced for several generations—particularly in the New Kingdom and Libyan Period. During the First Intermediate Period and earlier Middle Kingdom, the local governors duplicated the royal administration on a smaller scale with their stewards, priests, and henchmen. At least many of the officials had daughters in the royal harem.

No particular specialization was demanded in earlier times—thus Weni, of the Sixth Dynasty, whose training was as a steward, became in turn a judge, general, master of works, and hydraulic engineer. Ability as an organizer was apparently of more value than technical knowledge, and this remained true throughout Egyptian history: Amenhotep-son-of-Hapu, for instance, whose primary office was an administrative post in the army, was also the architect who moved "mountains of quartzite," as he put it, in erecting the colossal monuments of Amenhotep III.

THE VIZIER

This prime minister from the 12th Dynasty is wearing the characteristic robe for his position. It is a long piece of clothing that is knotted above his round belly—a sign of wealth.

As the origin and fount of all law, the king was the final court of appeal. Death sentences could apparently be confirmed only by him, and he must also have exercised prerogatives of mercy. Though his deputy was the vizier, nominally the king was at once the legislator, judiciary, and executive. But in such a state as Egypt, where the pattern of government was constantly repeated, precedent must have played a cardinal role, and a body of decisions with all the sanctity of holy writ must have been available to form the climate of royal opinion, if not actually to affect judgments in individual cases. Even in the reign of Thutmose III, decisions taken by a vizier who had lived some five centuries earlier, were still recalled.

There were also the *Instructions* which, as we have seen, several kings wrote for the guidance of their posterity. The king's creative power to make laws at his will evidently did not affect the main body of precedent. In the 13th century B.C., a lawsuit brought by a scribe before the king's vizier, regarding an estate near Memphis which had been given to his ancestor by King Ahmose three centuries earlier, went through a long process of litigation over several reigns, leading to claim, counterclaim, appeals, eviction, and eventual vindication.

This intricate case reveals that records of earlier judgments were filed in central archives over a long period, that bribery and collusion could be successfully challenged and *ex cathedra* decisions overcome by a kind of affidavit supported by sworn witnesses. While the case does little to elucidate the full extent and limits of the law in ancient Egypt, it does make clear that men and women were equal before it and enjoyed an equal degree of proprietorship.

In the New Kingdom, it was the officials of the palace who acted as a kind of privy council and helped the king to govern. They were the Egyptian equivalent of the *maryannu* who formed the military aristocracy of great states elsewhere. They are depicted walking in the funerary procession painted in the tomb-chapel of the vizier Ramose at Thebes, and are represented, like pallbearers, in the burial chamber of the tomb of Tutankhamun wearing mourning bands around their brows as they haul the catafalque of their dead lord. Included in the cortège would have been the two overseers of the treasury, concerned with the reception and allocation of raw materials and finished goods, tribute, plunder, and other commodities. Also important was the overseer of the granaries of Upper and Lower Egypt, whose responsibility was the harvesting, recording, and storage of the annual crops of wheat and barley.

There were several other court posts such as the chief steward, the master of the horse, the scribe of the recruits, the superintendent of works, the first and second heralds, the king's secretary and butler, besides a host of underlings, chamberlains, pages, and fan-bearers—though the title of "fan-bearer on the right of the king" was claimed as a great honorific by the highest officers in the land.

Two officials during the New Kingdom were of special importance. The first, a new post, was the viceroy of Kush, the king's deputy in Nubia and the Lower Sudan

TABLE OF OFFERINGS *(12th Dynasty) The funerary stele of Senpu and his entire family stands before the table of offerings, on which round loaves of bread are engraved. In front of the figures is a drain for the libations.*

169

as far as the Fourth Cataract. His seat of government was at Aniba, whence he was responsible for territories that stretched from Elkab in Egypt proper to Gebel Barkal in the Sudan. The viceroy appears to have inherited the title and office formerly held by the Prince of Kush in the later years of the Seventeenth Dynasty, but he differed from his predecessor in being an Egyptian and a nominee of the pharaoh, receiving his signet as a token of his delegated power. The office, like others in Egypt, however, had a tendency to be handed down from father to son.

The other important official was the first prophet, or high priest of Amun at Thebes, whose temples received such enormous endowments and gifts from grateful pharaohs that four senior prophets were required to administer its considerable revenues. Of these priests, the second prophet appears to have been a close relation of the king or his chief queen since the days of Ahmose. In later Ramessid times, the First Prophet became the virtual ruler of Upper Egypt, of which Amun was by then the state god. The last incumbents of the office were in turn sons of a predecessor, though the ultimate high priest before the appointment of Herihor was apparently dismissed from office by a rival.

This suppression began a contest that eventually resulted in a civil war, the eclipse of Western Thebes, the pillaging of the royal necropolis, and the loss of Nubia and Kush.

The chief official under the king, however, was still the vizier, whose office goes back to the dawn of history and persisted until the 4th century B.C. Generally, there were two viziers, one serving in Upper Egypt, the other in Lower Egypt. The vizier's responsibilities—in which he was assisted by a legion of scribes, stewards, runners, and guards—included not only a daily report to his sovereign on the state of the nation but also the delivering of judgments in his audience hall, the receiving and issuing of instructions to the various branches of central government, and the making and rescinding of appointments.

REWARDING WITH GOLD *(18th Dynasty) Seti I offers thanks to Hormin, head of the royal harem, for his exemplary services. During a lavish ceremony, the king gives him heavy gold necklaces.*

He was chiefly concerned with the collection of taxes in Upper and Lower Egypt, but he also mobilized the king's personal bodyguard, saw to the cutting of timber and general irrigation, directed village headmen as to summer cultivation, made a weekly inspection of the water resources, considered the state of the fortresses on the borders, took measures against raids by robbers and nomads, and saw to the fitting out of ships. He presided over important civil cases referred to him from lower courts, dealt with questions of land tenure and the witnessing of wills, and considered criminal cases requiring heavy sentences, all in his capacity as Chief Justice. He also received foreign embassies and supervised workshops and building enterprises, including the work on the royal tomb. No wonder that the pharaoh, in delivering the homily that it was customary to address to high officials when they took office, should say:

"Look to the office of the vizier. Be vigilant about what is done in it, for it is the mainstay of the entire land. As to the vizierate, it is not sweet, indeed, but it is bitter as gall. For the vizier is hard copper enclosing the gold of his master's house."

The king went on to warn the new incumbent against using his rank to further his own interests. He is to show favor to no one. He must be scrupulous in administering the law, neither favoring friends nor judging their cases more harshly because they were his friends, "for that would be more than justice."

Such officials were to be well rewarded; as *The Instruction for King Merykare* explains, a poorly paid official is open to corruption. In his reforming zeal after the Amarna interlude, King Horemheb decreed that he was appointing reliable men to the vizierate and adjuring them not to fraternize with other persons nor to accept bribes or gifts from them.

Those judges who performed their duties conscientiously were to be honored by being rewarded periodically by the king in person.

But if any member of the district councils was found to be practicing injustice, he was to answer a capital charge.

ROYAL VICTIMS
This is a detail from a decorated case found in Tutankhamun's tomb. Standing on his chariot, Tutankhamun crushes his Nubian enemies, who pile up before him.

The armed forces

The king, as the Narmer palette makes clear right from the start, was the protector of Egypt, producing concord at home and making the state enemies his footstool abroad. His divine might alone was sufficient to conquer: In the face of his superior right, his opponents became weak and submissive. In practice, the pharaoh was assisted in police and military matters by an army. During the later Old Kingdom, this probably consisted of local levies under their regional commanders, and it was but a short step from these to the feudal lords and their retainers that brought the miseries of civil strife to the kingdom at the collapse of the Sixth Dynasty. There must also have been a royal corps or bodyguard of Egyptian and Nubian troops stronger than any equivalent local force. The duties of such levies were concerned largely with police work on the frontiers; quarrying operations in Sinai, the Wadi Hammamat, and elsewhere; and in trading expeditions to Punt. They combined the duties of a labor corps and a protective force.

During the Middle Kingdom, immense fortress building on the frontiers became symptomatic of

WEAPON MAKERS
*On this New Kingdom
stele, weapon artisans are
making bows, arrows, and
chariot parts.*

the current military thinking. The frontiers of Egypt were to be strengthened against unauthorized entry. Trade with Asia and tropical Africa was to be strictly regulated. The massive mud-brick forts built in the region of the Second Cataract were extremely strong and, if resolutely defended, almost impregnable. The scenes of warfare in the Middle Kingdom tombs at Beni Hasan all center around attacks upon some such fortresses and probably refer to conditions during the First Intermediate Period. The private armies of this age of internecine strife were still tolerated until the reign of Sesostris III. The expeditions which the first three kings of the Twelfth Dynasty led into Upper Nubia were accompanied by the nomarchs of the Oryx and Hare nomes together with their contingents.

It is presumed that the central force of the pharaoh was just such a body of feudal levies, but organized on a larger scale, with a quota of Nubian volunteers around a nucleus of the personal retainers of the king. This army, which campaigned on a regular basis in Nubia—where it also garrisoned the trading-forts—was much more highly organized than the forces of former days.

The armies of the Old and Middle Kingdoms, however, have a thoroughly amateur appearance beside the large professional forces of the New Kingdom, with their chariotry, infantry, scouts, and marines. We have already referred to the heroic age that was ushered in with the horse-drawn chariot and the new social order that it fostered. A return was made to a mobile warfare, with its own peculiar rules

SATIRIZING THE SOLDIERY

Through the centuries, the Egyptian army won several conquests. This victory song attests to the fact: "This army comes home happy, we ravaged their country… This army comes home happy, we destroyed their fortresses. This army comes home happy, we cut their trees and their vines. This army comes home happy, we cut the throats of thousands of their troops. This army comes home happy, we captured a great number of soldiers."

Yet if we are to listen to the scribes who taught in the schools, a soldier's life was very difficult. To motivate their students who lazed around in front of the hieroglyphics, the teachers were both derisive and humorous. Therefore, they made satirical portraits of other professions—especially that of the soldier: At a very young age, a boy, they said, was placed in the king's stable, with help from his grandfather. "He hastens to capture the stud farm's stallions before His Majesty. If he caught handsome horses, he is overjoyed… and returns to town with them." With great joy, he sold his grandfather's heritage to buy a chariot. With his horse and carriage, he paraded through town, tumbled from his chariot, and received 100 lashes.

The fate of a foot soldier was even worse. Taken away when he was a small child, locked up in barracks, "his stomach is struck terribly hard, his eyebrows are split…he is stretched out and beaten like papyrus. Let us discuss his march to Syria. He carried his bread and water on his shoulders like a donkey. His load stiffens his neck… His vertebrae bend. He drinks brackish water.

"Does he arrive before the enemy? He is like a trapped bird, without any strength. Does he return to Egypt? He is like wood eaten by worms. Sick, he is bedridden. He is carried on a donkey and his cloths are stolen and his servant flees…"

and disciplines. The champion who distinguishes himself in single combat, or announces the day of battle, makes his appearance.

The age is notable for its paladins and their exploits: the two Ahmoses of Elkab; Djehuti, who took the town of Joppa by a stratagem; Amenemhab, who defeated a ruse of the prince of Qadesh by dispatching his decoy mare before it could throw the stallions of the Egyptian chariots into confusion.

With the chariot came new arms and armor, new methods of warfare, and a military aristocracy. The small standing army of the Old and Middle Kingdoms was expanded into a large professional organization with squadrons of chariots, each manned by a driver and fighter and armed with such new weapons as the composite bow, the heavy bronze falchion (a kind of broad, short sword) the battle-axe, and the light javelin impelled by a spearthrower.

Military standards enabled units to be readily located on the field of battle, and instructions could be signaled by means of the war trumpet. Engagements became more than the shock of armed bodies meeting in a general melée. Strategy and tactics became the concern of the pharaohs and their war councils, and if we are to believe the official accounts it was, for instance, the plan of battle devised by Thutmose III that was responsible for his great victory at Megiddo over a confederation of Asiatic princes (ca. 1456 B.C.).

Kings, or their sons, were nominated as in command of the armies or their chariot forces when they were mere children, as in the case of several of the sons of Rameses III, who died in childhood. Bakenkhons was in charge of the training-stable of Sethos I before his twelfth year.

The Egyptian forces, under the supreme command of the pharaoh or his deputy, were divided into four armies named after the principal gods. The highest staff posts in the army were open only to the educated man who might begin his career as a simple scribe acting either at home or in the field as a sort of pay clerk. From having charge of accounts and stores, he would pass to chief army clerk, concerned with keeping the war diary, with reports and general secretarial work. A further elevation would be the scribe of recruits, a very important post held, for example, by

Amenhotep-son-of-Hapu, who superintended conscription and the allocation of recruits to various services, either in the army proper or the public works for which the army supplied labor, such as the quarrying of stone, the working of the gold and turquoise mines, and the erection of great monuments.

The general staff was concerned more with logistics than strategy. Before a campaign, the pharaoh consulted a war council of general officers and his state officials, though the bold and successful plan is accredited entirely to the king. The general staff gained an unrivaled experience in the handling of large numbers of men and in complex organization and methods.

In the earlier part of the Eighteenth Dynasty, the armies were manned by native Egyptians and Nubian auxiliaries who followed the family calling. But the pick of the young men called up for service in the general corvée were also conscripted particularly for the labor force: "Every man is called up, and the best are chosen. The adult is made into an infantryman, and the youth into a cadet." A career in the army, in fact, was the only opportunity for an enterprising but uneducated man, either Egyptian or alien, to achieve a position of importance or affluence. By the reign of Amenhotep III, even foreign captives were being drafted into the Egyptian forces, and so winning their eventual freedom. From this time onwards, the Egyptian armies were manned more and more by foreigners—Libyans, Sudanis, Shardana and other Sea Peoples, and finally by Carian, Ionian, and Greek mercenaries. The Wilbour Papyrus lists a number of cultivators in Middle Egypt during the 12th century B.C. who bear foreign names and were evidently veteran soldiers who had been settled on the land.

In fact, an army career appealed so strongly to adventurous youth that the master-scribes had to paint a lurid picture of its drawbacks in order to keep their pupils at their dull tasks of learning to read and write. But despite what they had to say about the miserable life of the soldier, its rewards were considerable. Warriors who had shown bravery in the field were promoted to officers, given prisoners as serfs and decorated with "the gold of valor." Such awards took the form of massive flies in gold, gold or silver weapons, and jewelry of considerable intrinsic value.

Even the less distinguished solder shared in the cattle, weapons, clothing, ornaments, and other loot captured from luxurious Asiatic enemies. He was pensioned off with grants of livestock, serfs, and land from the royal domains, on which he paid taxes but which continued to be held by his family as long as they had an able-bodied male available for military service. Such soldiers formed a privileged class, devoted to the tradition of service in the armed forces. In times of peace, they dwelt in comfortable settlements. Experienced military scribes and officers were appointed to positions in the foreign service as ambassadors or district commissioners, and to such court posts as stewards of the royal estates, butlers, fan-bearers, police chiefs, and instructors to the young princes—or even major-domos to the king's daughters. Whenever the hereditary succession to the throne died out at the end of a dynasty, it was these warrior intimates of the king who stepped into his empty sandals.

A SCRIBE AT WORK
Sculpted in ordinary wood and painted in the traditional manner (the brown skin with which men were depicted, black hair, and white robe), this statuette of a scribe dates back to the Middle Kingdom.

The scribes

For all these posts in the highly centralized administration, officials were required who could read and write. The first necessity of any man who wished to follow a professional career was that he should be properly educated in one of the schools attached to the great departments of state such as the palace, the treasury and the army, or to the "House of Life," the scriptoria of the larger temples, where books were copied and inscriptions compiled.

Humbler village scribes would doubtless teach their own children and might also take a number of pupils from near relatives. The wealth of school exercises that has survived at Deir el-Medina and elsewhere suggests that the scribes found time to take advanced pupils as well as follow their calling. Education in Egypt was largely on the master and apprentice system.

The training of a scribe began at a very early age, and if we are to judge by the career of the high priest Bakenkhons in the reign of Rameses II, was completed twelve years later when he reached manhood.

The pupil began by learning by heart the different glyphs grouped into various categories, and from that he progressed to words in the literary language selected according to meaning. From this stage he went on to copy extracts from the classics, sometimes translating them into the vernacular language. Papyrus was too expensive for beginners to spoil, and potsherds and flakes of limestone (*ostraka*) had to serve instead. The writing of various glyphs demanded an ability to draw with the pen. Geography, mathematics, foreign words, articles of trade, traveling equipment, religious feasts, parts of the body, and so forth were learned incidentally in copying stock-letters, poems on the king and his residences, and the various exchanges in a literary controversy between two learned scribes. Learning without tears may have been the ideal in some respects, although the Egyptians also had a Tudor belief in the efficacy of corporal punishment: The pupil was told that if he was idle, he

would be soundly thrashed. It is not surprising that under such treatment, and obsessed with the tedium of learning, the schoolboy should have thought of running away to become a soldier or a baker or a farmer; repeatedly, by means of such homilies as *The Satire on Trades,* the teacher sought to make his pupils stick to their dull tasks, comparing the easy lot of the trained scribe with the miseries of other callings. The theme is usually that the profession of scribe leads to a comfortable, well-paid job, but some hint of the pleasure of learning for its own sake is given in the injunction to "acquire this high calling of scribe; pleasant and fruitful are your pen and papyrus roll, and happy are you the livelong day." There is evidence that some girls were taught to read and write, for profit as well as pleasure.

When the young scribe had graduated from school, he had his foot upon the first rung of a career in the higher ranks of the army, the treasury, or the palace. While a career open to all the talents was hardly possible in ancient Egypt, where the tradition was to appoint the son to the place of his father, from the pharaoh down to

ITEMIZED PROVISIONS
In this model of a well-stocked granary, a scribe is carefully taking note of the contents—date of storage of the provisions, quantity, and quality. The owner of the New Kingdom tomb in which the model was placed was therefore guaranteed to have everything he needed in the afterlife.

THE PRIESTS

Egyptian priests had little in common with today's priests. The world created by the gods was in unstable balance and was maintained through man's constant effort to satisfy the gods so that nothing would change. However, the deities demanded a son to nourish and protect their earthly souls. This son was Pharaoh, and he was in charge of the well-being of the gods, master of the cult.

Since it was impossible for him to be in all the temples at the same time, Pharaoh delegated his role to hundreds of priests. This involved a specific ritual that took place in the private world of the sanctuary. These priests were called "the purified," for, to serve the god, they had to wash themselves in cold water twice during the day and twice at night and shave themselves entirely.

An average size temple had about 50 people: six permanent priests and four alternating teams of servants. The rest of the time, the latter lived in their village. The temple's personnel were integrated into a strict hierarchy. At the top there was the great priest, a high-standing figure whose power was linked to that of the god he served. Generally appointed by royal favor, he received two gold rings and a symbolic stick. He was the one who would open the doors of the temple that harbored the divine statue before tending to it. He received help from several very knowledgeable priests: priests who read, priests who specified the hour and therefore the exact moment of the beginning of the cult, horoscope priests who established the calendar of lucky and unlucky days, cantors, musicians, female singers, offering-bearers, and a whole crew dedicated to maintaining the temple and its annexes, who worked its land and provided offerings. In short, it was a kind of small city that concerned itself with a god and was in charge of satisfying him.

the merest field laborer, it did sometimes happen that a man from humble circumstances attained high office. In the exhortation to be a scribe which the master set his pupil to copy, the rewards of successful graduation are enticingly set forth. "A man of worth is sought for, and you are found. The man that is skilled rises step by step until he has attained the position of a magistrate." It would help, of course, if he could follow his father in his chosen occupation, but occasionally an obscure man was able to rise by merit to a position of authority. Some of the high officers of state during the New Kingdom boast of their lowly birth, and though in most cases they exaggerate in order to flatter the king who had advanced them, nevertheless such a factotum as Senenmut did come from modest antecedents, his father having only a vague, and probably posthumous, title of "worthy."

A training as a scribe was also a necessary preliminary to a career in such professions as medicine, the priesthood, and art and architecture. A medical student would be apprenticed to a practitioner, almost always his father or some near relative, but an ability to read was necessary for learning the various prescriptions, spells, and diagnoses contained in medical papyri, whether the work in question was a quasi-scientific treatise on surgery and fractures such as the Edwin Smith Papyrus, or a specialist work on gynecology such as the Kahun Papyrus, or a mere collection of medico-magic recipes, nostrums, and incantations such as the Ebers Papyrus.

During the Old and Middle Kingdoms, the priesthood had been a largely amateur organization, the district worthy being the chief priest *ex officio* of the local god. During the New Kingdom, however, with the considerable resources that were lavished upon such state gods as Amun of Thebes, Ptah of Memphis, and Re-Herakhty of Heliopolis, the priesthood became a highly specialized profession. The chief priests were great secular administrators as well as ecclesiastics. Thus Amun had not only four prophets or high priests and a host of minor officiants down to bearers of floral offerings, but also a complete secular establishment, a chief steward and overseers of his granary, storehouses, cattle, huntsmen, peasants, weavers, craftsmen, goldsmiths, sculptors, shipwrights, draftsmen, recorders, and police—a veritable enclave within the pharaonic state.

All these posts and their subordinate offices had to be filled with trained scribes, though the degree of their proficiency varied.

It was through his command of writing in the hieroglyphic and hieratic scripts (and later in demotic) that the scribe for so long made ancient Egypt the most highly organized and prosperous state in the Near East. He was predominantly a civil servant concerned with keeping records of all kinds, but in addition to his accounts, reports, legal texts, letters, and mathematical and surgical treatises, he also produced a wide literature—novels, poems, lyrics, hymns, meditations, instructions and lamentations—which directly influenced some of the writings of the Old Testament. That these were not the least esteemed of their writings is clear from a eulogy on the ancient authors written by a scribe in the 13th century B.C.:

"Their monuments have crumbled in pieces. Their mortuary priests have gone; their tombstones are covered with sand; their chambers forgotten. But their names are pronounced because of the good books that they wrote and their memory is for ever more."

Artists and craftsmen

It is more difficult to determine whether the training of a scribe was demanded of artists and craftsmen, who are so largely represented as working anonymously in studios attached to the palaces and temples. It is clear that sculptors and painters need not have been able to read or write so long as they could copy on a large scale

THE CARPENTER
This painting from a tomb in Beni Hasan reveals the carpenter's skills. Using rudimentary tools, he was able to saw, adjust, and inlay wood.

what was drawn on a potsherd or papyrus by a master-scribe or draftsman. Models of hieroglyphs were supplied in plaster for ignorant workmen to copy at Amarna, and there is plenty of evidence from this same site that stock subjects and texts were copied mechanically from year to year even when they were out of date and, if corrected at all, only after they had been cut into the stone. During the Middle Kingdom, many *ex votos* were mass-produced at Abydos, for instance, by craftsmen who could not write, the inscription usually being feebly scratched on by a hand more used to wielding a pen than a chisel. From this and other evidence, it is usually argued that the artist was of little account, a despised and humble workman deviling away for a literate official who took all the credit. The fact is that, especially in the earlier periods, it was seldom that artists proclaimed their calling: They preferred to masquerade under such titles as the high priest of Ptah. Several court artists were given handsome tombs at Thebes by their grateful sovereigns. Parennefer (ca. 1350 B.C.) was honored by a tomb at Amarna as well as at Thebes, where he is prouder of his title of the king's cupbearer than that of chief craftsman of the king.

If the names of only a mere handful of ancient Egyptian artists are known and pictures of them very rare, and above all if we are unable to accredit nearly all the surviving works of art to particular artists, that is because the artist worked under the same anonymity that prevailed in the early Middle Ages. He was considered primarily as a craftsman, and sculptors and painters are often shown at work in the same studios as joiners, metalworkers, potters, and other artisans.

The individuality of the artist was of no importance. What mattered was his ability to render faultlessly the ageless conventions, which he had imbibed from his master and would impart in turn to his pupil.

But despite all the forces that operated to ensure that a statue or painting should repeat only the primal pattern, Egyptian art did move. The wonder is that it should change so much; it is often possible for the expert to date a specimen to within a few years by its stylistic features alone.

How could such artistic changes come about in the conservative and traditional milieu of the Egyptian art? In the early days, when the center of Egyptian culture was at the capital of Memphis, it was Ptah, the god who had brought all things into being by his creative utterance, who was also the creator of all artistic enterprises. His high priest bore the title of "Greatest of Craftsmen"—and it was such literate men who designed the buildings, their decoration, and their contents. It was they who guided the hands of the builders, stonemasons, painters, jewelers, joiners, and other artisans who made and embellished the works that they conceived.

Such humbler craftsmen were isolated in workshops attached to the palaces, the houses of the great feudal lords, or the temples of the gods to whom nearly all

THE ARTISAN'S
FURNISHINGS
In the tombs of the village of Deir el-Medina, excavators sometimes found moving relics of the humble furnishings that belonged to the workers and artisans. Chairs, stools, cases, and baskets were the basics. They did not own beds, but slept on mats spread out on the floor. A cushion made the head support more comfortable and prevented the sleeper from getting bitten on the head by scorpions.

their lives were dedicated. Communities of craftsmen resided at several of the sites of major construction as at Giza, Lahun, Amarna, and, most significantly, Deir el-Medina in Western Thebes.

This last-mentioned location was occupied by the workmen who hewed and decorated the tombs of the kings and their families at Thebes during the New Kingdom. The excavation of their walled village has recovered many articles and documents which tell us much of their lives and work. Generations of artisans and their families lived in this village, their employment being hereditary. They enjoyed a fair measure of independence and self-government, but the vizier or a king's butler visited the site from time to time to inspect progress, impart news, and listen to any requests or complaints. During the Twentieth Dynasty, these were not infrequent and mostly concerned irregularities in the supply of their rations. When protests had no effect, the workmen put down their tools. A strike in the last year of Rameses III caused special consternation.

The community was divided into two "crews," or gangs, each in the charge of a foreman and his deputy. A scribe kept their records and acted as their secretary. He also kept a diary of the work done, noting each day the names of absentees and the reasons for their non-attendance. Work went on throughout the year, but at the end of every week of ten days the men enjoyed a rest day; they also celebrated many festivals of the gods, some of these lasting for several days. Workmen were also part-time priests of the local gods and officiated in the village shrines.

The workmen were paid in kind, though payments of silver are also recorded at the beginning of a new reign. Their rations consisted of emmer wheat and barley for making the staple bread and beer.

The manual workers were given more generous allowances than the clerks and porters. In addition, they regularly received vegetables and fish and a supply of wood for fuel. Occasionally, salt, wine, sweet beer, and other luxuries were distributed.

Each family occupied a house built of mud brick on stone foundations. Intermarriage between members of the community was the normal practice. The callings that the various workmen professed—stonemasons, quarrymen, plasterers, draftsmen, painters, sculptors, coppersmiths, scribes—were hereditary. They had enough free time in which to cut and decorate tombs for their own use in the neighborhood of their village.

The workmen had a laboring force of servants and serfs to assist them and minister to their wants. These were literally hewers of wood and drawers of water—the former to supply fuel for the baking ovens of the village, the latter to bring up a constant supply of water on donkey-back from the Nile about 3 miles away. Laundresses were supplied to wash their clothes, and a few slave women to grind their corn.

Each gang had a fisherman to supply them with a stated quantity of fish every week. The community's affairs were managed by a village council which changed its composition from time to time, though usually one of the foremen and a scribe were members. Other representatives were the elder workmen and their wives. They settled disputes and awarded punishments.

In view of the popular idea that the monuments of ancient Egypt were built only by the blood and sweat of expendable slaves, it is sobering to learn that these artisans worked for four hours in the morning before knocking off for a meal and a

ARTIST MATERIALS
The artisans of the village of Deir el-Medina used limestone fragments, of which there were many in the Theban mountains, for their rough sketches— of columns, perhaps, or parts of the human body. They also used the fragments to write letters or stories and do accounting. The spatulas served to coat the walls of the royal tombs before decorating them.

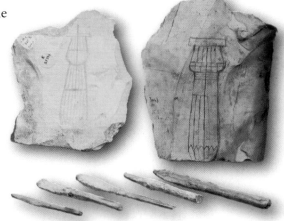

nap. The rest of their working day consisted of another four-hour stint in the afternoon. Even so, absenteeism was common.

Peasants and laborers

The peasantry of ancient Egypt formed the largest and most enduring component of the population but, because it was illiterate, has never spoken with its own voice. Instead, we have that view of the countryman which the more sophisticated townee, the scribe or the artist, has everywhere presented of him, as uncouth, clumsy, living close to the soil and his animals, doltish, and crippled with excessive toil or disease.

From the moment when the flood water came hissing through the parched channels at the beginning of the inundation, giving rise to the belief that the water snake in the cavern under Elephantine Island was on its way to Heliopolis in the north, the year began for the farmer and his family. His work included the draining of the marshy verges of the river, extending the cultivation, clearing the irrigation channels, removing wind-blown sand from fertile fields, and the laborious watering by hand of the higher-lying fields. The satiric scribe draws a woeful picture of him contending with drought, grubs, locusts, vermin, thieves, and the tax collector—but compared with the other cultivators of the eastern Mediterranean, his lot was favored. Each year he planted his seeds or dibbled his seedlings into virgin soil that had been freshly deposited and watered by the beneficent Nile. The plow was used not for breaking a hard-

BRICK MAKERS
After stomping on a mixture of earth, water, sand, and chopped straw, these men shaped bricks in rectangular molds. They then set them out to dry in the sun for a week or more.

pan and producing a tilth but merely for turning in the scattered grain. This was just as well done by driving animals over the fields to tread in the seed or by dragging a log over the ground.

Most of the labor was devoted to the irrigation of crops, whether in digging or cleaning water channels or in transporting the river by means of the *shaduf* or in pots slung on a yoke, since the *sakiyah* water-wheel operated by an animal was not introduced until Persian times.

For the most part, the peasants lived in their village around a nucleus of families or camped out with their flocks and herds under simple shelters among the pastures and rushy thickets of the Delta. It is probable that—like the artisans of Amarna, Thebes, and other residence centers—they lived fairly independent lives in their communities, their affairs managed by a headman and the village scribe, with a council of elders from the principal families.

POTTERS OR MASONS

The "wall masons," as the ancient Egyptians called them, spent much of their time molding the bricks used to build houses, garden walls, or city walls, which could be as much as 45 feet wide and 60 feet high. For houses, the wall masons stamped on a mixture of silt from the Nile, water, and a bit of sand and chopped hay. They then stirred it deeply with a pick. Despite the scorching heat, the water carriers would constantly go back and forth to keep the mixture wet, enabling the wall masons to pour it into as many rectangular wooden molds as bricks needed.

Once removed from the molds, the bricks were lined up on the sand to dry for a week in the sun. Afterwards, they had only to be stacked and transported to the work site on platforms hanging from a board. There, walls could be built quickly and at low cost; all that was needed to assemble them was some mortar.

The person called the "small mason" was in fact a potter. After having softened his clay with his feet, he placed a block of it on his wheel, which he would spin quickly to create vases, jars, cups, and—when he so fancied—a few statuettes. Once the modeling was completed, he polished and painted his pottery with slip (a clay solution of creamy consistency) before firing them in his mud kiln.

Pottery served many purposes, and the jars were even used to carry the potter's food and small items when traveling. A simple flat stone was all that was needed to close the jars to keep insects out. By covering this stone and the neck of the pot with an earth-based coating, a tight-sealing lid was created.

On the top of the jar handle, a scribe could not only note the place and date of its fabrication but also the contents of the jar. Once the jars were so itemized, it was easier for potters to travel.

But the impact of a more remote but more powerful authority was felt at certain times of the year, principally when the inundation flooded their fields and made cultivation impossible, and also when the harvest was ready for gathering and taxes had to be paid to the central state.

The essential wealth of Egypt was well understood to lie in its agriculture. Low Niles from time to time served to remind those in authority how dependent a large civilized nation was upon the skill and industry of its farmers. Nothing could therefore be allowed to stand in the way of securing a proper yield of produce each year. A great number of workmen not concerned with the cultivation of the land were yet wholly dependent upon the products of farms for their livelihood, such as weavers of linen and wool; butchers and leatherworkers; brewers, basket-, mat- and rope-makers; woodworkers, and so forth—not to mention the hosts of priests, scribes, and other officials necessary for running the state machinery.

In agricultural work, personal liberties and predilections were subordinated to the common weal. A time-honored institution for dealing with crises that demanded a concerted effort in a limited space of time was the corvée, whereby all the able-bodied citizenry were called up with their picks, hoes, and baskets to labor on such tasks as the maintenance of the irrigation system, the weeding of crops, or the gathering of the harvest. In this work, scarcely anybody was in theory exempt; even priests were conscripted, and high officials could be called upon to supervise the laboring force. Some kind of selection, however, appears to have been exercised in using the census returns for forming the local labor corps.

A similar system was expected to prevail in the Elysian Fields of the Osirian hereafter, where the wheat grew to a height of nine cubits, and even the king was not exempted from the operation of the corvée. To avoid such future inconvenience, the deceased provided himself with *shawabti* figures. These images would undertake the agricultural labor of the afterlife by virtue of a magic spell whenever he was called up and registered for work which had to be done in the otherworld. In real life, a sufficiently affluent Egyptian would be able to hire a proxy, possibly at a standard rate, and so avoid the operation of the corvée in his case.

SPOON FOR MAKE-UP
*(18th Dynasty) A Nubian
servant (the handle) bends
under the weight of his
burden (the unguent jar).
This spoon for make-up,
sculpted from wood and
meant to be used for grooming, probably belonged to
a noble or a god.*

It was the corvée that made major undertakings possible, although in the New Kingdom the army was largely conscripted for laboring in mines and quarries. The hydraulic works made necessary by the inundation were the main business of the corvée. After the flood waters had retreated, the old boundaries of fields had to be reestablished, and the surveyors then appeared to take measurements and replace any stone markers that may have been shifted, according to their cadastral records.

The second great encounter between the farmer and the central authority came at harvest time, when commissioners arrived to measure the standing crops and calculate what taxes they should yield. A little later, the tax collector, accompanied by a posse of police, would arrive to secure the imposts, or taxes. Censuses of cattle, geese, and other livestock would also be made and the yearly increase taxed accordingly. As no money in ancient Egypt existed in the form of coin until Persian times, all commerce was conducted by barter, and taxation was also exacted in kind. Besides the imposts collected on grain, cattle, and poultry, contributions were required from orchards, groves of palm trees, vineyards, weaving-sheds, hives, and every commodity that the earth provided and the craftsman manufactured. As far as the cultivator was concerned, his taxes were heavy; at least half of all produce went were taxed, and often he was left only with the bare necessities for himself and his family. It was these taxes, however, that maintained the rest of the population, and if they were not collected in their entirety, either because of crop failure or embezzlement, someone else went hungry—for instance, the workmen of the king's tomb at Thebes in year twenty-nine of Rameses III (ca. 1156 B.C.)

As elsewhere, tax-farming was employed as the most convenient way of gathering in the imposts, and such taxpayers ranged in importance from the managers of large estates and officials in charge of whole districts, through mayors of towns, to individual cultivators. All enjoyed the privilege of extracting from their plots produce in excess of the taxes required by the state.

In theory, the pharaoh owned all the land, though in practice, the management of the great estates was vested in such institutions as the departments of the palace, the state granaries, or the temples great and small. The temple of Khnum at Elephantine, for instance, had estates as far afield as the marshes of the Delta, from

SOBEK, THE CROCODILE-GOD

With a man's body and the head of a crocodile, the god Sobek was worshiped throughout Egypt. His temples harbored sacred crocodiles which were fed and heaped with jewels (earrings and bracelets) by the priests. When they died, the crocodiles were mummified and given sumptuous funerals.

Sobek was especially revered in the Faiyum, where an arm of the Nile spills into a lake teeming with crocodiles. In this place he was seen as the incarnation of the divine creator of the world. It was here that he gave his name to a city—Crocodilopolis. At Komombo, south of Thebes, where the Nile flood is celebrated,

Sobek assumed primordial importance because of his intimate ties with the river. He was said to laugh when the floodwaters arrived.

At Sais in the Delta, Sobek made vegetation bloom on both banks. Since crocodiles liked to leave the water and lie on the riverbanks, nothing could have been more natural than to associate their presence with the fertility of the places where they chose to rest. Sobek was the son of Neith, the archer goddess, who is sometimes depicted suckling two young crocodiles.

Though god of procreation and fertility, Sobek nonetheless had a character dreaded for the ferocity he showed towards enemies of the gods.

which it drew revenues and on which it paid taxes. As the king was the final owner of all land and property and industries, the laborers on these enterprises were referred to as "king's servants," even though most of them worked not directly on the royal estates but for the individuals and institutions to whom responsibility had been delegated by the pharaoh. Such laborers, the hewers of wood and the drawers of water, were registered in the census lists, and it was from such lists that the corvées were marshaled.

The lowest grade in this work force were the serfs or slaves, who were particularly numerous from the later Middle Kingdom until the end of the New Kingdom. They were mostly foreigners from Asia and Kush who had been sold into slavery or captured in war, and as early as the middle of the second millennium B.C. it is possible to see already established an institution which existed in the Near East until the end of the last century. Such people enjoyed fewer privileges than their fellows. They could not enter temple courts, being ritually impure, and it was only when the local god was brought from his shrine and paraded around his estate on a veiled litter during feast days that they could take a modest part in the worship. They were too poor to afford a tomb or burial in family plots, so their corpses were evidently thrown into the Nile for "the eater of the dead" to scavenge and so assimilate them to that primeval force that came out of the waters of Chaos in the form of a crocodile.

GARDENS AND PLOWING *(Valley of the Nobles, tomb from the 19th Dynasty) Sennedjem and his spouse plow their plot of land in the fields of Ialou. Osiris, the god of the dead, reserved these fields for the Egyptians after their death and judgment by the divine court, so that they could continue with their daily activities from the world of the living.*

IN THE TOMB
OF MERERUKA
(6th Dynasty) Mereruka,
a senior official in the royal
court, lavishly decorated his
mastaba in Saqqara. On one
of the walls of his 32 rooms,
a punishment scene serves as
a reminder of what would
happen to bad workers,
artisans, or peasants.

But the slavery system also required that in life they should be reasonably well treated. In addition to food and lodging, they received a yearly allowance of clothing, oils, and linen. Their working hours were reduced when the weather was hot. Captives were assigned as serfs to the temples and private estates and to the households of army officers who had distinguished themselves on the battlefield. But the demarcation between slave and citizen was fluid. The personal slave of a high-ranking Egyptian would be more affluent than most of the native peasantry. By Ramesid times, foreigners held important posts in the palace administration and in the army. A stela from the earlier Amarna days shows a Syrian mercenary soldier being waited upon by a native Egyptian. While slaves could be bought or sold, or hired out, the Wilbour Papyrus makes it clear that they could also rent and cultivate land on the same conditions as an army officer, priest, or other tenant farmer. A simple declaration by the owner before witnesses was apparently sufficient to make a slave into a "freeman of the land of Pharaoh," and one document has survived in which a woman adopted as her heirs the offspring of her dead husband and a female slave they had purchased, in preference to nearer relatives.

The satirist, in painting a woeful picture of the lot of the peasant, describes the tax collector as arriving on the farm with his apparitors, or subordinates, armed with sticks and palm-ribs. They demand corn and, when none is forthcoming because of drought or other misfortune, they stretch out the luckless peasant and thrash him thoroughly. This account reflects the scenes in the Old Kingdom mastabas of peasants being beaten at the whipping-post, and in New Kingdom tomb-paintings of farmers being bastinadoed, or beaten, by the police. Thus, it is claimed, even tenant farmers, as distinct from the mere serfs, received little or no consideration from their superiors and could be cruelly maltreated when they failed to deliver the full amount of the oppressive taxes imposed upon them.

There is also another side to the picture. Adjacent to such scenes, there are representations of a less abrasive relationship. A farmer, his wife, and sons greet the tax collector with a corn-dolly and refreshments. Field workers are shown during a break in their work, sitting under the trees and taking a pull from a water-skin, playing the flute, or just snoozing. A herdsman bringing cattle for registering is told by his companion not to waste time arguing with the scribe: "He is a fair man and will assess you properly; he is not hard on folk." A sage advises that the official should act considerately towards the cultivator: "If a poor man is in arrears with his taxes, remit two-thirds of them." Examples of such leniency are seen in actual accounts where an eight percent deficit in the harvest tax of one farmer is ignored; in the case of another, nearly half the quota of corn was not delivered, and eighty sacks of grain were allowed as seed for the following season.

The authorities, in fact, appear to have treated the peasant community with some respect. Many of them were veterans who had been settled on the land by grateful kings after their military service was over, though their sons might be called up to serve in their stead. The importance of not alienating such cultivators is seen in the stern measures which were introduced by Horemheb to stamp out the exploitation that had arisen during the preceding reigns.

While doubtless the system, like most human institutions, did not always operate with justice and efficiency, the general impression is that for the most part, it worked tolerably well. The cultivator had a weapon in his armory for use as a last resort. If a farmer was driven too hard, he could give up the cultivation of his fields and take to a hunting and marauding life like the bedouin of the Eastern Desert, as was often the case in Roman and Turkish times. Fields that once went out of cultivation could rapidly revert to desert.

The most wretched of the pharaoh's subjects were the criminals, some of them officials who had been found guilty of corruption; they were banished to the lonely frontier fortress of Tjel or forced to labor in the mines of Sinai and Nubia, often after losing their noses.

COUNTING
THE LIVESTOCK
It's the day to take inventory: Shepherds and herds parade before their master, who is comfortably seated under a pavilion and surrounded by scribes and servants. The master's minions use their sticks to punish negligent shepherds. Found in an 11th-Dynasty tomb, this painted wood model is a small jewel of precision and realism.

Epilogue

Throughout this book, we have intermittently referred to the ideology underlying ancient Egyptian civilization. But it remains impossible to grasp its development in depth without seriously studying the Egyptians' complex religious convictions. Unfortunately, we lack the space to do so. In fact, a methodical theological account of these beliefs is out of the question, since the dogma of Egyptian religion was never inscribed. The Pyramid Texts, Sarcophagus Texts, and later compilations give the impression that sacred books did indeed exist, but the goal of these works never confirmed faith in the divine: They were merely collections of prayers and formulas meant to assure the permanence of the person after his death, or else his assimilation by the demiurge.

The absence of a real dogma is not surprising for a society that accepted so many local gods. A single belief system can only be formulated and recognized in a monotheist context, and it is interesting to note that Akhenaten, the only monotheistic pharaoh, spoke of his *Teaching*. But this was never found again in the texts inscribed on the monuments that have survived.

Conversely, we have abundant information on the cult: Prayers, myths, rituals, forms of deities, and liturgical gestures are richly represented in temples and tombs and discussed in writings. The gods of ancient Egypt were generally the manifestation of two or three concepts of the world—tangible entities that were honored in local sanctuaries, the architecture of which is an image of the world at the time of the First Time, when the creator emerged from the waters of Chaos. In this house built on the primordial mound, the god existed from the start in the form of a sculpted image. Like all human dignitaries, he was served at his home by his servants (the priests), who relieved him of all impure household tasks and any contact that would dirty him. Magic protected him from all evil attack in any form in which it presented itself.

As early as the beginning of the New Kingdom, the construction of temples advanced considerably; large temples and their personnel became an important part of the state apparatus. They administered the religious foundations of the pharaohs or province governors and, as farmers of royal domains, assessed the taxes attached to these immense properties. Their granaries and storehouses were part of the public treasury, playing a key role in the economic organization of the country. Consequently, the property of the temple and its god were inseparable from that of the state. Moreover, the pharaoh had the title of first prophet to each god, the intermediary between man and the deity, as the presence of his statues at the entrance of the temples clearly shows. The members of the clergy were also theologians. Their adoration and reflection perpetuated the work of divine creation. Some of these cults, notably that of the sun god at Heliopolis, yielded great power and considerable influence for mainly political reasons; they dominated the thinking of the rest of the clergy. The cult of Amun in Thebes is an example.

The object of official religion was to favor the intervention of divine power in the name of the state directed by the pharaoh; at the same time, there existed several cults that had a clergy that was less intellectual and more charitable. They were more concerned with the personal well-being of the community of believers. These modest cults generally were directed at secondary deities without pretension, like the guardians of the home Bes and Thoueris or a spirit that lived at the top of a hill, a tree, the statue of a kin or an important man. The cult of those powers stemmed from popular piety; since only the humble classes observed them, they were generally not expressed in writing. But by chance, we have been left with a good number of late New Kingdom petitions from common people who had evidently had contact with a more literate person who could write for them; these texts indicate that there was a personal relationship

ANUBIS
(25th–26th Dynasty)
The jackal-god Anubis, painted on the outside of the mummy of a priest, is protecting the deceased. This inventor of mummification, this protector of the necropolises, always introduced the deceased into the afterlife as soon as he arrived by taking him gently by the hand.

between the god and the deeply religious person. They allude to physical and spiritual suffering that the god had eased, or to punishments inflicted in the form of disease, even blindness, that the believer deserved by his faults; this relegated the responsibility to divine mercy and help: "Forgive me for my many faults, I am a madman," one prays. "Give the breath to he who is afflicted and deliver me from slavery [...] for it is man's nature to sin and divine nature to forgive," another declares. "Come to me, deliver me in this ill-fated year," cries a third.

In these humble prayers, the piety and faith of the believer can be found in his invocations: "Herakhty, savior of he who implores you," "Amun, supreme judge of the miserable [...]. Beloved god who helps the most humble [...]. You who holds out a hand to the poor man and consoles those who are in a state of affliction."

These documents only partially cover a limited period, but they give us an idea of a religious current that had nothing to do with the complicated and intimidating structures of the official religion, with its power apparatus of priests, with its lavish offerings, hymns sung by choirs, its oracles and magic practices. This movement tells us that in ancient Egypt there was fundamentally simple faith that survived the changes in name of the gods and still exists today.

Glossary

Antika(s) Antiques or relics

Ashlar(s) Squared building stone

Baldachin Silk brocade interwoven with gold or silver threads

Bedouin Nomad(s)

Cadastral Adjective form of cadaster, a public record of the value and ownership of land for taxation purposes

Catamite Boy or youth in a sexual relationship with a man

Cartouche Scroll-like tablet, especially as an architectural feature

Centotaph Monument or empty tomb honoring a dead person whose body is elsewhere

Chthonic Of gods and spirits dwelling under the earth

Common Era Period since the year of Christ's birth

Congeries Assemblage; aggregation

Corvée Forced labor at the government's order

Dado Part of a pedestal between the base and the cap

Déblayeur Excavator; one who clears away

Demiurge Supernatural being imagined as creating the world under the direction of the Supreme Being

Demiotic Of or pertaining to the simplified hieroglyphics used in Egypt between 700 B.C. and 500 A.D.

Desiccation The preserving of food by drying

Dromos Columned entrance-passage to a temple or other building

Entrepôt Place for the storage or distribution of goods

Ex voto{s} Object left as an offering in fulfillment of a vow or in gratitude

Faience Glazed earthenware

Fellahin Egyptian farmers' dance

Heliotropian Of the ancient Egyptian city of Heliopolis

Hieratic Of or pertaining to abridged forms of hieroglphyics used by Egyptian priests

Imperium in imperio "Sovereignty within a sovereignty"

Kohl Cosmetic (powdered antimony sulfide) used for darkening the eyelids

Libation Liquid poured on the ground as a sacrifice to a god

Maryannu Chariot warriors of noble birth

Mastaba Tomb made of mud brick, rectangular in shape with sloping sides and a flat roof

Natron A mineral, hydrated sodium carbon

Nomarch Governor of a nome

Nome Territorial division in ancient Egypt

Paladin Knight or heroic champion

Philology Study and verification of literary texts and written records

Ramessid Of the period of the Rameses pharaohs

Regnal Of or pertaining to a sovereign, sovereignty, or reign

Sachedotal Of priests or the office of priests

Satrap(s) Ruler, usually a subordinate, despotic official of a dependency

Savant(s) Learned person or scholar

Serekh Very early symbol of Egyptian kingship, in the shape of a palace

Stela Wall or building surface bearing inscriptions or drawings

Stele (*pl.* stelae) Upright stone or pillar with an inscription, used as a grave marker or monument

Stratigraphy The arrangement of rocks in layers

Suzerain Sovereign or state exercising political control over a dependent state

Suzerainty Domain of a suzerain, or the authority thereof

Temenos Piece of ground around, adjacent to or surrounding a temple; a sacred enclosure

Vizier Chief minister of a sovereign

Wadi Water channel that is dry except during rainstorms

Index

Note: Page references in *italic* indicate photographs

Picture credits

Cover, (*background*) detail of the basalt sarcophagus of Nes-Shutfene (Ptolemaic era, Saqqara), MAGNUM/E. Lessing/Kunsthistorisches Museum, Vienna; (*foreground*) amulet with jeweled eye (polychrome faience, 20th–25th Dynasty), British Museum, London.

6/7, G. DAGLI ORTI; 10 top, G. DAGLI ORTI/Egyptian Museum, Cairo; 10 middle, G. DAGLI ORTI/The Louvre, Paris; 10/11 (background) HOA QUI/ALTITUDE/Y. Arthus-Bertrand; 11 middle, G. DAGLI ORTI/The Louvre, Paris; 11 top, G. DAGLI ORTI/Egyptian Museum, Cairo; 11 bottom, G. DAGLI ORTI/Egyptian Museum, Munich; 12 left, right, G. DAGLI ORTI/The Louvre, Paris; 12/13 (background), MAGNUM/E. Lessing; 13 top left, G. DAGLI ORTI/The Louvre, Paris; 13 top right, G. DAGLI ORTI; 13 bottom, RMN/H. Lewandowski/The Louvre, Paris; 14 left, G. DAGLI ORTI/The Louvre, Paris; 14 right, G. DAGLI ORTI/Egyptian Museum, Cairo; 14/15 (background), HOA QUI/ALTITUDE/Y. Arthus-Bertrand; 15 middle, G. DAGLI ORTI; 15 top, BPK, BERLIN/M. Busing/Egyptian Museum, Berlin; 15 bottom, 16 left, right, G. DAGLI ORTI/The Louvre, Paris; 16/17 (background), HOA QUI/C. Sappa; 17 top, G. DAGLI ORTI/Egyptian Museum, Cairo; 17 left, RMN/Chuzeville/The Louvre, Paris; 17 right, PELIZAEUS-MUSEUM, HILDESHEIM; 18 left, RMN/R.G. Ojeda/The Louvre, Paris; 18 right, IMAGE BANK/C. Brown; 18/19 (background), IMAGE BANK/G. Colliva; 19 top middle, J. LIEPE/Egyptian Museum, Cairo; 19 top right, G. DAGLI ORTI/The Louvre, Paris; 19 bottom left, G. DAGLI ORTI/Egyptian Museum, Cairo; 20, G. DAGLI ORTI/The Louvre, Paris; 21, DIAF/D. Ball; 23, CORBIS-SYGMA/S. Compoint; 25, Archives SRD; 26, G. DAGLI ORTI/BRITISH MUSEUM, London; 27, G. DAGLI ORTI; 28/29, G. DAGLI ORTI/Coll. part. Paris; 30, L'ILLUSTRATION; 31, ROGER-VIOLLET/L.L.; 32, L'ILLUSTRATION; 34 left, G. DAGLI ORTI/The Louvre, Paris; 34/35 (background), RMN/Chuzeville/The Louvre, Paris; 35 middle left, G. DAGLI ORTI/Egyptian Museum, Turin; 35 middle right, RMN/R.G. Ojeda/The Louvre, Paris; 35 top middle, G. DAGLI ORTI; 35 top left, G. DAGLI ORTI/Egyptian Museum, Turin; 35 top right, bottom, G. DAGLI ORTI/The Louvre, Paris; 36, HOA QUI/C. Sappa; 37, G. DAGLI ORTI; 38, TOP/H. Champollion; 40, HOA QUI/P. de Wilde; 41, HOA QUI/C. Sappa; 43, G. DAGLI ORTI; 44, DIAF/D. Ball; 46, G. DAGLI ORTI; 47, G. DAGLI ORTI/The Louvre, Paris; 48, RMN/Chuzeville/The Louvre, Paris; 51, HOA QUI/C. Sappa; 53, Y. KOENIG; 54, G. DAGLI ORTI/Egyptian Museum, Cairo; 56 left, 56/57 (background), G. DAGLI ORTI/The Louvre, Paris; 57 middle left, G. DAGLI ORTI/Egyptian Museum, Turin; 57 middle right, BPK, BERLIN/M. Busing/Egyptian Museum, Berlin; 57 top middle, RMN/Chuzeville/The Louvre, Paris; 57 top left, BRIDGEMAN ART LIBRARY/P. Willi/The Louvre, Paris; 57 top right, bottom right, G. DAGLI ORTI/The Louvre, Paris; 59, G. DAGLI ORTI; 60, G. DAGLI ORTI/Egyptian Museum, Cairo; 61, J. LIEPE/Egyptian Museum, Cairo; 62, G. DAGLI ORTI; 63, G. DAGLI ORTI/The Louvre, Paris; 65, 67, G. DAGLI ORTI/Egyptian Museum, Turin; 68, HOA QUI/C. Moreno; 69, BRIDGEMAN ART LIBRARY/Fitzwilliam Museum, Cambridge University; 70/71, Y. KOENIG; 72, 73, 74, G. DAGLI ORTI/The Louvre, Paris; 75, BRIDGEMAN ART LIBRARY/Brooklyn Museum of Art, New York; 76, G. DAGLI ORTI/Egyptian Museum, Turin; 77, G. DAGLI ORTI/Egyptian Museum, Cairo; 79, G. DAGLI ORTI/The Louvre, Paris; 80, J. LIEPE/Egyptian Museum, Cairo; 81, G. DAGLI ORTI/The Louvre, Paris; 82, BRIDGEMAN ART LIBRARY/Ashmolean Museum, Oxford; 83, G. DAGLI ORTI/The Louvre, Paris; 85, 86, G. DAGLI ORTI; 87, G. DAGLI ORTI/Egyptian Museum, Turin; 91, 92, G. DAGLI ORTI; 93, J. LIEPE/Egyptian Museum, Cairo; 96 top, G. DAGLI ORTI; 96 bottom, G. DAGLI ORTI/Egyptian Museum, Cairo; 97 top left, J. LIEPE/Egyptian Museum, Cairo; 97 top right, Egyptian Museum, Cairo; 97 bottom, G. DAGLI ORTI/The Louvre, Paris; 98 top, G. DAGLI ORTI/Egyptian Museum, Cairo; 98 bottom, J. LIEPE/Egyptian Museum, Cairo; 99 top left, G. DAGLI ORTI/Egyptian Museum, Cairo; 99 top right, bottom, G. DAGLI ORTI/The Louvre, Paris; 100 top, J. LIEPE/Egyptian Museum, Cairo; 100 bottom, G. DAGLI ORTI/Egyptian Museum, Cairo; 101 top left, J. LIEPE/Egyptian Museum, Cairo; 101 top right, ARALDO DE LUCA/Egyptian Museum, Cairo; 101 bottom, G. DAGLI ORTI; 102 top, RMN/H. Lewandowski/The Louvre, Paris; 102 bottom, G. DAGLI ORTI; 103 top, G. DAGLI ORTI/The Louvre, Paris; 103 bottom left, RMN/Chuzeville/The Louvre, Paris; 103 bottom right, 104 left, G. DAGLI ORTI/The Louvre, Paris; 104 right, G. DAGLI ORTI/Egyptian Museum, Cairo; 105 top left, G. DAGLI ORTI/The Louvre, Paris; 105 top right, RAPHO/P. Berenger/Egyptian Museum, Cairo; 105 bottom, G. DAGLI ORTI/Egyptian Museum, Cairo; 106, J. LIEPE/Egyptian Museum, Cairo; 107, G. DAGLI ORTI; 108, J. LIEPE/Egyptian Museum, Cairo; 109, G. DAGLI ORTI; 110, G. DAGLI ORTI/The Louvre, Paris; 111, G. DAGLI ORTI; 112, G. DAGLI ORTI/Egyptian Museum, Cairo; 113, G. DAGLI ORTI/The Louvre, Paris; 114, BRIDGEMAN ART LIBRARY/Brooklyn Museum of Art, New York, 115, G. DAGLI ORTI/The Louvre, Paris; 117, 118, 120 left, J. LIEPE/Egyptian Museum, Cairo; 120/121 (background), G. DAGLI ORTI; 121 middle left, middle right, top middle, top left, G. DAGLI ORTI/The Louvre, Paris; 121 top right, G. DAGLI ORTI/British Museum, London; 121 bottom, G. DAGLI ORTI; 122, 124, G. DAGLI ORTI/Egyptian Museum, Cairo; 125, RMN/H. Lewandowski/The Louvre, Paris; 126, G. DAGLI ORTI/The Louvre, Paris; 128, J. LIEPE/Egyptian Museum, Cairo; 129, G. DAGLI ORTI/Egyptian Museum, Cairo; 130, RMN/J.G. Berizzi/The Louvre, Paris; 131, TOP/H. Champollion; 132, BRIDGEMAN ART LIBRARY/British Museum, London; 134, J. LIEPE/Egyptian Museum, Cairo; 135, BRIDGEMAN ART LIBRARY/Brooklyn Museum of Art, New York; 136, J. LIEPE/Egyptian Museum, Cairo; 137, 138, G. DAGLI ORTI/Egyptian Museum, Cairo; 140, G. DAGLI ORTI; 141, G. DAGLI ORTI/The Louvre, Paris; 142, 143, G. DAGLI ORTI/Egyptian Museum, Turin; 144/145, G. DAGLI ORTI; 148, RMN/H. Lewandowski/The Louvre, Paris; 149, HOA QUI/Zefa; 150, G. DAGLI ORTI/The Louvre, Paris; 151, G. DAGLI ORTI/Egyptian Museum, Cairo; 152, DIAF/C. Senechal; 153, HOA QUI/C. Pavard; 154 left, ARALDO DE LUCA/Egyptian Museum, Cairo; 154/155 (background), J. LIEPE/Egyptian Museum, Cairo; 155 middle left, G. DAGLI ORTI; 155 middle right, J. LIEPE/Egyptian Museum, Cairo; 155 top middle, top left, G. DAGLI ORTI/Egyptian Museum, Cairo; 155 top right, RAPHO/Fathy/Egyptian Museum, Cairo; 155 bottom, 156, G. DAGLI ORTI/Egyptian Museum, Cairo; G. DAGLI ORTI/The Louvre, Paris; 159, RMN/H. Lewandowski/The Louvre, Paris; 162, 163, G. DAGLI ORTI/Egyptian Museum, Cairo; 164, J. LIEPE/Egyptian Museum, Cairo; 165, G. DAGLI ORTI; 166, RMN/H. Lewandowski/The Louvre, Paris; 167, G. DAGLI ORTI/Egyptian Museum, Turin; 168, RMN/C. Larrieu/The Louvre, Paris; 169, RMN/Chuzeville/The Louvre, Paris; 170, G. DAGLI ORTI/The Louvre, Paris; 171, G. DAGLI ORTI/Egyptian Museum, Cairo; 172, 174, G. DAGLI ORTI/The Louvre, Paris; 175, RMN/H. Lewandowski/The Louvre, Paris; 177, BRIDGEMAN ART LIBRARY; 178, 179, G. DAGLI ORTI/The Louvre, Paris; 180, G. DAGLI ORTI; 182, RMN/C. Larrieu/The Louvre, Paris; 183, 184, G. DAGLI ORTI; 185, J. LIEPE/Egyptian Museum, Cairo; 187, G. DAGLI ORTI/Luxor Museum.